Informing Faculty
Development
for Teacher Educators

SOCIAL AND POLICY ISSUES IN EDUCATION: THE UNIVERSITY OF CINCINNATI SERIES

KATHRYN M. BORMAN, *SERIES EDITOR*

Children Who Challenge the System
edited by Anne M. Bauer and Ellen M. Lynch

Contemporary Issues in U.S. Education
edited by Dolores Stegelin

Effective Schooling for Disadvantaged Students: School-based Strategies for Diverse Student Populations
edited by Howard Johnston and Kathryn M. Borman

Home Schooling: Political, Historical, and Pedagogical Perspectives
edited by Jan Van Galen and Mary Anne Pitman

Investing in U.S. Schools: Directions for Educational Policy
edited by Bruce A. Jones and Kathryn M. Borman

Minority Education: Anthropological Perspectives
edited by Evelyn Jacob and Cathie Jordan

IN PREPARATION

Assessment Testing and Evaluation in Teacher Education
edited by Suzanne W. Soled

Basil Bernstein: Consensus and Controversy
edited by Alan R. Sadovnik

Critical Education for Work: Multidisciplinary Approaches
edited by Richard D. Lakes

INFORMING FACULTY DEVELOPMENT FOR TEACHER EDUCATORS

Edited by

KENNETH R. HOWEY

NANCY L. ZIMPHER

The Ohio State University

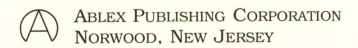
ABLEX PUBLISHING CORPORATION
NORWOOD, NEW JERSEY

Printed in the United States of America

Library of Congress Cataloging-in-Publication Data

Informing faculty development for teacher educators / edited by
  Kenneth R. Howey, Nancy L. Zimpher.
      p. cm. — (Social and policy issues in education)
  Includes bibliographical references and index.
  ISBN 1-56750-119-2 (cl.). — ISBN 1-56750-120-6 (pbk.)
  1. Teacher educators—In-service training—United States.
2. Education—Study and teaching (Higher)—United States.
I. Howey, Kenneth R. II. Zimpher, Nancy L. III. Series.
LB1737.5.I54 1994
378.1'25—dc20   94-8871
                                          CIP

Ablex Publishing Company
355 Chestnut Street
Norwood, New Jersey 07648

THIS BOOK IS DEDICATED TO OUR COLLEAGUES IN THE
URBAN NETWORK TO IMPROVE TEACHER EDUCATION (UNITE)
AND TO THOSE WHO HAVE MADE THIS NETWORK POSSIBLE

TABLE OF CONTENTS

1

INTRODUCTION

KENNETH R. HOWEY
NANCY L. ZIMPHER

The Ohio State University

This volume brings together a diverse group of scholars to address a topic that has not received the attention it deserves: the continuing professional development of faculty members who educate prospective teachers. The topic nonetheless is important. The case for more and better professional development for teacher educators can be argued on several fronts. An examination of the traditional triad of professorial responsibilities—teaching, research, and service—illustrates the need to enable these individuals more effectively. For example, recent assessments of the nature and quality of instruction in higher education in general (Boyer, 1987) and in teacher education specifically (Goodlad, 1990) are not kind. Published scholarly work represents the efforts of only a relatively small percentage of teacher educators (RATE, 1988); we reserve comment on the quality of much of this work. Although institutional expectations and conditions seriously constrain many teacher educators in this regard, there are additionally challenges to how scholarly studies of different types are undertaken. What constitutes valid scholarship? Where? With whom? In what manner should it be undertaken? The pressure to focus on practice-oriented research with teachers in schools continues to build (The Holmes Group, 1990). Service by teacher educators has been neither widespread nor effective, at least in terms of direct contributions to improving elementary and secondary schools in urban and rural areas where problems are the greatest. Many observers acknowledge no role in this regard for faculty members in schools and colleges of education (Howey, 1993). The possible contributions of higher education/ teacher education, for example, are not considered in such major school reform initiatives as the Edison Project, Nabisco's Next Century Schools, and The New American Schools Development Corporation.

It is also apparent that conditions and events calling for change by many teacher educators are accelerating. For example, changes advocated in teacher education include more potent and more protracted programs of preservice preparation incorporating such features as: student cohorts, portfolio documentation, collaborative planning and instruction, the development of teaching clinics, instructional cases, outcome-based measures, and more robust and more sustained relationships than maintained previously with teachers and administrators in elementary and secondary schools. These evolving expectations compound a situation in which many teacher educators apparently are already finding it difficult to address present challenges. In addition, these heightened expectations, or at least altered responsibilities, are evolving in a context of shrinking resources and a climate of increased scrutiny for teacher education.

Given this context, this book takes a broad-based view of professional development for teacher educators and focuses on endeavors that can be integrated as fully as possible into ongoing responsibilities. Although the central concern is how we as teacher educators might enhance our pedagogical abilities, this book also discusses how we might nourish our collective commitment as a faculty to an ethos and a culture—to a learning community, if you will—that can also maximize our growth as scholars and our ability to serve a variety of clients better than at present. This multidimensional conception of professional development also addresses the corporate commitment necessary to achieve a *program* of preservice preparation, wherein our responsibilities as role models and mentors and our relationships with our peers would often be more sustaining and more public than they typically are at present. In addition, this volume addresses the particular challenges confronting clinical faculty members, their responsibilities, and the relationship between faculty members in schools and colleges of education and those in elementary and secondary schools who assume these evolving clinical roles in many instances.

There is one other contextual factor that deserves mention at the outset. The problem is not just how teacher educators can be enabled to prepare teachers better but rather how to prepare teachers for difficult-to-teach in contexts. The two editors of this volume have contributed to the Research About Teacher Education (RATE) studies sponsored by the American Association of Colleges for Teacher Education (AACTE) since this project began eight years ago. In this regard we have become increasingly cognizant of the challenges involved in recruiting and preparing teachers for urban schools. As teacher educators we are also aware, first-hand, of the challenges to professional schools of education in their efforts to redress the problems attached to these urban schools.

Given this context and this view of faculty development, we invited a number of colleagues we respected to a series of meetings to consider what a small network of schools and colleges of education in urban settings might do collectively to address the concerns cited above. In determining a joint agenda, we acknowledged our own professional development as teacher educators as essential, and in some instances as a prerequisite to assisting our colleagues in schools. Several scholars prepared papers for our meetings; their papers serve as the basis for this volume.

In Chapter 2 we discuss the general strategy that the two of us presented to our colleagues for improving the quality of preparation for teachers in urban settings. We propose a multi-faceted professional development agenda to be advanced by leadership cadres of three or four individuals at each school or college of education. The dean or the director of education in these institutions engages with other faculty leaders in a sustained leadership development program designed to do the following:

1. Improve the organizational functioning and professional culture of schools and colleges of education;
2. Initiate systematic faculty development and especially the improvement of teaching in schools and colleges of education;
3. Improve in a major way programs preparing teachers for urban settings; and

4. Develop a clinical faculty that will, in turn, also serve as catalyst for improving urban elementary and secondary schools.

These leadership teams engage in a continuing cycle of intensive professional development. The members allocate part of their time, in turn enabling their colleagues' professional development and the restructuring of programs for preparing urban teachers. In this chapter, we discuss the rationale for these leadership cadres and outline the four types of leadership preparation provided. We make explicit the distinctive properties of a network as we have defined it.

We outline for the reader how this network relates to the leadership development activities. We present a conception of job-embedded professional development. Professional development activities are integrated into the professors' ongoing responsibilities, and often are distinguishable from those responsibilities only by intent and later analysis of them. The orientation to professional development emphasizes inquiry into our individual and collective practice. So that such activity may be fostered and sustained, changes in both institutional ethos and cultural norms as well as in individual values and beliefs will be necessary in many instances. Hence, we also discuss how the leadership teams and the resources of the network contribute to institutional capacity and focus on culture, climate, and organizational functioning to enable the desired professional development.

In Chapter 3, Robert Menges draws on his wealth of experience in faculty development generally to help establish a basis for the development of teacher educators. He draws upon his affiliation with the Center for the Teaching Professions at Northwestern University and the National Center for Research to Improve Postsecondary Teaching and Learning at Penn State. Once again, as his chapter title connotes, a major theme is the promotion of inquiry into one's own teaching. Menges begins his chapter by reviewing the literature on studies of college teaching. He examines what has been learned from this literature and provides specific strategies for moving students from *grade-oriented* to *learning-oriented* behaviors. In order to help conceptualize how faculty development might proceed in these respects, he specifies a limited number of theoretical perspectives that can guide inquiry into our teaching abilities and foster the further development of those abilities. These perspectives derive from the social, cognitive, and motivational literatures.

Menges next reviews the literature, as sparse and uneven as this is, on professional development activities designed to improve teaching in higher education, including such innovative undertakings as cognitive apprenticeships. He points out the paucity of research and theory undergirding many of these activities and provides suggestions to rectify this. Menges suggests looking to role and status concepts from sociology, information-processing approaches from the cognitive sciences, attribution concepts from motivational theory, and what we have learned about students in higher education from multiple developmental theories.

He also briefly reviews common support mechanisms for aiding faculty development. He especially argues for self-initiated investigations of pedagogical issues and problems. Inquiry into personal theories of teaching is one form of professional development that he illustrates. Menges emphasizes a feedback-seeking framework strongly consonant with constructivist principles of teaching and learning. He concludes his chapter by providing illustrative scenarios of inquiry activities that exemplify such a model.

The author of Chapter 4 is Bill McDiarmid, co-director of the National Center for Research on Teacher Learning. Dr. McDiarmid has a history of scholarship into teaching in higher education. He is especially interested in faculty members' understandings of subject matter and in the subsequent forms of teaching and learning that occur as a result of differences in understanding this subject matter. McDiarmid focuses on the arts and sciences as preparation for teaching, but, as with Menges, there are obvious implications for all teacher educators. He examines the problems inherent in the arts and sciences and discusses how such problems might be overcome.

After responding to Bill's original draft chapter, we asked him to incorporate a few suggestions for faculty development and faculty instruction as a result of his review of the literature in this area. His response in personal correspondence to us captures a major concern that he raises in his chapter:

In trying to lay out some of the implications of the research I reviewed, I found that the most salient issue was not specific changes in approaches to teaching but rather the changes necessary in values. So rather than specify and elaborate on recommendations for practice, I analyze the impediments to change. I sincerely believe that university faculty who put student learning and understanding center stage find ways to teach that lead to better opportunities to learn. Useful and thoughtful suggestions for better college teaching—premised on connected, meaningful learning—have been around for years. These suggestions have fallen on deaf ears.

McDiarmid reminds us that much of the education of prospective teachers occurs with members of the arts and sciences faculty; these faculty members commonly call for reforms of precollegiate teaching but remain remarkably uncritical of their own work. On the other hand, people who have observed in the arts and sciences classes, such as Boyer (1987), are sharply critical of this work. The receptive accrual model of teaching is all too common in these classrooms; doubtless it is one of the primary reasons why a recent study of elementary and secondary teachers (Cohen, Peterson, Wilson, & Ball, 1990) found that they lacked "connected and conceptual" understanding of the subject matter they were expected to teach.

McDiarmid begins his chapter with a review of studies of teaching in higher education. He contrasts the stable practices found there over time with the vast changes that have occurred in information and in how information has come to be transmitted during this century. Next he advances several arguments to underscore teachers' need to learn about the subjects they teach. He provides multiple illustrations of how teachers communicate, not only consciously but also unconsciously and as a matter of course, their understanding of the subjects they teach.

McDiarmid emphasizes studies that examine how undergraduates learn; this subject matter in turn demands that we give attention to the opportunities for learning that these students encounter. Although a substantial body of research on college teaching exists, some of which Menges reviews in Chapter 3, investigations of students' understandings are far fewer. McDiarmid draws our attention to these studies including those undertaken in physics, chemistry, mathematics, writing and literature, and history. He underscores the importance of looking at students' learning by quoting Arons (1990):

Deficiencies in assimilation and understanding of the concepts remain concealed from us physics teachers partly because of our own wishful thinking regarding the lucidity of our presentations and partly because conventional homework problems and test questions do not reveal the true state of student thinking and comprehension. It is tempting to believe that adequate performance on conventional end-of-chapter problems indicates understanding, but, in fact, it does not. (p. 38)

McDiarmid's review of this small but growing body of literature complements and contrasts with Menges's chapter, which focuses on general pedagogical tactics. McDiarmid's focus is subject-specific; it emphasizes in-depth qualitative studies that can mine a complex phenomenon such as the understandings with which students enter and leave the classroom.

McDiarmid concludes by examining the implications of this research for practice. Although he suggests multiple directions, they are anchored in the personal note to us that we quoted earlier. His recommendations support the strategy that the two of us set forth in Chapter 2, for confronting cultural norms and organizational practices that distract faculty members from attending more closely to students' ideas and understandings.

The broad strategy for faculty development is concerned with overall program improvement as well as individual instructional enhancement. In Chapter 2, we draw attention to several factors that require attention if we are to achieve more laboratory oriented and clinically oriented teacher preparation. In Chapter 5, Kay Merseth enlarges on a laboratory-oriented program. She examines three evolving instructional technologies—microteaching and simulations, hypermedia, and cases—and their particular relevance to different conceptual orientations that can support and guide coherent programs of teacher preparation. As director of the Roderick MacDougall Case Project at the Harvard Graduate School of Education, Merseth has first-hand experience especially in developing and using instructional cases.

Following on the divergent perspectives presented in Chapters 3 and 4, Merseth acknowledges that prospective teachers need to acquire both principles and techniques that they can adapt to a variety of contexts. She argues that "thinking like a teacher" also demands creating one's own knowledge in the face of uncertain and often unanticipated and ambiguous situations. Merseth reminds us, however, that deep differences exist in terms of how teaching is viewed. For example, learning to teach can be viewed primarily as academic, practical, or technical. Employing as an analogue the work of a weaver, she demonstrates how the "warp" of different conceptual orientations undergirding programs provides firm threads, across which the "woof," consisting of thoughtfully selected instructional methodologies, is woven to develop rich patterns of understanding about teaching and learning by prospective teachers.

Merseth elaborates on five different conceptual orientations in order to prompt us to think about the how of educating teachers; we view this topic as especially suited for faculty development activities. These five conceptual bases for programs of teacher preparation are the academic, the technical, the practical, the personal/developmental, and the social/critical. In her provocative analysis of the best fit between technologies and conceptual underpinnings, Merseth reveals how microteaching and computer-assisted simulations are particularly consistent with technical skill development and hypermedia designs with a practical orientation. One use of cases from her perspective is to assist professionals in "using judgment, analysis, and strategic action to untie the 'knots' of teaching." Merseth illustrates how cases encourage the development of multiple perspectives and interpretations of a situation; such endeavors especially help teachers to be sensitive and responsive to our multicultural society.

Merseth's chapter reviews the multiple purposes that have been addressed by pioneers in the case method in education, such as the writing of personal cases to enable self-understanding or the enhancement of a critical perspective. She concludes by examining the implications for faculty development that emerge when the various orientations intersect with the different methodologies. In this regard she calls for rethinking and redesigning how teacher preparation programs historically have been conceived.

As we set forth an inclusive faculty development agenda, a priority was the definition, development, and further preparation of *clinical* faculty members, including both those in schools and colleges of education and experienced teachers in elementary and secondary schools who work primarily in the classroom. A major endeavor of clinicians working with prospective teachers is to develop in these novice teachers the ability to reason soundly about teaching and learning, to justify decisions about teaching with data from multiple sources, and to ensure that their intentions are principled. For this reason we asked Victor Rentel, one of the few scholars who have attempted to enhance teachers' practical reasoning, to review the literature on this topic. We asked him to examine implications for faculty development, and especially for faculty members who work in the classroom. In

Chapter 6, Rentel emphasizes why this particular intellectual perspective is present not only at the core of effective teaching, but also in learning to teach:

> Constructing sound rationales for teaching—the ability to explain action on the basis of *warranted* belief, sound evidence, and adequate backing (Fenstermacher, 1986; Green, 1971, 1976) leads to improved pupil reading levels associated with the Reading Recovery™ program (Pinnell, Fried, & Estice, 1990).

Preparing teachers for the highly acclaimed Reading Recovery™ Program served as the context for Rentel's research into teachers' reasoning. He first provides a definition of teachers' reasoning by contrasting it with formal conditional reasoning and underscoring the abstract and pragmatic rules of inference that teachers use in relation to particular goals, contexts, and relationships. He illustrates how various disciplines over time have constructed their own distinctive forms of practical reasoning; in this vein he reviews studies of such reasoning in clinical medicine and in international affairs.

Rentel then examines studies of teachers' reasoning undertaken before, during, and after teaching episodes. Thus in his review he examines how pedagogical reasoning occurs in the complex and dynamic contexts in which teachers teach as well as how it occurs during planning for teaching. Formal written plans, according to Rentel, appear to be a subset of more comprehensive images of teaching, and serve as *scripts* for further activity. Differences in this regard between more expert and experienced teachers and novice teachers can be especially informative to teacher educators with implications for their own professional development.

Again, the central consideration in this chapter is how teachers learn to engage effectively in practical or pedagogical reasoning as central to their clinical development. To address this point, Rentel reviews studies of training students to understand and employ conditional reasoning for different types of formal reasoning, such as in psychology, law, and medicine. He then reviews the research he undertook with Pinnell (Rentel & Pinnell, 1989) in attempting to promote pedagogical reasoning in teachers. This work resulted in a validation of some of Shulman's (1987) categories of pedagogical content knowledge and also in the delineation of additional categories. This research reveals that the premises employed by teachers change over time: examination of means–ends relationships increases and the focus on the teachers' responsibilities is stronger.

Rentel, as McDiarmid stressed in his chapter, emphasizes the powerful mediating influence of subject matter and underscores the need for deep understanding of subject matter in learning to reason about teaching and to represent subject matter in pedagogically effective ways.

Obviously we have some way to go in helping teachers improve the quality of their reasoning about teaching. Thus, Rentel, on the basis of his own research and his review of reasoning across a number of fields, concludes his chapter with an examination of implications for changes in teacher education and hence teacher educators. Like Merseth, he calls for clinical experiences carefully articulated with case analysis, wherein students can control and study situational variables at their own pace. In this context, students and faculty members (both clinicians and others) can grapple with the problems, dilemmas, action premises, and hypotheses embedded in cases. Rentel concludes, as do others in this volume, that those aspects of teaching wherein teachers "construct and reconstruct their thoughts in conformity with the teaching process and context" are an argument for preservice programs analogous to medical internships and residencies. Surely they call for a larger and more complex role for clinical faculty members than typically is found today.

In Chapter 7, Catherine Cornbleth and Jeanne Ellsworth take a broader view of the issues associated with clinical preparation than does Rentel. They examine a variety of issues and problems attached to the concept of a clinical faculty and to the type of professional development that seems appropriate to realizing this concept more fully than at present. On the basis of their work at the Buffalo Research Institute on Education for Teaching (BRIET) and their familiarity with a number of other clinical faculty programs evolving across the country, Cornbleth and Ellsworth are especially well qualified to address these problems. They define clinical faculty members as those:

> whose primary university teacher education responsibilities are other than serving as a cooperating teacher or supervising preservice teachers (or simply teaching a single course without further involvement in the teacher education program), and who hold a university faculty title, receive remuneration, and/or receive other university benefits such as a parking permit, library privileges, or office space.

Their chapter has a threefold purpose: (a) to examine how clinical faculty members might contribute to the improvement of teacher education; (b) to explore the implications of a clinical faculty in terms of role relationships with academic faculty members, and what this implies for faculty development; and (c) to consider the impact of a clinical faculty on teachers' broader professional lives and careers.

In order to help explain the move toward clinical faculties today, the authors examine a variety of current factors that encourage this idea and provide a brief historical overview of clinical faculty initiatives. In their analysis of contemporary factors that provide impetus for the development of clinical faculties, they examine underlying assumptions about this phenomenon. These range from the need to upgrade field experiences by improving the teachers in schools who work with prospective teachers to fully engaging outstanding teachers in a redefinition of initial teacher preparation; the latter was the authors' intent at SUNY Buffalo. Their review of several contemporary programs containing clinical faculty initiatives and of the differences and similarities among these programs are helpful in understanding this re-emerging phenomenon. The authors examine the implications of the development of a clinical faculty for professional development, both for the clinical faculty and for those who work with the clinical faculty.

The historical perspective provided by Cornbleth and Ellsworth is also helpful because prior reform efforts left a residue that affects contemporary perspectives. Bolster (1967) provides particular insight in his account of his experience as Harvard University's first clinical professor, with a dual assignment at Harvard and at Newton High School in the mid-1960s. Bolster addressed what appears to be an unresolved problem in many current clinical faculty initiatives:

> Our problem is not that the worlds of the university and the school cannot be joined, but rather that by positing the existing institutional arrangements for the clinical training of teachers we have necessarily limited the potential effectiveness of the clinical professorship by insisting that it be created by means of minor *ad hoc* modifications of the existing structure . . . (1967, p. 96)

Cornbleth and Ellsworth conclude by analyzing some of the tensions that are present in efforts to develop clinical faculties, including such problems as role overlap or lack thereof, role relationships, and issues of autonomy, power, and authority. Again, one can derive implications for the professional development of both clinical and nonclinical faculty members. These authors remind us that the challenge in developing a clinical faculty should not be underestimated. Elementary and secondary teachers who enter these new roles and relationships from a "lower status" organization and without appropriate support can be very much at a structural disadvantage. Transformational change is probably necessary if these initiatives are to succeed, as outlined in the strategy for change presented in Chapter 2 and repeated as a theme throughout the volume.

REFERENCES

Arons, A. B. (1990). *A guide to introductory physics teaching.* New York: Wiley.

Bolster, A. S., Jr. (1967). The clinical professorship: An institutional view. In W. R. Hazard (Ed.), *The clinical professorship in teacher education* (p. 96). Evanston, IL: Northwestern University Press.

Boyer, E. (1987). *College: The undergraduate experience in America.* New York: Harper & Row.

Cohen, D. K., Peterson, P. L., Wilson, S., & Ball, D. (1990). *Effects of state-level reform of elementary school mathematics curriculum on classroom practice* (Research Report 90–14). Washington, DC: National Center for Research on Teacher Education.

Fenstermacher, G. (1986). Philosophy of research on teaching: Three aspects. In M. Wittrock (Ed.), *Handbook of research on teaching* (3rd ed., pp. 37–49). New York: Macmillan.

Goodlad, J. I. (1990). *Teachers for our nation's schools.* San Francisco, CA: Jossey-Bass.

Green, T. (1971). *The activities of teaching.* New York: McGraw-Hill.

Green, T. (1976). Teacher competence as practical rationality. *Educational Theory, 26,* 249–258.

Holmes Group, The (1990). *Tomorrow's schools: Principles for the design of professional development schools.* East Lansing, MI: Author.

Howey, K. R. (1993). *Recent reform and restructuring initiatives in elementary and secondary schools: Implications for preservice teacher education.* Unpublished manuscript, The Ohio State University, Columbus.

Pinnell, G. S., Fried, M. D., & Estice, R. M. (1990). Reading Recovery™: Learning how to make a difference. *The Reading Teacher, 43*(4), 282–295.

RATE (Research About Teacher Education). (1988). *Teaching teachers: Facts & figures II.* Washington, DC: American Association of Colleges for Teacher Education.

Rentel, V., & Pinnell, G. (1989). *Stake that claim: The content of pedagogical reasoning.* Paper presented at the National Reading Conference, Austin, TX.

Shulman, L. (1987). Knowledge and teaching: Foundations of the new reform. *Harvard Educational Review, 57,* 1–22.

2

LEADERSHIP TEAMS AND NETWORKING: A STRATEGY FOR FACULTY DEVELOPMENT

KENNETH R. HOWEY

The Ohio State University

In this chapter I outline a strategy for a comprehensive approach to professional development for teacher educators. Faculty development has been a patchwork, haphazard enterprise in higher education generally, as Menges illustrates in Chapter 3. It has been similarly limited in teacher education, even though there is a considerable need here for faculty development. As was stated in the introduction, many problems are revealed by even a cursory examination of how well faculty members fulfill the historical triad of professional responsibilities—teaching, research, and service. This is not to say that many teacher educators have not excelled in each domain; surely they have. Others have not, however. I would simply assert that there is room for considerable growth. Multiple factors explain why the abilities and endeavors of many teacher educators are less than they should be, but lack of attention to our continuing professional development is a major cause.

This chapter proceeds as follows. First, I present slices of reality in the lives of teacher educators, into which I believe professional development must be integrated more fully than at present. The variety of issues and problems that affect teacher educators have been addressed less effectively than they might have been in many situations in the past, and the future presents even greater challenges. Thus, I also briefly review future projections pertaining to teacher preparation and their implications for faculty development. After this contextual overview I outline a strategy for developing increased institutional capacity and alleviating problems in the workplaces of teacher education professors so that professional development might be facilitated. The particular strategy that I present calls for the development of leadership cadres with a four-fold focus. Leadership teams of faculty members and administrators from schools and colleges of education engage in intensive leadership development activities, which attend in interrelated fashion to: (a) organizational renewal; (b) a broad-based conception of faculty development; (c) program redesign, as well as research and evaluation into these programs; and (d) the attachment of a clinical faculty to the schools and colleges of education engaged in testing this strategy.

This leadership development is projected in the context of a small network of urban schools and colleges of education. Thus, the unique elements of a network that can contribute to faculty development are also articulated in this chapter. I emphasize the urban mission because we must better prepare teachers who can teach all children effectively, especially those who live in poverty.

Concomitant with the development of leadership cadres for the schools and colleges of education is the development of clinical faculty members in urban elementary and secondary partnership schools. These clinical faculty members eventually will assume leadership responsibilities in their schools parallel to those undertaken by the leadership teams in the cooperating schools and colleges of education.

The conception of faculty development presented here is deeply rooted in the ongoing daily activities of teacher educators, and is characterized by continuing, critical inquiry.

SLICES OF THE TEACHER EDUCATOR'S LIFE: THE CONTEXT FOR PROFESSIONAL DEVELOPMENT

Let me begin here on a personal note. I believe that in many respects I am a good teacher. Over time I have accumulated some evidence of this fact. Yet I would readily admit that I still have a great deal to learn about teaching; surely there are many ways in which I could improve my instruction. In writing this chapter and reflecting on my teaching and my efforts to improve my teaching, I recalled a number of factors. For example, except in isolated instances concerning promotion and tenure, I have never systematically observed another professor in the institutions in which I have taught. In my field studies I have had the opportunity to observe a fair number of professors teaching in other institutions, but again, not on a sustained basis or with the explicit intent to improve my teaching. Nor have I ever been observed by a colleague (again, with one exception, during the promotion process); much less have I engaged in any systematic discourse with a colleague about a specific lesson I have taught. On a number of occasions and in a variety of settings I have discussed teaching generally with associates. Although I have engaged my students in various forms of peer and microteaching and in recording their teaching episodes in elementary and secondary schools, I have not carefully examined my own teaching as represented on videotape.

I have taught in a considerable variety of classrooms, and at times have teamed with elementary and secondary teachers. Occasionally I have taught elementary and secondary pupils. More typically, however, my school-based instructional activities are intended for elementary and secondary teachers and take place after these teachers have taught all day. This teaching has occurred in various settings ranging from lunchrooms and auditoriums to what appeared to be large closets. Often I bring a variety of resources and materials, but on some occasions I have been severely constrained by the setting and the lack of resources. I have worked with a group of teachers over an entire year. At times I am convinced that I have begun to make inroads into mutually derived goals with respect to improving teaching and learning for young people. However, the actual effect of my efforts in these teachers' classrooms is quite unclear in the final analysis. Perhaps their true thoughts can be put into perspective with an anecdote. Recently when my wife and colleague, Nancy Zimpher, and I were shopping for groceries, we were startled by the exclamation "There she is, there she is! That's the professor I've been telling you about!" The speaker was pointing toward Nancy and elbowing her husband, but before we could claim any satisfaction with this vocal and enthusiastic acknowledgment, she went on: "She's that professor with those crazy nylons that I've been telling you about."

As I recalled many advising activities, my perception was that I am patient, reasonably committed to my students, and willing to devote the time necessary to work through problems, whether monitoring a program of studies for the forthcoming quarter for a beginning student or clarifying once again the conceptual basis for a doctoral thesis. Yet as I thought about this aspect of my activities, it was clear that I have never systematically attempted to explore how my relationships with students outside class could be enhanced in any way. I have not sought my students' reactions, in any formal or regular way, to the nature and effects of my advising. I can recall occasions on which I worked with cohorts of prospective teachers over periods of one to two years. I worked with one cohort that met regularly with me and with a doctoral student from counseling psychology who helped me and the cohort to improve our interpersonal abilities. This was the only incident that I could recall, however, in which my interaction with a group of students was examined systematically.

I recalled that most time committed to scholarly efforts had been spent on organizing and sharing the results of prior inquiry; that is, in writing. I found that the time I devoted to this, usually alone, was disproportionate to the time I spent on what was to be studied and how best to study it, especially in thoughtful discussion with colleagues. On different occasions I have devoted sustained periods of time to evolve joint research and development with colleagues across academic units. These have proved to be considerable challenges and have not lasted long. In at least two projects, I have attempted to work with teachers in schools on action research projects. My ruminations about these latter endeavors led me to conclude that I have much to learn in these areas. Two of my most lasting recollections of these efforts are that they required a great deal of time and that often, despite my attempts to achieve as much parity as possible in these relationships, they took on the tenor of graduate advising. Especially vivid are the recollections of the time required merely to find a parking place on returning to campus and of my mixed feelings toward my colleagues, who were conducting their instruction and scholarship more comfortably on the campus.

As a teacher educator, I suspect that I am probably fairly representative as to the time and effort I have spent on improving my teaching, advising, and scholarship. I do not doubt that faculty members vary as to the scope and the quality of the effort they devote to these endeavors. Surely many have devoted much more time and effort to improving themselves then I have—others, less. My major point in these personal recollections is that in a role characterized by a multiplicity of demands, my own personal professional development rarely is a primary factor in my many activities. (This is not to deny or underestimate the byproducts of learning associated with several of these activities.) In summary, I have not been especially thoughtful or structured in my own growth and no one else has directed me in this respect.

CONTEXTUAL DIFFERENCES NEED TO BE ATTENDED TO

I am aware that major differences also exist within and among institutions in terms of expectations for faculty members, as well as among individuals within institutions. For example, some people, especially in major research institutions, identify themselves strongly with an external network and spend considerable time away from the institution. Clark (1985) accordingly characterizes the view of select professors in higher education as follows:

> This high cosmopolitanism is even found in the upper reaches of the not-so-rich humanities, where a conference on structuralism one week in New York for the academic jet-set might be followed by a conference on poststructuralism the following week in Stockholm or Bellagio—a hectic pace hilariously depicted by David Lodge in his recent book *Small World.* (p. 39)

Although such instances are not common in teacher education, major research universities vary considerably as to the spectrum of national and international arenas in which teacher educators engage. Teaching loads range from one to three courses per term; supervising responsibilities typically are assumed by doctoral students or adjunct appointees. In addition, faculty members in these institutions are engaged in an array of activities including serving on advisory boards of major research and development projects, reviewing manuscripts, serving as external reviewers to other institutions, critiquing research proposals submitted to agencies, serving on committees for major professional associations, and assuming key roles in the governance of their colleges and universities. This is to say that widely respected faculty members have opportunities and responsibilities which many other teacher educators do not. In summary, instructional loads vary within these institutions, and the spectrum and the locus of faculty activities are broad and diverse.

Clark (1985) also provides a characterization, acknowledged as stereotypic, of the state or regional college professor:

> We do not need to stray very far from the leading universities before teaching becomes a true "load," jumping to twelve hours a week and leaving little or no time for research. In the public comprehensive colleges, teaching is undergraduate centered, with perhaps some master's level instruction but not a Ph.D. student in sight. Pay is less than in the universities, and professors know they are in second- and third-level institutions, ones of "some status" in the institutional hierarchy.
>
> Generally, the state college of today was a teachers college in the recent past and is now somewhere midstream between that blighted shore and the promised land of university status. The midstream location may be nigh-permanent, however, since existing universities have already pre-empted the high ground on the far shore and state plans insist that the newcomers stay out of Ph.D. programs and away from major research. Some respondents referred to an inchoate institutional character—"the place has not come to terms with itself"—that confuses their own professional culture. (pp. 39–40)

I have encountered such institutions myself in studying the types of institutions that prepare teachers. In recent case studies, the chairperson of one teacher education faculty told me, with some pride, how he oriented new faculty members:

> I tell them [new faculty members] if you come here you're going to work. These are all people who have recently been in college and in Ph.D. programs and typically in a large university where their major professors have two hours of class a week. And I tell them, look, you're going to be here at 7:30 or 8:00 every morning and you're not going to leave until 4:30 or 5:00. You're going to be flooded with students all day long. If you're not supervising, you're going to have students in your office, so you're not going to be able to do any extended preparation during the day. You're not going to be able to check any papers during this time. If you think you're going to do research, you're going to have to do that on Saturdays and Sundays. I tell them this is the kind of institution we are. Don't come here if you think you're going to have the kind of life

you've seen in a large university because you may not even have
time to eat dinner some days. (Howey & Zimpher, 1989, p. 107)

From my perspective, such a portrayal often contains too
much truth. This slice-of-life introduction is intended to portray
in a firsthand and (I hope) graphic fashion the context for more
thoughtfully conceived professional development endeavors than
exist at present. Whatever the mission and size of the institution,
it is likely, especially if it's a publicly supported institution, that
there are fiscal constraints to achieving these endeavors. Such
problems have multiple effects. Schuster and Bowen (1985), for
example, depicted higher education generally as follows, and conditions have worsened since that time:

> Whereas changes in compensation are easily measurable, changes
> in the work environment are not. Nonetheless, deterioration in the
> faculty's working conditions is plainly evident, from diminishing
> clerical support to increasingly obsolete instrumentation, from neg-
> ligible travel budgets to poorly prepared students. And, for many
> faculty members—few of whom expected to acquire great wealth in
> academic life—the erosion of conditions in the workplace has been
> particularly galling. (p. 15)

The author of this chapter is a member of the research team
that annually collects the Research About Teacher Education
(RATE) data. In 1991, in a sample stratified by type of institution, the RATE study examined the context and conditions in
which preservice education is conducted in the United States. A
litany of concerns similar to those cited above was reported by
people primarily involved in preparing teachers. I could summarize their sentiments as having to do more in less time with fewer
resources and with less to say about it.

Although the perceptions of these faculty members and administrators in the RATE study revealed a great many challenges,
many respondents reported that there existed the capacity to
move forward, although not easily and certainly not in all
instances. Institutional capacity generally was summarized as
follows:

> Across strata, almost sixty percent of the faculty (59.4%) rated
> their general institutional capacity as good or excellent. There are
> major differences by institutional type, however. Slightly more than
> seventy percent (71.7%) of those in the smaller bachelor's institu-
> tions rated their institutional capacity good while only forty-eight
> percent of those in the master's institutions did similarly; doctoral

institutions were in the middle (60.2%). However, overall almost a
third of the respondents rated their capacity for change as three
on a five point scale, or C on an A through E scale, and ten percent viewed institutional capacity as only marginal. (RATE, 1992,
pp. 8–9)

FUTURE DIRECTIONS FOR PROFESSIONAL SCHOOLS OF EDUCATION

I hope that the relatively large proportion of respondents who
reported a good or fair capacity for change reflects the reality of
their energies and intentions. It is not only a confluence of factors, internal and external, which makes the job of many teacher
educators difficult, it is also charting the directions in which
teacher education must move so that schools of education will
become more fully professional and will prove themselves able to
assist with the problems confronting elementary and secondary
schools. Accordingly a number of ambitious agendas have been
established for those in teacher education. The Holmes Group
(Sykes, Judge, & Devaney, 1992) is notable for its vision for
schools and colleges of education. Howey (1992) identified eight
general goals toward which progress must be made if professional schools of education are to thrive in the immediate future.
He argued that professional schools of education must do the following:

1. Demonstrate that they can contribute in a more direct
    and more viable manner to resolving problems and mak-
    ing improvements in K-12 schools, especially schools in
    poor neighborhoods;

2. Develop a clinical faculty that can guide novice teachers
    with strategies more potent than are typically employed,
    and that are consistent with the best of contemporary
    understanding about learning to teach;

3. Further develop a corpus of scientific findings to guide
    how one learns to teach and to conduct much of that
    scholarship in schools and in collaboration with teach-
    ers and school administrators;

4. Demonstrate that pedagogical content knowledge as well
    as knowledge of content exists in programs of teacher
    preparation;

5. As a corollary, demonstrate that campus-based teacher
    education has a laboratory and a clinical capacity
    beyond that of the lecture hall;

6. Demonstrate that entry-level teachers can acquire the
    understandings, abilities, and dispositions to work with
    the growing plurality of pupils in many U.S. schools. (In
    addition, these pressure points combine to emphasize
    that the professional "life space" in preservice teacher
    education is inadequate at this time.) Therefore, those
    concerned with initial teacher education also must

7. Demonstrate that initial teacher education can continue
    in a substantive and structured manner into the entry
    year of teaching; and, finally, can

8. Achieve more coherent, more closely interrelated, and
    more potent programs of teacher preparation on campus
    as well as in schools. (1992, p. 4)

These challenges appear to be—and are—somewhat overwhelming. Bold strategies are needed if we are to achieve goals
such as those enumerated above. It is clear, as I attempted to
illustrate at the outset, that we cannot make an already difficult
endeavor even more difficult in efforts to enable teacher educators and to improve the education of beginning teachers. It would
seem, however, that the odds favor doing just that.

PRINCIPLES GUIDING PROFESSIONAL DEVELOPMENT

I embrace certain principles with regard to professional development for teacher educators. These undergird the strategy that I
outline in the remainder of this chapter. First, in order not to
make a difficult job even more difficult, the professional development of teacher educators must be embedded and integrated
deeply in their ongoing activities. To an outsider, this type of professional development often would be discernible from ordinary
activities only with an understanding of the purposeful, critical
attention given to the nature and effects of these activities.

Second, we must develop an institutional capacity that simply
does not exist in many places, despite the limited optimism
reported in the RATE data. Ways of doing things in these schools
and colleges of education must change so that faculty members
can be enabled in a sustaining and pervasive manner. Our strat-

egy calls for a redirection of effort by key persons on these faculties to address these needed changes and to assist their colleagues more directly. Our proposal hinges on the ability to develop a cadre of leaders with responsibilities for working with their colleagues on a set of interrelated functions.

Third, in what is (or at least should be) a community of scholars, the emphasis in much of this professional development must be on broadening our conception of scholarship, as Boyer (1990) aptly illustrated.

Fourth, professional development itself also must be defined in robust and manifold terms rather than in a narrow and technical sense. It must focus on our growth as role models and mentors, as curriculum designers and developers, as teachers and advisors, as diagnosticians and clinicians, especially with regard to our students and their development over time, as well as on our roles as scholars and pedagogues.

Fifth and finally, a critical perspective must be central to these activities; our efforts must be focused on redressing conditions in this society that foster a growing underclass, conditions that cannot be excused, and conditions that to a large degree can eventually be overcome only by a better education for all children.

Ginsburg (1988) provides an excellent example when he asks what types of issues and concerns a teacher educator devoted to critical paraxis would bring to the recommendations offered in various recent reform reports. He illustrates this critical perspective as follows:

> We should probe concerning how the social class, gender and racial composition of teacher education students, university instructors, and "professional" or "lead" teachers would change if these proposals were implemented. In Texas, for instance, the implementation of standardized testing as a criterion for entry into and exit from teacher education programs has had the effect of screening-out a higher proportion of Black and Hispanic than White candidates, and has threatened the continued existence of some programs that attract a predominantly "minority" population. Similar trends of decreased racial minority entry into teaching have been noted for the US more generally. We know, furthermore, that the class and racial composition of research universities is different from other institutions of higher education and graduate programs tend to be more masculinized than undergraduate programs. Will the "professional" or "lead" teacher category contain a higher proportion of White, male, relatively economically advantaged educators compared to instructors? (p. 205)

I turn now to a professional development strategy based on the five principles stated above. This strategy is tied to a concept of leadership development embedded in and supported by a small urban network. The focus is on the urban context for a number of reasons; one reason is that only 15 percent of our graduating students state a preference for teaching in urban areas, where the challenges and problems in the education of youth are often the greatest (RATE, 1989).

THE URBAN NETWORK: A STRATEGY FOR SYSTEMIC CHANGE

The civic responsibility of universities in many cities have not been fulfilled, according to Harkavy and Puckett (1991):

> In the last decade of the 20th century, it is clear that America's urban universities no longer can afford to ignore the plight of their cities and local neighborhoods. For 75 years, urban universities have functioned largely as if they were in, but not of, the city. They have done so to the detriment of themselves and the nation. Contributing precious little to the amelioration of social conditions that have steadily eroded the quality of urban life, engaging in long standing policies of neglect and halfhearted engagement, and exacerbating urban deterioration through narrow, shortsighted strategies of campus development, urban universities have been, to put it mildly, poor neighbors. (p. 8)

Urban schools and colleges of education have a particular obligation to the quality of urban life. It is a firsthand, manifold commitment to the quality of education for youth in these cities. The quality of education provided to these young people, especially to the growing underclass in this country, is central to the survival of our cities and to the well-being of our larger society. The moral and civic responsibility of persons in schools and colleges of education is derived from the following premises:

1. The very nature of our social fabric, our quality of living, and our sense of social justice are tied inextricably to the character and quality of our elementary and secondary schools, and especially to the quality of public schools in our major urban areas.
2. The quality of these schools ultimately hinges on the quality and dedication of teachers in these schools and

on the nature and quality of the culture and conditions in which teaching and learning occur.

3. The quality of teachers and of the teaching that occurs in these schools is related directly to the quality of their preparation as teachers.

4. The nature of how teachers are (or at least should be) prepared also speaks directly to the culture that evolves in elementary and secondary schools and, to some degree, to the conditions that we created in which teaching and learning occur.

5. Teacher preparation must be anchored deeply in the intellectual foundations of the university and in professional schools and colleges of education. At the same time it must be tied directly and continuously to the realities and problems of elementary and secondary schools.

6. Finally, this integrated notion of teacher education calls for an authentic partnership between persons in schools and colleges of education and persons in elementary and secondary schools. Those of us in schools and colleges of education cannot advocate major changes in elementary and secondary schools from the lecture hall or in a journal article. We have a concomitant responsibility to exemplify a more diverse and more powerful array of instructional methodologies on campus, while working closely with our partners in specific urban elementary and secondary schools with concentrated faculty resources and for sustained periods.

So that we can achieve these goals and practice what we preach, major systemic changes are needed in schools and colleges of education. As Deal and Chatman (1989) cautioned, deep structures and practices cannot be reformed; they must be transformed. To transform an organization "is to alter its fundamental character or identity." Examples of such change are obviously rare. Yet a small network of institutions preparing teachers in the United States and Canada, which are located in urban areas, have dedicated themselves to such systemic change, with a focus on professional development. These institutions in the Urban Network to Improve Teacher Education (UNITE) have excellent reputations, but their faculties acknowledge that if they are to contribute significantly to the quality of schooling in cities, they have a long way to go.

The goal of this network is to make possible the following in a sustained and interrelated manner: (a) enlarging the capacity for change in our schools and colleges of education, (b) enhancing the quality of our instruction, (c) improving the quality of our programs for preparing urban teachers, and (d) enabling our fundamental working relationships with teachers in urban elementary and secondary schools.

The basic element of the strategy for transformational change is the development of leadership teams of three or four key people in each of these institutions who have highly specialized and differentiated, yet complementary, responsibilities. The network of institutions as it is configured will also serve as a powerful catalyst for systemic improvement. Both the leadership team, in terms of the functions it performs, and the network, as I have defined this concept, are strategies for change in higher education, which have been employed only rarely. The proposed network intends to test whether these two strategies combined, over a reasonable length of time, have the power for transformation, that is, the fundamental alteration of structures, norms, and practices that are long-standing, but nonetheless in many ways limit progress in teacher preparation.

THE LEADERSHIP TEAMS: THE WEBBING
OF THE NETWORK

Administrators in higher education, including deans of schools and colleges of education, typically receive little, if any, leadership preparation for the roles they assume. Deans typically have associate deans to report to them in a staff relationship; the latter are responsible for such discrete matters as graduate or undergraduate studies, research, budget, and personnel. In this regard these people could be viewed as a leadership team.

In the present context, the notion of a leadership team includes faculty members and in some instances school personnel who have a major responsibility for restructuring programs and faculty development. Leadership teams within the network are composed of the dean or director and two or three acknowledged faculty leaders, along with a leader from a cooperating urban school or school district. As a group they engage regularly in intensive leadership preparation throughout the life of the project. This leadership preparation draws on the talents of a variety of scholars in the network, who have achieved success in organizational change, faculty development, teacher education, clinical preparation, and urban education. These are also individuals who in many instances have achieved success in some of the most difficult school settings in the United States and Canada. The interactive nature of these leadership teams is illustrated in Figure 2-1, below.

These leadership teams serve as the webbing of the network. They meet regularly, sometimes in intensive development activities and at other times in open-ended discourse and shared problem-solving activities. They also communicate with their counterparts in the other institutions in the network, both via E-mail and in computer conferences. These means also allow them to interact with expert consultants both inside and outside the network. Members of the leadership team visit other sites as well as host visitors to their site.

The leadership development focuses on the four interrelated functions stated at the outset:

1. organizational well-being and organizational capacity for sustained and directed change;
2. faculty professional development, with an initial focus on improved teaching and the evolution of more contemporary instructional contexts, materials, and facilities;
3. redesign of programs preparing teachers for urban settings and the development of designs for more systematic research and evaluation of these programs;
4. selection and preparation of clinical faculty members. (Clinical faculty members are defined here as outstanding classroom teachers who have a partial or limited-time appointment to the college and who assume responsi-

FIGURE 2-1   The Leadership Team: An Interactive Model of Transformational Leadership

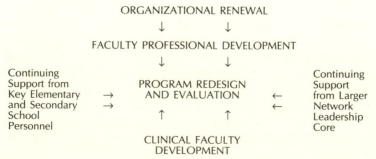

ORGANIZATIONAL RENEWAL

FACULTY PROFESSIONAL DEVELOPMENT

Continuing Support from Key Elementary and Secondary School Personnel   →   PROGRAM REDESIGN AND EVALUATION   ←   Continuing Support from Larger Network Leadership Core

CLINICAL FACULTY DEVELOPMENT

bility for the clinical and/or internship preparation of a number of preservice students.)

Each of these four interrelated functions are undertaken by at least one member of the leadership cadre at each institution. The insights and experience of key teachers and administrators in partnership schools are also drawn upon especially in the latter three functions. Although space limits an extensive elaboration of the nature of the leadership training, I can describe briefly some of the key constructs that guide leadership development in each domain. I also discuss some of the key questions that will guide the leadership development activities. According to the project design, the leadership cadres enable faculty development that is embedded as often as possible in their daily activities. Such development also focuses as often as possible on helping them inquire into various aspects of their practice, with emphasis on matters of social justice and enabling learning by all youth.

LEADERSHIP DEVELOPMENT TOWARD TRANSFORMING THE ORGANIZATION AND CULTURE OF THE SCHOOL OR COLLEGE OF EDUCATION

The leadership opportunities in each domain are shared not only among members of the leadership team, but with others on the faculty as well. Understandably, however, the dean or director has a major responsibility in this, the first domain. Transformational change calls for transformational leadership. Sergiovanni (1990) illustrates aspects of this form of leadership when he contrasts fairly common bureaucratic or transactional leadership with what he defines as moral authority or more transformative leadership.

> In transactional leadership, the leader and the led exchange needs and services in order to accomplish independent objectives. Leaders and followers assume they do not share a common stake in the enterprise and thus must arrive at some kind of agreement. The wants and needs of followers are traded against the wants and needs of the leader: a bargain is struck. Positive reinforcement is exchanged for good work, merit pay for increased performance, promotion for increased persistence, a feeling of belonging for cooperation, and so on. This bargaining process can be viewed metaphorically as a form of, what I have termed, leadership by bartering.

In transformative leadership, by contrast, leaders and followers are united in pursuit of higher-level goals common to both. Both want to become the best . . . eventually, transformative leadership becomes moral because it raises the level of human conduct and ethical aspiration of both the leader and the led. When this occurs, transformative leadership takes the form of leadership by bonding. Here the leader focuses on arousing awareness and consciousness that elevates school goals and purposes to the level of a shared covenant that bonds together leader and follower in a moral commitment. Leadership by bonding responds to such human needs as the desire for purpose, meaning, and significance in what one does. This stage is characterized by cultural and moral leadership. (pp. 31–32)

Sergiovanni's developmental stages of leadership, from bartering to building to bonding, are among several constructs that can be employed in further developing the leadership capacity of deans, directors, and others on the leadership team. In the Urban Network a shared vision of whole-cloth change in our schools and colleges of education is embraced, and it bonds the network. This strategy for change has four dimensions, as articulated above. Changes in these areas are viewed as a precondition to providing major assistance to urban elementary and secondary schools and to enabling learning by all young people—the ultimate goal of the network. Throughout the leadership development activities and the subsequent professional development activities for faculty members, the emphasis will be on critical examination of our own instructional practice as teacher educators and of the conditions of our workplace. Examples of questions that support activities in this domain include the following:

1. How is discourse or (better) a discourse community about teacher education promoted and sustained across departments and divisions and with our colleagues in schools?
2. How is inquiry into how we function, as an organization and as a community, promoted and acknowledged as a legitimate form of inquiry?
3. How are faculty members who are vested heavily in partnership schools supported and rewarded in the institution for the research and development they undertake there?
4. How are "boundary spanners"—people with appointments in our schools and colleges of education as well

as in elementary and secondary schools—entitled, supported, and protected in regard to workload?

5. How might the concept of transformational leadership and its effects be measured over time.

LEADERSHIP DEVELOPMENT FOR THE IMPROVEMENT OF TEACHING AND LEARNING

We have much to learn about instructional practice in teacher preparation as well as in faculty development, which can enable exemplary P-12 teaching. Considerable agreement exists, however, with regard to the general attributes of effective learning, including learning by prospective teachers. The Urban Network hopes to promote teaching and related instructional activities by faculty members that will result in learning that often can be characterized as active, exploratory, often self-regulated, at times group-supported and interdependent, conceptual, and having a problem-solving and problem-posing orientation.

In addition, teaching and learning in programs that prepare teachers must increasingly employ contemporary technologies such as computer conferences, which can accommodate personal schedules, individual rates of learning, and different locations for learning. In this area, the opportunities for growth and development by faculty members are manifold.

In Chapter 5, Kay Merseth discusses new technologies and the extent of their congruence with different orientations to learning to teach. Recently I reviewed the literature on novice teachers' developmental patterns (Howey & Zimpher, 1993). The studies examined make it clear that learning to teach in the realities of elementary and secondary school classrooms is an uneven proposition at best. A sequence of well-conceived laboratory and clinical activities is needed; such activities would precede full-time classroom responsibilities and would allow the novice teacher to understand, incrementally and in a critical manner, the many layers and facets of teaching and learning.

Obviously we have made only limited progress in this respect, but the vision to guide such practice is being articulated increasingly. Howey (1992) argued as follows for a broader vision:

We have a responsibility to exemplify a broader and more powerful range of instructional activities and teaching approaches in the preparation of teachers on campus than witnessed at present. The seeds for the disposition to continuously inquire into one's instruc-

tional practice and to support that practice with principled reasoning and with decisions that are data-based and theoretically
grounded need to be nurtured in pedagogical laboratories, teaching clinics, and through the utilization of instructional cases in a
campus setting. Prospective teachers should, employing various
conceptual lenses, view dozens of hours of video representing both
principles which guide the teaching profession and the pervasive
problems teachers will encounter. Some advances are being made
in this regard (Merseth, 1991). These preservice teachers should be
able to do this in a context in which complex phenomena can be
represented from multiple perspectives, through several media, and
at a time and in a manner conducive to their learning. They should
be able to critically inquire in a setting and at a pace that fosters
such activity. At present, critical examination of instructional practice is generally neither fostered well in the lecture hall nor the
teacher's workplace. It could also be argued that until we can send
larger numbers of teachers into the workplace better disposed
toward critical examination of their practice, the character and culture of the teachers' workplace will not change. (pp. 30–31)

Studies of learning and of learning to teach suggest that we
need contexts in which at least some aspects of complex phenomena such as teaching and learning can be represented in
multiple media and through multiple perspectives. The learner
must be able to regulate the pace and monitor his or her learning, both alone and with others. As Rentel emphasizes so
cogently in this volume, teachers' reasoning—that is, teachers'
decisions that are supported by thoughtful and data-based reasons—are a hallmark of good teachers. The ability to critically
examine one's teaching by employing video playback and by
incorporating the perspectives of students in the class seems not
only to be germane to novice teachers, but also to be a powerful
form of professional development for faculty members in teacher
education. One could envision a developmental sequence of
teaching clinics. Rather than placing novice teachers under the
spotlight in a critical analysis of their own instruction early in
their program, would it not make more sense to allow these preservice students continuously to first observe and then participate with teacher education faculty members, both on campus
and in clinical settings, in the analysis of those faculty members'
teaching?
Faculty members who not only can model various aspects and
dimensions of effective teaching but also can articulate in a vari-

ety of ways why they did what they did in the course of instruction, are needed on campus as well as in schools. This would seem a reasonable starting place in thinking through laboratory and clinical preparation. In a second phase, novice teachers could examine their teaching alone and with other novices. Thus, they could gain further confidence and acquire baseline analytic skills before the third phase, in which they assume broader responsibilities; in this phase their own teaching would be examined with greater scrutiny and sophistication by clinical faculty members.

Methods derived from the many studies with a cognitive science perspective focus on strategies to enable self-directed and self-regulated learning. They are being incorporated slowly but surely into the classrooms of elementary and secondary teachers. These self-directed principles also are relevant to a group because most teaching and learning occurs in groups. Drawing on principles of effective group functioning and cooperative learning, one can examine how a group is responsible for all its members and can enable them to learn. Greater attention to the social and cultural dimensions of teaching and learning must be given in clinical settings with faculty members who can model effectively the powerful social dimensions of learning.

When the focus is on one's instruction and on how learning actually occurs, not only individually but in a group (as McDiarmid emphasizes in Chapter 4), the studies of developmental patterns among college-age students and prospective teachers provide yet another source of data to enhance the professional growth of faculty members. For example, the literature on the psychosocial development and general socialization of students in higher education has hardly been examined in the context of teacher education and learning to teach.

These are only a few examples illustrating how inquiry into aspects of teaching and learning can serve as grist for the further development of faculty members. The possibilities for further inquiry are manifold. I acknowledge the major mediating influence of subject matter and the importance of the situated nature of learning in efforts to improve the instruction of faculty members. Even so, a broad repertoire of general pedagogical understandings, basic instructional tactics, and pedagogical moves is intertwined with, and enriches, pedagogical maneuvers that appear to be particular to the situation. To employ an analogue, every play in basketball involves a complex set of interactions

and, in certain respects, unique interactions and results. Even
so, the action has distinctive parameters, just like those which
occur in distinctive episodes or plays in the classroom. In addition, the many adaptations and improvisations that take place
during each play are rooted in and necessarily enabled by a
broad repertoire of fundamental skills. Athletic skills are practiced over and over and are examined repeatedly on film, often
reduced to minute detail. Good teachers employ the same supportive structure. Methods of questioning, probing, and extending that inculcate active and self-directed learning, creation of a
climate, an ability for dialectic or group interdependence, and
many other essential skills are not so much derived from particular contexts as adapted to those contexts.

On the basis of the numerous individuals I saw teaching in my
case studies, I would argue that some teacher educators lack
even the most basic repertoire of instructional activities. Effective
strategies for involving students in the social construction of
knowledge individually, in dyads, in small groups, in charette
activities, and even in the large group, for example, are uncommon. I observed infrequently strategies that not only highlight
key concepts but also, and more fundamentally, showed how and
what students were thinking in relation to those concepts. I saw
only rarely the representation of major ideas and core concepts
in multiple ways. I believe that developing and refining a repertoire of general tactics for representing subject matter and for
actively engaging students with that subject matter is a reasonable point of departure for instructional improvement. I think
that bringing faculty members together across disciplines can
help us to learn how various aspects and dimensions of teaching can be examined critically. My position is that a balance
must be struck between core and transcending pedagogical
understandings and abilities and those distinctive to a specific
discipline.

In efforts to improve our own teaching, I reiterate that critical
inquiry into practice is essential. Thus, I report here some of the
questions that were generated in meetings with members of the
network.

1. What does teaching for conceptual understanding
    involve? What are important general pedagogical strate-
    gies that transcend subject matter and discipline and
    that enable conceptual learning?

2. What characterizes intellectual discourse in an instruc-
    tional setting in higher education (as opposed to recep-
    tive-accrual learning)? What are its purposes and effects
    and how can these be measured?

3. What activities and abilities enable active, self-moni-
    tored, and self-motivated learning for adults (prospective
    teachers) both as individuals and in groups?

4. What developmental similarities and differences among
    adult learners mediate performance?

5. What social and cultural dimensions of college class-
    room setting and program context mediate teaching and
    learning?

6. In what ways can teacher educators and, for that mat-
    ter, the general professoriate inquire into their own
    teaching and attendant learning, especially while engag-
    ing their students in this process?

A MULTIFACETED CONCEPTION
OF PROFESSIONAL DEVELOPMENT

As the remaining chapters in this book suggest, this emphasis
on improved teaching will be the primary but hardly the only
focus in faculty development in the proposed project. I see this
as our departure point; sustained attention to improving the
quality of teaching and instruction offered by campus-based
teacher educators is viewed as a precondition or at least a corollary to helping elementary and secondary teachers improve their
instructional practices. Also, in attempting to improve our own
pedagogical abilities, we would be well advised to draw on the
pedagogical wisdom of experienced elementary and secondary
teachers.

Although initially we focus on our own professional development, appraising our own teaching practice as critically as possible, we also address a number of other functions in our professional development. Dennis Theissen, one of the participants
in the network, shared with me in personal correspondence the
following conception of professional development. It reflects the
broader and longer range agenda for faculty growth that we hope
to establish.

The "faculty" in faculty development is an inclusive concept, encompassing those in faculties of education and in schools (cooperating teachers, clinical faculty) who work closely with beginning (preservice and early years) teachers. "Development" refers to, at least, three areas:

1. Classroom—what faculty members do with their students (how and what they teach, in which contexts, and for what purposes).

2. Corridors—how faculty members, within their respective organizations, work with each other to support each other's development, to improve programs, to transform their "teaching" culture, and to reorient how they do business.

3. Streets—how faculty members work with colleagues in other organizations—in school–university partnerships, in joint action research projects, in mutual efforts to improve the clinical experience for example.

For the most part, the above framework builds on the assumption that we must simultaneously address individual, collaborative, and (intra and inter) organizational development if we want to make significant changes in what we do. Each arena has its own range of necessary capacities (skills and knowledge), many of which overlap. But to reach the bold heights we want, we need to consider and to push all three areas of development within the community of teacher educators. The leadership teams will have to address the classroom, the corridors, and the streets.

LEADERSHIP DEVELOPMENT FOR PROGRAM DESIGN AND ASSESSMENT

Recent investigations into programs of teacher preparation reveal a loosely coupled series of activities more often than thoughtful designs that interrelate activities (Goodlad, 1990; Howey & Zimpher, 1989). These studies also have identified specific program attributes; thus, they contribute to construct development of what constitutes a *program* of preservice preparation. One priority in the network will be to identify leaders in each of the participating institutions who can assume primary responsibility for ongoing program development and for research and evaluation into these programs. These program leaders will have the opportunity to observe and learn from the variations across programs represented in the network. We will engage in capacity building in the network institutions by further developing faculty members' abilities and interests in program design and assessment. Clinical faculty members from cooperating schools also will assume key roles in program redesign.

To illustrate what we mean by the concept of program, as opposed to a series of relatively independent courses culminating in student teaching, we offer the following tentative definition. We derived this from our case studies of programs of teacher education, with the purpose of eventually defining more potent and more coherent programs.

> Programs have one or more frameworks grounded in theory and research as well as practice; frameworks that explicate, justify and build consensus around such fundamental conceptions as the role of the teacher, the nature of teaching and learning, and the mission of schools in a democracy. These frameworks guide not only the nature of curriculum as manifested in individual courses but, as well, questions of scope; developmental sequence; integration of discrete disciplines; and the relationships of pedagogical knowledge to learning how to teach in specific laboratory, clinical, and school settings. Programs embedded in such frameworks clearly establish priorities in terms of key dispositional attitudes and behaviors desired for students. These are enabled and monitored in repeated structured experiences. These core teacher understandings, values, and abilities become themes that bind the program together.
>
> Programs also reflect consideration of ethos and culture building and the critical socialization of the prospective teacher. The nature and function of collegial relationships is considered both between and among faculty and students as well as with those who assume responsibilities for teacher preparation in K-12 schools. Various short-term student cohort arrangements and other temporary social systems such as inquiry teams, cooperative learning structures, or political action committees are repeatedly integrated into the formal curriculum. Conceptually coherent programs underscore collective roles as well as individual course responsibilities. Programs also contribute to more mutual endeavors in research and evaluation beyond the individual course level. Finally, programs provide considerable guidance both in terms of the nature and pattern of preprofessional or preeducation study and also extended experiences in schools in the nature of induction programs. (Howey & Zimpher, 1989, p. 242)

The following are among the many questions that could guide our inquiry into programs preparing teachers:

1. To what extent are programs of teacher preparation guided by explicit conceptions of teaching, learning, schooling, and learning to teach? To what extent are those conceptions embedded in theory, craft wisdom,

scholarship, and scientific findings? To what extent are they manifested over time in basic design considerations of scope, sequence, integration, and articulation? To what extent do they contribute to an explicit, coherent design for programmatic research and development?

2. How are alternative conceptions of teaching, learning, schooling, and learning to teach manifested in shared beliefs among teacher education faculty members and students? How are these conceptions related to interaction patterns between and among them inside and outside the classroom?

3. To what extent are major thematic goals articulated in terms of core attitudes and abilities desired in preservice students? What progression of activities contributes to the development of schemata whereby prospective teachers acquire such understandings and abilities? Given our emphasis on preparing teachers for urban settings, what thematically should be manifest in our programs in relation to race, culture, and gender or to the multiple effects of poverty, for example?

4. What defines intellectual rigor in programs of teacher preparation? What is the nature of subject matter? How is it represented and engaged in by prospective teachers not only in class but also in a variety of laboratory and clinical settings? As addressed earlier, what is the nature of intellectual discourse? What characterizes out-of-class assignments? What are standards for evaluation and how are they implemented? Are identifiable "milestone" assignments, benchmark experiences, and rites of passage built into programs to contribute to intellectual rigor?

5. What contributes to the culture and the hidden or informal curriculum that constitutes a critical aspect of programs? Can short-term cohorts or groups be structured purposefully for varying lengths of time to achieve such purposes as collaborative learning, political action, group inquiry, collective case study, or intrapersonal development? What symbols, rituals, and organizational properties give distinctiveness to a program and its culture?

6. What is distinctively urban about a program preparing teachers for urban settings beyond placement in such

settings? What subject matter, what activities, and inter-action with what individuals are essential to under-standing and succeeding in the urban context?

LEADERSHIP DEVELOPMENT FOR THE PREPARATION OF CLINICAL FACULTY MEMBERS

Despite recent insights into the nature of learning and learn-ing to teach, contributed especially by the cognitive sciences but also by studies of the social and cultural nature of classrooms and schools, the preparation of clinical faculty members remains limited. Teachers in these roles are provided with little, if any, clinical preparation, little release time, and minimal reimburse-ment. Clinical practice too often is embedded in a behavioristic orientation, wherein clinical supervision consists of observing and reinforcing relatively discrete indices of teaching effective-ness. Teaching is viewed more as a performing art calling for demonstration and external critique than as a highly clinical and intellectual endeavor calling for sustained discourse about and defense of teaching decisions and actions. To redress this situa-tion, the network hopes to provide more contemporary and more powerful clinical preparation for those who work with prospective teachers in the laboratory and in the field. This preparation will be planned and conducted jointly between leaders on campus and leaders in elementary and secondary schools.

Numerous literatures can be employed in designing a program of studies for clinical faculty members which extends beyond the single orientation course now offered (if even that much is offered) by most institutions. These literatures include teacher socialization studies, the expert-novice studies of teaching, vari-ous constructs articulating patterns of development in teachers and in young adults generally, studies of beginning teachers' beliefs and their anticipatory socialization, and, of course, the earlier mentioned literature on teachers' reasoning, which is cen-tral to the project.

Cornbleth and Ellsworth's chapter addresses additional critical issues in cultivating a clinical faculty and discusses how we can build on the abilities and insights that experienced teachers bring to this role. Howey and Zimpher (1993) suggest that care-fully delineated preservice teacher portfolios, anchored in what we are learning about dimensions of novice teachers' develop-ment, would be a staple of clinical instruction. Such conceptu-ally based portfolios would help these clinicians over time to monitor the following elements, among others, in their preservice teachers:

1. Changes in their beliefs about schooling, teaching, learning, and coming to know; moving (it is hoped) from a perception of teaching largely as telling and from an emphasis on control and performance to conceptions of active learning that are both self- and group-monitored, with an emphasis on development rather than on performance;

2. Changes in the locus of their concerns; again, from a preoccupation with cosmetic appearance and performance as a "teacher" to a focus on causal relationships that might help explain students' behavior, especially their intellectual and social functioning in regard to how they learn;

3. Changes in their reasoning about teaching; from unexamined assumptions and unsupported justifications to decisions and actions that are subjected repeatedly to public discourse and are supported by multiple forms of data, with full consideration of the ethical consequences;

4. Changes in novice teachers' efficaciousness (not merely sense of efficacy). Pupils are the basic source of knowledge about teaching efficacy; thus the progression here for the novice teacher would be from relatively intermittent and uneven self-assessment to a continuing pattern of feedback from pupils about multiple aspects of classroom interaction; evaluation would be blended with and indistinguishable from instruction. (pp. 62–63)

The following sample questions could guide inquiry into clinical preparation and clinicians' work with beginning teachers.

1. How can the preparation of prospective teachers be understood and fostered by expert clinicians as a process of progressively sophisticated problem solving?

2. In a related vein, how can the preparation of prospective teachers be fostered by clinicians as a series of complex practical arguments that evolve over time into highly reasoned principles and warrants? Again, what type of clinician–novice teacher interactions are needed and can be designed to promote these processes and purposes?

3. How can the multiple effects of socialization, planned and unplanned, in the preparation of prospective teachers be understood more clearly?

4. How can a variety of powerful contextual factors that mediate the preparation provided to prospective teachers be understood more clearly and receive more attention?

THE DEVELOPMENT OF CLINICAL FACULTY AS A CONTRIBUTION TO URBAN SCHOOL RENEWAL

The development of key clinical faculty members at selected school sites designated as partnership schools, portal schools, or professional development schools will serve as the nexus between teacher preparation and school improvement. In these targeted schools, cadres of the teacher preparation faculty will work with these clinical faculty members as well as with the broader school faculty to focus on the education of both beginning and experienced teachers in a school characterized by a commitment to ongoing renewal. Typically, after a period of two to four years, the cadre of teacher education faculty members and the cluster of preservice students assigned to the schools will be rotated to another site, but they will leave behind a leadership team composed of three or four clinical faculty members. This team will serve as the stimulus for continuing school renewal and for job-embedded faculty development, just as the leadership cadres on campus have this continuing responsibility.

School renewal, and surely the transformation of an institution over time, are ongoing activities. A static state is never reached. The ideal is never realized. The goal is to develop institutional capacity; the keys to this are collective skill and commitment to constant renewal. The primary strategy that we advocate is that much of this skill be vested in leadership teams of teachers working with administrators. Although such teams might be more common in elementary and secondary schools than in schools and colleges of education, they are still uncommon.

Thus, we envision a team of teachers in place at each of the urban partnership schools, parallel to the leadership teams on campus. They too will have specialized abilities beyond their excellence as classroom teachers in such specific areas as the improvement of teaching, action research, case studies of students, organizational functioning, and curriculum development.

A major part of their instructional assignment is teaching pupils, but some of their responsibilities entail working collegially with other teachers at the school site. Again, the intent is that continuing professional development at these urban elementary and secondary school be embedded as much as possible in ongoing activities during the instructional day. If the clinical sites serve as the nexus for the partnership, the clinical or consulting teachers, some of whose time is reallocated to working with their colleagues, serve as the linchpin. They provide a new capacity and function as a catalyst for ongoing school renewal. Thus, the nature and the quality of preparation provided for these clinical faculty members are especially critical. The network draws on the best of contemporary knowledge and on outstanding educators inside as well as outside the network to design a leadership program together with teachers in the targeted urban elementary and secondary schools. One example of leadership preparation for teachers, which we piloted, is represented in Figure 2-2.

This figure is merely illustrative. We continue to experiment and revise the domains of knowledge in which we engage teacher leaders. Recent adaptations, for example, include a growing emphasis on documentation and measurement, the nature of leadership in a collegial context, and a more manifest vision of job-embedded professional development than when we began our explorations.

THE POWER OF A NETWORK

Individuals in the institutions planning the network have deliberated about what a network might achieve that individual institutions cannot achieve alone, or at least not easily. First and foremost, this concept should be defined. In analyzing the concept of networking, Devaney gives the following advice:

> Don't think "networking." Think "net-working": weaving a net. Like a fisherman knotting strings by hand. Or a spider spinning connections and following those pathways. Making and using nets of personal connections is as legitimate and vernacular as recommending your dentist to a friend, or asking Uncle Si to help you find a job when you're brand new in town.
>
> This simple, useful social process, long studied by social scientists just for the commonfolk ingenuity and efficiency of it, has in the last decade or so been adapted for ulterior purposes—the deliberate dissemination of the results of organized research and devel-

FIGURE 2-2 Domains of Knowledge for Teacher Leaders

	Local District Needs	Interpersonal and Adult Development	Classroom Processes and School Effectiveness	Instructional Supervision, Observation, and Conferences	Disposition toward Inquiry
Rationale	Teacher leaders possess knowledge of how to assess, interpret, and prioritize local districts' and teachers' needs and concerns.	Teacher leaders possess an understanding of theories and frameworks which describe how adults develop and how teacher leaders develop personally, foster (challenge and support) teachers' development, and exert leadership.	Teacher leaders possess knowledge of contemporary lines of inquiry with regard to classroom processes and school effectiveness, and they can translate that knowledge into useful practice in schools and classrooms.	Teacher leaders possess knowledge of models of clinical supervision and processes that support effective descriptions of classroom practices, analysis and feedback regarding those data, and the provision of instructional support for continuing classroom improvement.	Teacher leaders are guided by a reflective and inquiry-oriented posture to improve classroom and school practice, including processes of individual and interactive reflectivity and collaborative action research.
Focus	Describe the needs assessments; review frameworks for effective staff development programs (purposes and formats); review research on common problems of teachers and schools.	Theories of personal, cognitive, moral, and psychosocial development; leadership theories and notions of power and authority; interpersonal relations/human strategies.	Reviews of research on teachers' effectiveness, schools' effectiveness, classroom management, and models for instructional improvement; reviews of alternative conceptions of effective teaching; review descriptions of and research on instructional improvement packages.	Reviews of clinical supervision models; reviews of compendia of observation instruments; review of narrative scripts; review approaches to giving feedback and coaching.	Overview of practice-centered inquiry and collaborative action research; reviews of action research projects; reviews of research critiques.
Activities	Conduct district tours of the community; construct community, school, classroom sociograms; use cases to relate district policies to practical local dilemmas; simulate parent conferences.	Collect data on teacher's personal profile, using inventories and profiles; complete leadership inventories; complete sentence stem exercises; analyze moral dilemmas; engage in small-group interpersonal activities.	Complete personal inventories of teaching style and behavior; complete analytic inventories of school contexts; write imaginary letters to beginning teachers about effective training; complete training through instructional improvement program (Hunter, PLS, TESA, classroom management, and cooperative learning).	Design personal models of clinical supervision; observe teaching in classrooms (in situ); engage in peer teaching and analysis; design category/sign systems; record observations from videotapes; create and analyze cases.	Formulate action research designs; conduct action research studies; complete reflectivity packets (critical events, logs and diaries, self-interviews); complete self-inventories about classroom practice; conduct and attend research conferences.

Reprinted by permission. Copyright by the American Association of Colleges for Teacher Education. N. L. Zimpher, "A Design for the Professional Development of Teacher Leaders." Journal of Teacher Education, 39(1):56.

opment, or to try to bring about change in organizations and institutions. The private, haphazard, spontaneous process has become public, organized, on purpose. (1982, p. 9)

Huberman (1982) also identifies attributes of this concept:

1. Networks serve as alternatives to the established system. (Among other things members of this small network will be committed to respond to colleagues elsewhere on a regular basis, especially employing contemporary technology—E-mail and computer conferencing are prime examples but phone and FAX also serve this function.);
2. Networks provide support as well as sharing;
3. Networks generally have among their leaders persons who function as effective facilitators;
4. Networks typically involve voluntary participation and egalitarian treatment of members (In this network we seek a genuine partnership across our institutions and with those in elementary and secondary schools.);
5. Networks provide their members with shared purpose and commitment. (p. 91)

In regard to the last of these attributes, the members of the network have met on several occasions to create a shared vision. This vision is a whole-cloth effort at change. We will re-examine our organizational patterns and cultural norms with regard to preparing teachers. We will focus on improving our own teaching and instructional capacity. We are committed to achieving more potent and protracted programs of preparation for urban teachers. We plan jointly, with our colleagues in schools, to make possible a clinical faculty that is grounded in our best understandings of good schooling, teaching, learning, and learning to teach. Finally, we are dedicated to achieving a more powerful interaction between teacher education and school renewal.

SPECIFIC PURPOSES OF A NETWORK

At the outset we emphasized the labor-intensive nature of teacher preparation and the increasingly limited resources attached to most institutions preparing teachers. We identified the specific purposes of a network in planning this project. Our intent is to enable the *combined* resources of a network to address this situation. A major investment of time and resources by each institution participating in the network calls in turn for the realization of major goals. Thus, in addition to the benefits of a network listed by Devaney and Huberman, the following potential assets of participation in a network have been specified:

1. A network that is selective in its membership and distinctive because of its ambitious agenda acts as a catalyst for change among its members. Visibility, mutual pride, friendly competition within a shared agenda, and increasing openness to examination by others are derivatives of a well-conceived and well-conducted network, and thus enable desired change.

2. The highest quality resources, not only within the network but wherever they might exist, are more accessible and more affordable to a network. The network is committed not only to sharing but also to providing intensive professional development by the very best persons who can be found in regard to various aspects of organizational renewal, faculty members' professional development, program design, and clinical preparation.

3. The network will coordinate demonstration and participation sites where faculty members from different institutions can visit for varying lengths of time and can assume a variety of roles. Coordinated efforts across the institutions should afford firsthand encounters with "best practice" relative to aspects of faculty development, program design, clinical preparation, and partnership schools.

4. Institutions will serve as external auditors to one another. The visits will take place not as the actions of mandated external reviewers, but rather as invited boards of visitors, who will provide expert assistance as well as external assessment.

5. Badly needed development of instructional materials can be coordinated across institutions. Most schools and colleges of education are resource-poor in instructional materials and facilities, even in comparison with elementary and secondary schools. Case materials representing the major problems that teachers encounter, for example, might be developed in concert across institutions because individual campuses have limited capacity to engage in this seriously needed developmental activity.

6. As a corollary, we have much to learn about how best to prepare teachers, especially for urban settings. A coordinated program of development and research, as opposed to isolated studies, can be initiated within a network. Such priorities could include study of the multiple effects of a case approach to aspects of instruction, or perhaps the impact of a specific form of clinical preparation for experienced teachers who work with preservice teachers. A program of research addressing needed priorities can be established, especially if multiple sites have common elements of teacher or clinician preparation.

7. Joint Ph.D. programs, or at least components of programs, can be designed to prepare future teacher educators more effectively.

8. Finally, many of the changes needed to advance teacher preparation call for more enlightened policy. One example is a policy that provides the partial release of clinical faculty members from some of their instructional responsibilities to work with both preservice and beginning teachers in the earliest years of teaching. It is hoped that a network can influence policies to enable such practices more strongly than individual institutions have succeeded in doing.

In summary, the network will address these four pervasive problems in a comprehensive design for faculty development:

1. organizational and structural elements and cultural norms that constrain the goals articulated in this proposal;

2. the limited range of teaching methodologies and the uneven quality of teaching and related instructional activities that are provided to prospective teachers in schools and colleges of education;

3. the scarcity of systematically designed programs of urban teacher preparation—of programs that are conceptually coherent, research-supported, and characterized by inquiry into their efficaciousness; and

4. the limited and sometimes questionable preparation provided to the clinical faculty members who are responsi-

ble for educating and evaluating prospective teachers in this important aspect of preparation.

To achieve these interrelated goals we embrace a multidimensional view of faculty members' professional development, as will be discussed further in the remaining chapters. An outgrowth will be more coherent and more conceptually based programs designed for the preparation of urban teachers. Our intent is to develop a cadre of teacher educators with specific abilities and responsibilities as program developers and programmatic researchers. The development of a variety of preservice student cohorts, brought together for various periods to achieve a variety of purposes, should engage faculty members in new role relationships with their students. We believe that an investment in such activities, especially if studied over time, should enhance our capacities as role models, mentors, and advisors. The development of conceptually anchored portfolios, as described earlier in this chapter, could greatly increase our abilities as diagnosticians and clinicians, considerably beyond present practice in assessment of students. The development of teaching clinics, with the incorporation of portable video equipment that can focus on our students as well as on ourselves, is only one of several ways in which teaching can be improved through inquiry into our practice.

Our principal focus initially is to improve ourselves as teachers. In this undertaking, preservice students will engage in critical discourse with us about the teaching and learning in which they have engaged. This conception of teaching underscores their responsibility for learning and involves them legitimately in an examination of our classroom activities. Such activities would move us away from narrow conceptions of teacher-directed instruction and limited assessment of faculty members by students. The development of faculty members as scholars can be enhanced in a variety of ways, for example through the development of instructional cases, the design of portfolios whereby one can reflect on one's own teaching, and the study of the effects of a more coherent program design.

Throughout this volume, we wish to emphasize a critical perspective and inquiry. We must model such an approach if we desire a sustaining critical perspective in the teachers we educate. Throughout the professional development activities, emphasis will be placed on issues of race, culture, and gender, and on other problems attached to preparing teachers specifically for city classrooms. This always will be a priority. Garcia (1991) speaks to the perspective, especially in our academic setting, that we must cultivate:

> A Copernican view of teaching—the view that the universe of teaching and learning consists of vast galaxies of cultures and human groups—abandons the fiction that the hub and center of the teaching universe is the middle-class American culture. The Copernican view calls for a radically different perspective based on the cultural diversity of American society. It calls for viewing all cultures as coexistent, abandoning paradigms that speak of cultures as "underdeveloped," "overdeveloped," and "primitive." It discards educational labels that describe nonwhite, non-middle-class students as "culturally deprived," "disadvantaged," or "culturally deficient." Bilingualism becomes an asset rather than a liability and Black English becomes another dialect of American English rather than substandard English. Embracing a Copernican reorientation to the universe of teaching and learning can serve to liberate teachers and assist them in transcending the narrow confines of their cultures. (p. 9)

REFERENCES

Boyer, E. (1990). *Scholarship reconsidered: Priorities of the professoriate*. Princeton, NJ: Carnegie Foundation for the Advancement of Teaching.

Clark, B. (1985). Listening to the professoriate. *Change, 17*(4), 39-40. Reprinted with permission of the Helen Dwight Reid Educational Foundation. Published by Heldref Publications, 1319 18th St., N.W., Washington, DC 20036-1802. Copyright 1985.

Deal, T. E., & Chatman, R. M. (1989). Learning the ropes alone: Socializing new teachers. *Action in Teacher Education, 11*(1).

Devaney, K. (1982). *Networking on purpose*. San Francisco, CA: Far West Laboratory.

Garcia, R. L. (1991). *Teaching in a pluralistic society: Concepts, models, strategies*. New York: Harper Collins.

Ginsburg, M. (1988). *Contradictions in teacher education and society: A critical analysis*. New York: Falmer Press.

Goodlad, J. I. (1990). *Teachers for our nation's schools*. San Francisco, CA: Jossey-Bass.

Harkavy, I., & Puckett, J. L. (1991). The role of mediating structures in university and community revitalization: The University of Pennsylvania and West Philadelphia as a case study. *Journal of Research and Development in Education, 25*(1).

Howey, K. R. (1992). Teacher education in the United States: Trends and issues. *The Teacher Educator, 27*(4), 4.

Howey, K. R., & Zimpher, N. L. (1993). *Patterns in prospective teachers: Guides for designing preserving programs.* Unpublished manuscript, The Ohio State University, Columbus.

Howey, K. R., & Zimpher, N. L. (1989). *Profiles of preservice teacher education: Inquiry into the nature of programs.* Albany, NY: SUNY Press.

Huberman, M. (1982). Making changes from exchanges: Some frameworks for studying the teachers' centers exchange. In K. Devaney, (Ed.), *Networking on purpose.* San Francisco, CA: Far West Laboratory.

RATE (Research About Teacher Education). (1989). *Teaching teachers: Facts & figures III.* Washington, DC: American Association of Colleges for Teacher Education.

RATE (Research About Teacher Education). (1992). *Teaching teachers: Facts & figures VI.* Washington, DC: American Association of Colleges for Teacher Education.

Schuster, J., & Bowen, H. (1985). The faculty at risk. *Change, 17*(4), 15.

Sergiovanni, T. J. (1990). *Value-added leadership: How to get extraordinary performance in schools.* New York: Harcourt Brace Jovanovich.

Sykes, G., Judge, H., & Devaney, K. (1992). *The needs of children and the education of educators* (Occasional paper #6). East Lansing, MI: The Holmes Group.

Zimpher, N. L. (1988). A design for the professional development of teacher leaders. *Journal of Teacher Education, 39*(1).

3

PROMOTING INQUIRY INTO ONE'S OWN TEACHING

ROBERT J. MENGES

*Northwestern University and National Center
   on Postsecondary Teaching,
   Learning and Assessment*
Evanston, IL

Professors of education are experts on teaching and on its improvement. We advise kindergarten, elementary, middle, and high school teachers, as well as administrators. We establish graduate programs in higher education, create specializations in instructional development and staff development, and supervise dissertations on instructional innovation and faculty development. Our studies of teaching, however, usually deal with someone else's teaching. We rarely study our own institutions or use our own departments, courses, and instructional approaches as laboratories. Not surprisingly, when universities create centers to study and improve teaching, our expertise is sometimes shunned.

Nevertheless, education faculty members are not without influence on programs for improving postsecondary teaching. A significant number of positions in teaching centers at colleges, universities, and professional schools are staffed by people with graduate degrees in education. These individuals are active in professional associations, and they are major contributors to the scholarly literature. Some graduates of pioneering programs, such as those from the University of Massachusetts School of Education, are now senior figures in professional development, and students they have trained are beginning to appear among the second-generation leaders.

Now it is time to bring our expertise home. It is time to heed the advice we give to K–12 teachers and administrators and to other departments and programs in postsecondary education. It is time to create our own research-based professional development programs. In short, it is time for research to inform professional development for teacher educators.

The timing of these efforts is propitious for other reasons. Prominent critics are accusing colleges and universities of emphasizing research to the neglect of teaching, of rewarding most heavily activities that do not directly advance our institutions' teaching missions. Critics say that our institutions claim to be oriented toward the development of students, but that often they behave more like institutions dedicated to research.

The ideal of dedicated teachers who are also scholars at the cutting edge of a discipline does not fit the reality of higher education. Actual faculty life is quite different. Most faculty members spend most of their time in instructional activities, and most original scholarship is produced by a minority of members of the profession. Pressure to engage in both teaching and scholarship leaves nearly everyone frustrated. Many faculty members are frustrated because the research they feel obligated to publish diverts them from work they want to pursue with students. Others are frustrated by responsibilities to students, which they feel rob them of time for original scholarship.

A few authoritative voices argue that teaching and scholarship should be reconceptualized so that each is defined in ways that provide a better match between what is expected of faculty members and what faculty members actually do. One major advance toward redefining scholarship is the Carnegie Foundation's publication *Scholarship Reconsidered* (Boyer, 1990). Boyer distinguishes four kinds of scholarship: discovery, integration, teaching, and application. Work that meets high standards in any of these areas, he argues, is properly regarded as scholarship. In this view, academics could attain scholarly recognition even though their job descriptions or personal inclinations leave little time for *discovery*. Their contributions might involve synthesizing previous discoveries, reflecting on pedagogical issues, or evaluating methods for applied community service. At many colleges and universities, discussions of these new conceptions of scholarship have begun. Revised policies and procedures for identifying and rewarding effective teaching are sure to follow.

Teaching as well as scholarship deserves redefinition. In a recent committee report at my own university, we asserted,

> Everything the University does involves teaching. A professor's activities may involve different audiences and different methods, but in one way or another, properly construed, the whole enterprise—research, graduate training, and undergraduate instruction—consists of teaching. In research and other creative activities, faculty members are involved in teaching their peers and in addressing various aspects of our culture. In training graduate students, faculty are teaching their successors not only how to conduct independent research but also how to transmit knowledge to others. In dealing with undergraduates—teaching in the classroom, instructing in the laboratory and studio, advising in the office, and working with living groups and co-curricular activities—faculty lead students toward the knowledge and creative thinking that are essential to full membership in society. (Committee on the Evaluation and Improvement of Teaching, 1991, pp. 16–17)

This expanded view of teaching brings actual faculty work more closely in line with the avowed missions of our institutions.

We have no guarantee, of course, that merely expanding the meanings of scholarship and of teaching, as the examples seem to do, will solve these dilemmas of faculty work. Yet we must proceed to discuss what we know about teaching our students effectively, about how we ourselves learn and develop as professional educators, and about how this knowledge can be turned into programs that promote reflection, inquiry, and improvement in instructional activities and programs. The purpose of this chapter is to further that discussion.

STUDENTS AS LEARNERS: WHAT WORKS TO PROMOTE LEARNING?

I like to assure teaching assistants and new faculty members that their students will learn if teachers attend to three things. Teachers must ensure that students are exposed to the subject matter, they must give students practice in dealing actively with the subject matter, and they must provide students with feedback about that practice. I believe that higher education is fairly successful with the first of these elements. We choose our subject matter carefully and we ensure that students are exposed to it through reading, lectures, discussion, and other techniques. I believe we are less successful at ensuring active practice with subject matter. For passing grades on tests and assignments, we may require no more than repetition and recall. Students can be successful without processing information or transforming subject matter in ways that promote application to new and varied tasks. With regard to feedback, I believe we are seriously inadequate. In many courses, graded work is the major or sole form of feedback; yet feedback from graded work is likely to be too general and too long delayed to foster additional and better learning.

WHAT MAKES A DIFFERENCE FOR LEARNING?

The three-component framework—exposure, practice, feedback—does not do justice to all the subtleties of college teaching, but it can guide our search for factors that make a difference for learning. Keeping these components in mind will be helpful as I summarize some conclusions from research. I draw on reviews by the National Center for Research to Improve Postsecondary Teaching and Learning (McKeachie, Pintrich, Lin, Smith, & Sharma, 1990), Dunkin in the third edition of the *Handbook of Research on Teaching* (1986), Pascarella and Terenzini (1991), and Menges and Mathis (1988). These reviewers generally agree about effective practices for promoting learning by students. From these and other sources I have synthesized the following six conclusions.

Class size makes a difference.   Teachers prepare differently and behave differently in large classes than they do in small classes. For instance, they are likely to prepare more carefully and to explain more clearly in large classes, while relying more strongly on spontaneous discussion in small classes.

Much depends on instructional goals. If the goal is that students acquire knowledge of subject matter, no disadvantages may accrue to the large class. Indeed, research shows that knowledge is gained as well as in large lecture classes as in small discussion classes.

However, in those experiments involving measures of retention of
information after the end of a course, measures of transfer of
knowledge to new situations, or measures of problem solving,
thinking, attitude change, or motivation for further learning, the
results tend to show differences favoring discussion methods over
lecture. (McKeachie et al., 1990, p. 81)

The teacher is likely to talk more in large classes, although
talk by the teacher predominates in virtually all classes. A study
of 40 classes (averaging 47 students) found that about 80 percent of classroom time was devoted to talk by the professor,
mostly at the level of factual knowledge. More than 80 percent of
questions—and questions accounted for only about 4 percent of
class time—were at the lowest level of cognitive complexity. Students did not respond at all to about one-third of teachers' questions (Ellner, Barnes & Associates, 1983). Thus, typical classes
offer a great deal of exposure to subject matter but little practice
and feedback.

Teachers who advocate the discussion method may need help
in acquiring or refining skills that promote students' participation. They may need to learn how to elicit more participation and
how to ensure that such participation is meaningful. They may
need to learn how to formulate questions in ways that stimulate
discussion appropriate for the objectives they have in mind
(Andrews, 1980). They may need to learn how to be silent after
posing questions because eliciting students' responses when the
question is complex requires longer pauses than teachers typically provide (Ellsworth, Duell, & Velotta, 1991).

Benefits of a small class do not come about automatically.
They originate not with the number of students as such but with
what can happen when there are fewer students. Our emphasis
should be on teachers' and students' activities that enable learning. Some of these enabling activities are discussed in the following sections.

Students' interpersonal activities make a difference.   It comes as
no news to educators that students' engagement and involvement
are important for learning. New knowledge meaningfully affects a
learner's existing cognitive structure only when that knowledge is
processed, and processing is facilitated by engagement. New
skills are unlikely to transfer beyond the situation in which they
were learned unless engaged learners practice them in a variety
of circumstances.

One way to ensure that students deal actively with subject matter is to require that they teach it. As McKeachie et al. (1990) put it:

> The best answer is the question, What is the most effective method of teaching? is that it depends on the goal, the student, the content, and the teacher. But the next best answer is, Students teaching other students. There is a raft of evidence that peer teaching is extremely effective for a wide range of goals, content, and students of different levels and personalities. (p. 81)

Although peer teaching is not equally successful for all students, it is most likely to be effective when groups are working toward cooperative goals and when individuals also are accountable for learning. I suspect that another major reason for the success of peer teaching is that this approach forces the teacher into a new and less dominating role. The teacher cannot dominate class discussion if discussion is occurring simultaneously in multiple groups. Further, such an approach forces the teacher to become attentive to students' interpersonal skills and to assist those students who need to acquire the skills.

Whatever the particular form—peer teaching, collaborative learning, or small-group inquiry—students teaching students requires the active processing of new information rather than passive absorption. Students also must become socially engaged with peers rather than remaining isolated in a mostly silent and predominately intellectual relationship with the instructor. Those activities increase students' practice with subject matter.

Systems of individualized instruction make a difference.   Individual learners may not receive much attention under conventional lecture and discussion methods. These methods are teacher-paced: All students are exposed to the same content at about the same speed. If instruction is to be individualized, it must take account of the differences in rate and thoroughness with which learners acquire and process information. It must consider differences in the range of examples and the extent of practice that learners need in order to comprehend and transfer complex learning.

In the 1960s, Keller (1968) proposed a teaching method that would recognize such differences and maximize the change of success for all students. In practice the Keller plan, sometimes called the Personalized System of Instruction (PSI), presents students with small units of material, usually one textbook chapter or less, and a written guide with objectives and questions for study. When students think they have mastered a unit, they take a brief test. Then they are permitted to move to the next unit. If the first test is unsuccessful, a parallel test must be taken after further study. Lectures are used primarily for enrichment and motivation; attendance is not required. Tests are administered by tutors, usually students who completed the course recently. Tutors also suggest ways in which students can remediate poor performance.

Preparing a course for PSI requires more time than does conventional preparation, but PSI incorporates several features consistent with good teaching: Objectives are clear; testing is frequent and repeatable, so that test anxiety is reduced; students interact with peers (tutors), who provide immediate feedback, as well as with the course instructor; students gain practice in judging their readiness for testing; and they demonstrate success before moving to new material. Under these conditions it seems likely that students will work more efficiently as well as more independently.

Research shows that learning, retention, and satisfaction are significantly higher under PSI than under conventional instruction (Kulik, Kulik, & Cohen, 1979). Research on various components of PSI (Kulik, Jaska, & Kulik, 1978) emphasizes the mastery requirement. Small units and frequent quizzes with immediate feedback also appear to be important; self-pacing is related more to students' morale than to achievement. Some students complete PSI courses faster than others, as much as twice as fast. When the effectiveness of the Keller Plan/PSI and of conventional instruction are compared, the results are clear. Dunkin (1986) observes that PSI is "so consistently found superior that it must rank as the method with the greatest research support in the history of research on teaching" (p. 759).

PSI has been used by thousands of teachers in many fields and in most parts of the world. Nevertheless, its popularity declined during the 1980s, and I see no indication that the decline will be reversed. The reasons that PSI has become less popular despite extensive evidence of its effectiveness have much to do with the new roles that the method requires of faculty (Menges, 1994).

As an instructional method, PSI improves the ways in which students are exposed to course content and increases the frequency of feedback.

Students' tasks make a difference.   One effect of peer teaching is to structure interpersonal academic tasks in ways that influence acquisition of knowledge and cognitive skills. One effect of PSI is to structure subject-matter tasks into manageable units, facilitating learning through assessment of well-focused academic tasks. In this section I discuss academic tasks in greater detail, viewing them as ways of attending explicitly to particular cognitive operations.

Doyle (1983, 1991) posits several components of the kinds of academic tasks that teachers set for students. An academic task: (a) involves particular cognitive operations, (b) requires certain resources, and (c) results in a particular product. Consider an example in which the academic task is a quiz. Students are likely to prepare cognitively by reciting major points (operations) in a textbook chapter (resources) so that they can recognize the correct multiple-choice option (product). Again, consider the example of an essay contrasting two works of art. Students are likely to prepare cognitively by noting particular characteristics of these works and by translating their reactions from the visual to the verbal (operations). They then compare these art works with other images (resources) and fashion their prose into sentences and paragraphs (product). A final component of academic tasks is the significance of the task in the scheme of classroom rewards, specifically the contribution of the task to course grades.

Four basic types of academic tasks are included in Doyle's formulation: memory tasks, procedural tasks, comprehension tasks, and opinion tasks. Reciting major points—my example—requires only memory. My example of the essay on art could be comprehension or opinion, depending on the criteria used to grade students' products.

Little systematic research has been conducted on academic tasks in postsecondary education, although a study by Blake and Dinham (1991) shows the potential value of such research. Seven college teachers were each interviewed four times during an academic term about (among other things) the tasks they assigned to students. It became clear that their tasks were designed to bring students into contact with the subject matter in a way that leads to engagement and synthesis. Blake and Dinham observe that these tasks can be understood as fostering "studenting," in Fenstermacher's sense:

> The teacher does not convey or impart the content to the student. Rather the teacher instructs the student on how to acquire the

content from the teacher, text, or other source. As the student becomes skilled at acquiring content, he or she learns. (Fenstermacher, 1986, p. 39)

Studying academic tasks set by teachers can reveal much about what teachers expect student to gain from exposure to the subject matter, how they expect students to process and otherwise transform subject matter (practice), and in what ways they prefer students to display their learning for grading and comment (feedback). The process of evaluation is a very sensitive one; Blake and Dinham (1991) note how students "negotiate with teachers to reduce the ambiguity and risk" of evaluation (p. 19).

The topic of academic tasks leads directly to issues of assessment, evaluation, and grading.

Grading practices make a difference.   In the economic system of the classroom, grades are hard currency. It is no surprise that students regulate their behavior in order to maximize "earnings." Nor is it surprising that when grade-oriented behaviors and learning-oriented behaviors conflict, most students choose the former.

After an extensive review of research on the effects of testing on students, Crooks (1988) concluded that methods of testing affect both how students study and the level of their motivation. He found that objective tests are more likely to elicit a surface approach than a deep approach to studying. In addition, grading on a curve forces some students to be compared unfavorably with others, even when their progress has been substantial. These students are likely to develop low expectations for future success and low motivation for subsequent studying. Also, increased cheating is a likely result of competitive, impersonal grading.

Tests and other graded tasks operationalize course goals. As McKeachie et al. (1990) point out, goals conveyed in this way are

very compelling for the students. Thus, if teachers say that they are concerned about developing skills and strategies for further learning and problem solving and that they hope to help students develop cognitive structures that will form a foundation for continued learning and then give tests that require memory of individual facts, definitions, and isolated information, students will memorize the facts, definitions, and information on which they expect to be tested. In so doing they will use memorization, repetition, and other learning strategies unlikely to be useful for achieving the higher-order cognitive objectives we have proclaimed. (p. 95)

Teachers should use assessments that match their declared goals. For some goals, short-answer quizzes are suitable. Indeed, the success of PSI may be due primarily to the quizzing it requires (Kulik, 1987); quiz questions direct students' attention and focus their energy. The frequency and the repeatability of PSI quizzes permit correction of mistakes about course content and refinement of study practices.

Short-answer quizzes, however, are unlikely to be sufficient. PSI teachers, no less than teachers of other courses, are challenged to assess not only memorized information but also the full range of intended course outcomes. Unfortunately, assessing higher order goals is likely to be labor-intensive; for example, it requires papers and essays rather than multiple-choice questions.

Professional development offices should help faculty members examine the congruence between their declared course goals and their grading practices. We serve faculty members by helping them to develop and implement innovative assessments that are feasible, that are appropriate for higher order learning objectives, and that expand opportunities for active practice and timely feedback.

Teachers' behaviors makes a difference.   Some college teachers are more successful than others in stimulating learning and satisfaction among students. We know what differentiates more effective from less effective teachers, and it appears that at least some of these distinguishing characteristics can be acquired.

More and less effective college teachers have been identified on the basis of several criteria: students' course evaluations, learning of subject matter, colleagues' and administrators' ratings and nominations, and so on. Students' course evaluations are most widely used as criteria, and they are generally satisfactory for that purpose; numerous studies show positive relationships between these perceptions by students and achievement in the course. Carefully constructed student evaluation forms usually reveal that several factors underlie effective teaching. These factors include skill in presentation, rapport, and interaction with students, course organization, course difficulty and workload, and feedback to students (see Cohen, 1981). Feldman (1989) notes that the largest correlations occur between achievement and the following dimensions of instruction: "preparation and organization;

clarity and understandablenes; stimulation of interest; high standards and motivation of students; encouragement of discussion and openness to others' opinions; and elocutionary skills" (pp. 625–626). As for student satisfaction, greater importance may lie with rapport and interaction, including interaction outside the classroom (Pascarella & Terenzini, 1991).

In a study by Murray (1983), teachers who had received high, medium, and low student evaluations were observed in their classrooms. These teachers differed in a number of ways, particularly in clarity, enthusiasm, and rapport. Because observation categories consisted of specific behaviors, findings are useful for feedback and consultation with teachers who find their student evaluations to be less positive than they wish. Behaviorally oriented studies such as this may lead to more immediate improvements in teaching than do studies of teachers' beliefs or personality traits.

A large body of research supports generalizations about teaches who successfully stimulate students' achievement. Reviewers Pascarella and Terenzini (1991) conclude:

> Student subject matter learning seeks to be enhanced when teachers (1) have a good command of the subject matter and are enthusiastic in its presentation, (2) are clear in their explanation of concepts, (3) structure and organize class time well, (4) present unambiguous learning stimuli to students (for example, use examples and analogies to identify key points, signal a topic transition clearly), (5) avoid vagueness terms and language mazes, and (6) have good rapport with students in class (are open to student opinions and encourage class discussion and the like) and are accessible to students in non-classroom settings. (p. 110)

These conclusions are particularly helpful for understanding how classroom performance can promote effective exposure to subject matter. They move us toward a model of instruction that can help individual teachers develop their own authentic styles.

The Need for Theory

Most of the research to which I have referred is directly relevant to practical decisions about teaching and its effectiveness, but I have not commented about how these studies clarify or extend theoretical issues. Because I believe that theory-based research is likely to yield stronger results and to be more useful than inquiries without connections to theory (Menges & Svinicki, 1991), I describe below several theoretical perspectives that are appropriate for studies of instruction in postsecondary education. These are the social perspective, the cognitive perspective, the motivation perspective, an integrated cognitive/motivation perspective, and the learning sciences perspective.

The social perspective.   The interpersonal context of teaching and learning defines the social perspective. In most postsecondary teaching and learning settings, the context is inevitably social. It is also relatively unstable and unpredictable because neither teacher nor students control it fully. Tiberius and Billson (1991) describe conceptual frameworks that are compatible with the social perspective, such as group process theory, communication theory, and cooperative learning. They identify several research-based characteristics that promote students' learning and growth in social settings, including mutual respect, effective communication and feedback, and a sense of security in the classroom.

In a companion essay, Billson and Tiberius (1991) offer guidelines to help teachers further each of these characteristics in particular courses. Guidelines for mutual respect, for example, include suggestions about establishing a climate of egalitarianism and tolerance with regard to gender, sexual orientation, and ethnicity. Among guidelines for effective communication and feedback are techniques for eliciting competing views or unconventional opinions for the purpose of stimulating class discussion and techniques for providing timely feedback, including feedback from fellow students. Guidelines for increasing security and trust include suggestions for reducing unnecessary status distinctions between teacher and students and for dealing with group norms constructively by discussing them openly in the classroom.

The social perspective, according to Billson and Tiberius (1991), consists of "viewing the teaching-learning process as an alliance, conceiving of the classroom as a group situation, and taking full account of the social context of educational experiences we share with students" (p. 107). Therefore they contend that the appropriate metaphor for instruction is dialogue or conversation rather than information transmission.

These guidelines are legitimate inferences from theories that underlie the social perspective, but in general their effects have not been verified empirically in higher education settings. Formulating them as verifiable propositions would not only contribute to improvements in instructional practice but also would contribute to the clarification and extension of theories.

The cognitive perspective.   The cognitive perspective deals both with the nature of course content and with strategies by which students learn that content. Weinstein and Meyer (1991) emphasize that students should possess knowledge not only about material being studied but also about themselves as learners, about course context and learning tasks, and about learning strategies that are available and how they can be used. Instructors, in parallel fashion, should know their own strengths and weaknesses; they also should know about their students, students' learning, and strategies for teaching and learning course content.

In a companion chapter, Svinicki (1991a) offers principles for effective college teaching derived from cognitive theories. She asserts, for example, "During learning, learners act on information in ways that make it more meaningful" (p. 30). This principle implies that "both instructor and student should use examples, images, elaborations, and connections to prior knowledge to increase the meaningfulness information" (p. 30). The principle has received considerable support from empirical studies and could well be used as the basis for workshops on teaching. Classroom research on the kinds of images, connections, and so on used by students in various fields would be instructive.

A special challenge for research and practice is to decide what place in the curriculum should be occupied by instruction specifically about learning strategies and their relation to particular disciplines. When students understand these strategies, they are more likely to integrate their experiences across courses in various disciplines.

The motivation perspective.   Drawing on several theories of motivation, McMillan and Forsyth (1991) present a heuristic model of college students' motivation. Motivation, they contend, is a function of students' needs and expectations. Thus learning is more likely (a) when it meets important needs and (b) when expectations for success are high. Inquiries based on these theories should look into the determinants of needs and expectations, and the interaction between these needs and expectations.

Forsyth and McMillan (1991) offer practical proposals for motivating students, each of which is based on particular motivation theories. Because the need to achieve is enhanced where motivation is intrinsic, they advise that extrinsic motivators be minimized. The weakest possible extrinsic motivators should be used in order to affirm students' responsibility and self-determination. To increase expectations for success, instructors are advised to refer whenever possible to circumstances that are controllable by students.

> Minimize references to the causal importance of uncontrollable factors, such as mood, inspired guessing, time of year, luck, the ease or difficulty of the particular unit, the presence of poor items on the test, and so on. Instead, emphasize the causal impact on performance of effort, note-taking skill, diligence, preparation, and other factors. Irrespective of performance, students who think they control the causes of their outcomes experience more positive emotions than students who think their performance is caused by uncontrollable factors. (Forsyth & McMillan, 1991, p. 59)

The research agenda for motivation theory should determine how advice such as this applies to particular students in particular postsecondary courses.

An integrated cognitive/motivation perspective.   No single theory provides a lens through which reality can be viewed fully and completely. Theories provide alternative lenses, and it is up to teachers to ingrate them in a useful way. Researchers, too, attempt this integration. McKeachie (1990) argues that both cognitive and motivation variables must be considered in any theory that hopes to account for "student learning that will last and be used for further learning after formal college/university education has ended" (pp. 128–129).

The National Center for Research on Improving Postsecondary Teaching and Learning developed a self-report questionnaire for students that taps both learning strategies and motivation. The Motivated Strategies for Learning Questionnaire (MSLQ) includes scales in three areas. Motivation scales deal with such topics as self-efficacy, test anxiety, and intrinsic/extrinsic goal orientation. Cognitive scales deal with learning strategies such as rehearsal strategies and elaboration strategies. Resource management scales deal with time and study management, peer learning, help seeking, and so on.

MSLQ research found both motivation and cognitive scales to be related to student outcome (performance on examinations, essays, papers, labs, and course grade). Regarding motivation scales, for example, students who have high expectations for success, and who believe that their own behavior (rather than the behavior of others) accounts for their grades, performed higher on all four measures. As for cognitive scales, students who reported using rehearsal and organization strategies performed better on examinations and had higher grades, but the use of these strategies was not related to essay or laboratory performance (Pintrich, 1989). Across a number of studies, motivation and cognitive variables interacted in a positive way, although high motivation provided little increment to performance for students who already used strategies of elaboration and organization (McKeachie, 1990). McKeachie also describes interesting differences across disciplines, especially in relationships between test anxiety and performance.

The MSLQ was piloted as part of campus programs to improve teaching. Faculty members studied MSLQ profiles of their classes in order to understand their students' cognitive strategies and motivation characteristics. Teachers received some tips that apply to students with various characteristics, and they passed along to students suggestions for self-instruction about motivation and study practices (Johnson, 1990). The MSLQ also can be used to assess changes over time under particular educational treatments.

This perspective keeps both cognition and motivation in view, thereby providing a more nearly complete explanation of effective instruction. Teachers play important roles in both the cognitive and the motivation perspectives.

> In the case of cognitive theory, the teacher is helping the student to create meaning and to monitor learning. In motivation theory, the instructor works with the student to recognize his or her own potential, to select personal and realistic goals, and to feel secure in the classroom. (Svinicki, 1991b, p. 118)

This integrated perspective includes both roles played by teachers. The MSLQ is a convenient mechanism for researching these interesting conceptual relationships.

The learning sciences perspective.   Researchers in the emerging field of the learning sciences draw from cognitive psychology, linguistics, artificial intelligence, computer science, and other disciplines to understand learning more fully and to draw implications for learning. Learning scientists rely more strongly on research into cognitive processes, but they also apply knowledge of motivation, particularly intrinsic motivation. Intrinsically motivated learners experience their study tasks as authentic and realistic rather than as artificial. Learning scientists incorporate the benefits of social interaction by asking learners to solve problems in cooperative groups and then to reflect on the problem-solving processes they used. Often learning scientists experiment with computer-based technologies as a means of moving toward these instructional goals. (For further discussion of work in the learning sciences, see Collins, Brown, & Newman, 1989.)

A particularly rewarding line of inquiry compares the knowledge of experts with that of novices in particular domains of practice. These studies reveal two kinds of expert knowledge: domain knowledge and strategic knowledge. Domain knowledge includes facts, concepts, and procedures relevant to the domain. It is explicit and can be taught fairly readily. Strategic knowledge is typically tacit and includes the heuristics that experts use to solve problems, the controls by which they select appropriate problem-solving strategies and decide when to use them, and particular cognitive strategies such as those discussed in the above section on the cognitive perspective.

When learning scientists plan instruction, they emphasize care in sequencing experiences for leaners. In particular they argue that learners' experiences should move from relative simplicity toward greater complexity, from relative similarity to greater diversity, and from the global or more conceptual toward the local or more detailed.

Context—that is, how instructional events are situated—is especially important. Knowledge is always situated, "being in part a product of the activity, context, and culture in which it is developed and used" (Brown, Collins, & Duguid, 1989, p. 32). Learning scientists use the familiar notion of apprenticeship to define and investigate situated cognition. In this connection, they offer the term *cognitive apprenticeship*. Cognitive apprenticeships "try to enculturate students into authentic practices through activity and social interaction in a way similar to that evident— and evidently successful—in craft apprenticeship" (1989, p. 37).

These researchers describe a college mathematics class that focuses on strategies for solving problems, on ways of generalizing those strategies, and, to put it more grandly, on the culture of mathematics. The correct answer to a problem under discussion is almost incidental because the class is not governed by the search for solutions. Instead, what the class does is developed by students rather than directed or declared by the teacher. Students are active learners; their relationships with the professor are like those of apprentices.

Much of this seems reminiscent of Dewey, albeit Dewey in light of recent cognitive research. It is different from Dewey, however, in two important ways. First, the teaching methods advocated in the learning sciences are better articulated than Dewey's. Second, the technologies used to assist students' learning are far more advanced than Dewey might have imagined.

Several teaching methods are believed to be helpful in moving novices toward the knowledge, skills, and strategies displayed by experts. They "give students the opportunity to observe, engage in, and invent or discover expert strategies in context" (Collins, Brown, & Newman, 1989, p. 481). Researchers elaborate six methods.

1. In *modeling*, students observe an expert who models the processes necessary for completing a task. The processes are made explicit by (for instance) the expert's talking aloud.

2. In *coaching*, students complete a task. The coach comments in ways intended to move their performance closer to expert performance.

3. In *scaffolding*, students are supported in their early learning by the teacher's prompts, hints, guiding questions, partial modeling, and other techniques appropriate for the learner's level. These supports gradually are *faded* until learners are on their own.

4. In *articulation*, students verbalize the processes they are using perhaps by thinking aloud while solving a problem; thereby they make explicit the knowledge, skills, and strategies that guide their actions.

5. In *reflection*, students hold up their performance and their processes for comparison with those of experts or other students, thereby refining their internal cognitive models of expertise.

6. Finally, in *exploration*, students are confronted with new domains in which they must frame problems and attempt solutions. They are explicitly taught strategies needed for successful exploration.

Creating cognitive apprenticeships that employ these methods requires individualization far beyond the resources of most educational institutions. The learning sciences attempt to show how computer-aided learning can implement at least the first three of these six methods: modeling, coaching, and scaffolding/fading. Implementation is becoming technologically feasible with today's computers and with the software now under development. It is less clear whether educational organizations are flexible enough to accommodate this technologically based approach.

Massive changes in educational organizations would be required if computer-aided learning were adopted to the extent required by cognitive apprenticeships. Collins (1991) enumerates several shifts that typically occur in schools where computers have been adopted in a significant way. Instruction shifts from the whole class to small groups and from lecture and reciting to coaching. Attention is redirected from better students to weaker students. Students become significantly more engaged in their activities. Assessment shifts from tests to progress and effort. Social structures become less competitive and more cooperative. No longer do all students learn the same things; instead, different students are learning different things. Verbal thinking is no longer always primary; students begin instead to integrate visual thinking with verbal thinking. (Of course, introducing technologies into schools usually has other effects as well, negative as well as positive, but that is a topic for another occasion.)

All of these shifts are consistent with the good teaching practices mentioned earlier in this chapter. They are inconsistent, however, with many of our usual operating procedures, with the conventional roles and identities of educators, and with many beliefs held by students, teachers, and lay citizens. In higher education we have avoided confronting these inconsistencies because hardware and software have been inaccessible or inadequate. As accessibility and adequacy increase, the confrontation cannot be postponed much longer.

CONCLUSION

We know a great deal about effective instruction in postsecondary education, and some of that knowledge is based on theories. Yet our knowledge is not precise enough to be prescriptive, that is, to tell us exactly what Professor W should do with Student X in Course Y in order to reach Goal Z. Our knowledge is sufficient, however, for improving instruction in many courses. It is also rich with opportunities for systematic inquiry and research.

TEACHERS AS LEARNERS: WHAT WORKS
TO IMPROVE TEACHING?

A decade ago, Judith Levinson-Rose and I undertook a review of research on improving college teaching (Levinson-Rose & Menges, 1981). An updated review on the same topic has been completed by Maryellen Weimer and Lisa Lenze (1991), my colleagues at the National Center on Postsecondary Teaching, Learning, and Assessment. Largely on the basis of these reviews, I will summarize what we know about the five interventions that are used most commonly to improve teaching: workshops and seminars; individual consultation; grants for instructional improvements; resource materials, such as books and newsletters; and colleagues helping colleagues. (Portions of this section are drawn from Menges, 1991a.)

We have considerable information about the incidence of particular faculty development activities at various types of colleges and universities. Eisen and Hill (1990) surveyed faculty developers at 70 institutions. Erickson (1986) surveyed four-year institutions; Centra (1978) gathered data from two-and four-year colleges. Three articles focus on community colleges: Smith (1981) conducted a national survey, Hansen (1983) studied institutions in Illinois, and Richardson and Moore (1987) studied community colleges in Texas. Two studies from outside the United States have been reported: Konrad (1983) surveyed 25 Canadian universities, and Moses (1985) queried 17 academic development units in Australia.

Of course we need to know more than the incidence of teaching improvement activities if we are to invest resources wisely and plan programs responsibly. We need to know a great deal about the conditions under which particular interventions are successful. This section emphasizes assessments of the effectiveness of interventions.

EVIDENCE APPROPRIATE FOR ASSESSING INTERVENTIONS

What should we expect of our efforts to improve college teaching? When teachers attend a workshop, view a class on videotape, or conduct a classroom research project, what effects should be expected? How can those effects be documented reliably? Where do we look for evidence of effectiveness? What should that evidence include?

Five levels of evidence are used by both the 1981 and 1991 reviews as a framework for discussing the literature. As shown

FIGURE 3-1   Levels of Evidence for Assessing Interventions to Improve Teaching

1. Teacher's satisfaction (from self-report):
   Participants offer opinions about the intervention.

2. Teacher's knowledge (from tests or observations):
   Pre- and posttests or observations document changes in teacher's knowledge.

3. Teacher's behavior (from observer):
   Classroom observations show changes in teacher's skills.

4. Students' satisfaction (from self-report):
   Students' evaluations document changes in teacher's performance.

5. Students' learning (from tests or observations):
   Tests or observations reveal changes in students' learning.

Adapted from Weimer & Lenze, 1991. Copyright ©1991, Agathon Press. Used with permission.

in Figure 3-1, evidence ranges from information about the teacher (including teachers' satisfaction, teacher's knowledge, and teacher's behavior) to information about the learner (student's satisfaction and student's learning). It also ranges from information gathered in the training setting (for example, evidence from teachers at a workshop) to information in the setting where the teacher's learning is applied.

INTERVENTIONS TO IMPROVE TEACHING

Each intervention (workshops, consultations, grants, resource materials, colleagues helping colleagues) is discussed separately below with reference to these five levels of evidence.

Workshops.   The ubiquitous workshop or seminar is the most common approach to improvement of teaching. Workshops and seminars vary a great deal in content, duration, method, and target audience. There is little variance, however, in how they are evaluated. Rarely does assessment go beyond the first category of evidence—that is, participants' satisfaction.

From accumulated research we can conclude that faculty/staff developers are capable of designing and delivering workshops and seminars which leave participants satisfied. Studies containing evidence about teachers' knowledge, teachers' behavior, and students' learning are too few to show a reliable pattern of results. Thus, little progress has been made toward a research base for designing workshops that employ the most effective methods for a given audience pursuing a particular topic. Levinson-Rose and Menges (1981) discuss several problems of research design that mar otherwise promising studies of workshops, seminars, and short courses.

Some people might argue that elaborate evaluations are unnecessary, that simply experiencing workshops is sufficient justification for the time and effort they require. After all, workshops and seminars bring faculty members together in pleasant circumstances to discuss issues about curriculum, teaching, and learning which they might not address otherwise. If workshops have only superficial effects, however, they may accomplish little more than keeping the faculty development staff busy. That outcome is no more defensible than requiring professors to produce publications that almost nobody reads. We must be alert to alternative approaches for improving teaching that have greater impact at comparable cost.

Consultation.   Many teaching centers employ specialists who consult with individual faculty members about their teaching. Consultations might be stimulated by course evaluations, a classroom visit, a videotape, or by issues raised by either the teacher, the consultant, or an individual who refers the teacher to the consultant. The distinctive characteristic of a consultative interaction is its individualized, focused nature: "looking at, interpreting, analyzing the individual teacher-client's unique teaching behaviors in a collaborate, investigative fashion" (Weimer & Lenze, 1991).

Most evidence about consultation programs is limited to faculty members' satisfaction; it is not surprising that teachers who invest themselves in this activity report that it has been useful. A few studies find changes in classroom behavior when the consultation involves videotapes or records of classroom interaction. The largest and most important body of research on consultation comes from the literature on students' ratings. About 30 studies have examined the effects on subsequent teaching of feedback from ratings by students. In these studies, some teachers get no feedback, others receive written reports of students' evaluations; in a few studies, some also receive consultation about their ratings. In a meta-analysis of this literature (Menges & Brinko, 1986), we found only modest effects on students' subsequent ratings from feedback ratings alone. The effect, however, was almost four times as great when ratings were accomplished by consultation. Results are less clear in the few studies that examine the effects of feedback on students' achievement and affect.

Although research on consultation constitutes the beginning of a useful research base, it is not yet adequate for tailoring specific consultation programs to particular faculty members.

Grants for instructional projects.   Administrators often point proudly to grant programs as evidence of their institution's commitment to high-quality instruction. These programs typically invite faculty members to compete for funds that support faculty time and travel, auxiliary staff, instructional equipment and materials, and other resources aimed at improving instruction. Not surprisingly, recipients say they are pleased to have received a grant, and persons who administer programs feel that the programs are successful (see Eble & McKeachie, 1985). Reports of satisfaction are virtually the only systematic evidence we have regarding these programs, with the following interesting exception.

Jacobsen (1989) compared students' evaluations before and after a grant period for three groups of faculty: those who received a grant, those who applied but were unsuccessful, and those who did not apply. Jacobsen found no change in students evaluations of courses in the college as a whole. Instructors with grants received higher initial evaluations than their colleagues, but their evaluations did not improve during the grant period. In fact, the only improved evaluations were made for teachers who applied but did *not* receive a grant, a finding for which Jacobsen had no ready explanation.

Another reason for skepticism about grant programs, particularly those which support the release of faculty members' time from other duties, comes from research with new faculty. Boice (1991) found that junior faculty who planned to use long blocks of summer and vacation time for concentrated work on research and writing rarely completed their plans. The most productive juggled many activities simultaneously in a disciplined way. For example, they scheduled regular periods of writing even if those periods were brief. Presumably they would handle instructional innovations in a similar way.

In summary, grants undoubtedly yield instructional innovations that would not have occurred otherwise. Yet the research does not make clear what the optimal size or duration of such grants should be or what kinds of faculty activities are supported most effectively by grants.

Resource materials.   Discussions about teaching appear in newsletters, journals, monographs, books, and many nonprint outlets.

Some publications are disseminated widely by professional organizations or research agencies. Others are aimed at local campus audiences. Many contain examples and suggestions by authors who presumably expect their work to be read, pondered, and applied in teaching situations.

Resource materials are numerous and varied: newsletters, such as *The Teaching Professor*; general-interest journals, such as *College Teaching*; discipline-specific journals, including *Teaching Sociology* and *The Journal of Chemical Education*; and numerous periodicals and books from publishers such as Jossey-Bass. These items apparently enjoy strong, sustained support.

It is evident that resource materials are purchased and presumably are read, but I have found no studies of their influence on faculty members' knowledge and behavior. Indeed, the general subject of elective reading by professionals and the relationship of such reading to their practice seems to be nearly unexplored by researchers. The National Center on Postsecondary Teaching, Learning, and Assessment is planning inquiries on the topic. Campus-based studies also are appropriate, perhaps through interviews or focus groups. Because producing these resources consumes considerable staff time and because distribution can be expensive, research would be helpful in finding ways to increase their cost-effectiveness.

Colleagues helping colleagues.   Most academics place high value on their autonomy, so it is not surprising that peer-based activities are appealing. In peer programs, colleagues serve as resources for one another. They discuss course materials or talk about class visits, videotapes, or particular issues such as problems encountered in teaching large classes.

The popularity of this approach is relatively recent; the category did not appear in the 1981 review. Weimer and Lenze (1991) point out that such programs grew in number during a time when funding decreased. Peer-based programs do not require a permanent staff or large budgets. Once a sufficient number of individuals volunteer their time—and as few as two people are sufficient—the program can begin.

Pairs of faculty members, not necessarily from the same discipline, might focus on a course that one of them is teaching. (During the next term, the partner's course is examined.) Classes are visited; the teacher and the partner each interview students about their experiences in the course. Both write brief essays at the conclusion of their participation as a way of summarizing what they have learned (Katz & Henry, 1988). The New Jersey Master Faculty Program, founded by Joseph Katz, is probably the most extensive implementation of this approach (Golin, 1990): Nearly 200 faculty in 21 private and public New Jersey colleges were part of the program through the early 1990s.

Colleague support programs produce almost universal satisfaction among participants, but research has not addressed the other effects. The most interesting evidence in New Jersey may lie in the essays written by participants. Unfortunately, however, no large-scale pre/post comparisons can be made from the available data. As with other interventions discussed here, colleague support programs can be considered to be validated by research only if we regard faculty satisfaction as an adequate index of success.

THE NEED FOR THEORY

In preparing this chapter, I planned to look separately at studies of interventions that are theory-based. A number of conceptual and theoretical frameworks are potentially appropriate for such research: role and status concepts from sociology; information-processing approaches from the cognitive sciences; ideas on verbal and nonverbal communication from the communication sciences; incentive and attribution topics from theories of motivation; and, from developmental theories, characteristics that are hypothesized to change during the adult years. Unfortunately, the literature on interventions to improve teaching is just beginning to pay attention to theory. For example, Sherman, Armistead, Fowler, Barksdale, and Reif (1987) propose a developmentally based theory of teaching excellence, and Sprague and Nyquist (1991) review developmental theories that they believe are pertinent to the development of teaching assistants.

As one approach to theory-based research, consider an assessment model derived from attribution theory. Steiner, Dobbins, and Trahan (1991) present a model for assessing (a) the performance attributions made by trainees—new employees receiving initial training—for their own behavior and (b) the attributions made by trainers for the trainees' behavior. The model includes contextual variables, outcomes (both skill and affect), and individual difference variables, such as self-efficacy. The authors suggest how this model might be put to empirical test, and they offer propositions that could be tested. With regard to trainees, for example, they predict, "Poorly performing trainees will exert less effort in training when they attribute their past failures to stable rather than unstable factors" (p. 280). With regard to trainers they predict, "Trainer behaviors which are directed at the factor that trainees attribute their training performance to will result in higher levels of trainee satisfaction and greater behavioral change" (p. 281). Research based on the model could asses the presence and the effects of self-serving biases—that is, the likelihood that those who are being trained will attribute their performance (when successful) to characteristics of themselves (internal trainee factors) and that those who are doing the training will attribute trainees' performance to the effectiveness of the instruction (a factor external to trainees).

Although this study was not set in higher education, it is relevant to some faculty development activities, such as individual teaching consultations. I believe it could stimulate further fruitful investigations.

CONCLUSION

Research does not strongly support our faculty and staff development enterprise. As Weimer and Lenze (1991) put it, research provides "feeble and inconclusive support at best" (p. 330). This does not mean that these interventions do not work or cannot work, but the research so far is inadequate for producing reliable conclusions about their effectiveness. This is more a commentary on our failure to conduct research than an indictment of faculty development practices. This literature, as Weimer and Lenze say, is a literature of practice rather than a literature of research. We share descriptions of what works, but decisions about what works are based more often on intuition than on empirical data.

PROFESSIONAL DEVELOPMENT SPECIALISTS, MEMBERS OF SUPPORT STAFF, AND ADMINISTRATORS AS LEARNERS

In addition to students and teachers, the campus community includes other groups important to instructional improvement, particularly professional development specialists, members of support staff, and administrators.

PROFESSIONAL DEVELOPMENT SPECIALISTS

At some institutions, professionally staffed programs for improving instruction have been in place for more than 20 years. As a field, faculty/staff development boasts national and international conferences, professional associations, and an extensive professional literature. Nevertheless, the profession has been studied little. Except for some descriptive work, not much is known about the activities that its members pursue for their own professional growth.

There is no reason to think that professional development specialists learn differently from other members of the faculty. Like faculty in general, they work with adults and with young adults in several roles: as agents of change, as facilitators of learning, and as evangelists for the highest ideals of postsecondary education. No less than faculty members, they will benefit from inquiry into their own practice.

SUPPORT STAFF MEMBERS AND ADMINISTRATORS

Support staff and administrators too often are ignored in programs for professional development. Members of support staff may be regarded as marginal to these programs, a most unfortunate and uninformed view. Administrators may be seen mainly as the source of vision and of resources for professional development programs. They become targets of blame when their visions and resources are inadequate. They are viewed less often as developing professionals themselves.

In some countries, particularly in the United Kingdom, there exists a "unified" approach to faculty/staff development (Partington, 1991). Those programs sensibly contend that educational outcomes can be enhanced and that many operational problems can be avoided when departmental secretaries, laboratory technicians, library staff members, and others who support instructional activities participate together in professional development efforts. Rather than working only with faculty members and across departments, programs deal with both the faculty and the staff—that is, with everyone who works in a particular unit. This level of intervention and the organizational knowledge it requires are important areas for further investigation.

A unified approach naturally touches administrators in any unit it affects, but administrators also can be served directly through activities intended expressly for them. A growing literature discusses the roles and responsibilities of administrators in higher education. (See, for example, Bennett & Figuli, 1990; Boyer, 1990; Tucker, 1984; Wheeler, Seagren, Egly, & Beyer, 1990). Additional knowledge from studies in organizational behavior, leadership, and performance evaluation contributes to a subspecialty that focuses on development of administrators in higher education.

CONCLUSION

Learning and development among professional development specialists, support staff members, and administrators is an area ripe for research. Experiences and activities of professional development specialists might be examined fruitfully within the framework of professionalization because this profession is one that is still emerging. Also needed are assessments of programs that serve the faculty, the support staff, and administrators as a unified group rather than as separate audiences.

METHODS FOR PROMOTING INQUIRY INTO ONE'S OWN TEACHING

What is inquiry into one's own teaching? Such inquiry engages faculty members in relatively systematic investigations, preferably self-initiated investigations, of pedagogical issues and problems. In this section, I present some advantages of the inquiry approach, discuss conditions that increase the likelihood of inquiry, and suggest several ways in which inquiry might be conducted.

ADVANTAGES OF THE INQUIRY APPROACH

At best these inquiries are self-initiated, the result of stimulation from within rather than the consequence of requirements from without. Issues for inquiry are defined and refined most effectively by the teacher, and it is the teacher who should choose methods of investigation. Put another way, the motivation for inquiry is intrinsic, and the process of inquiry should be its own reward.

This view fits well with the importance of autonomy as a traditional professorial value. College teachers value freedom to decide how their time is used and how their energies are directed. The inquiry approach recognizes faculty members' autonomy and therefore is likely to have greater long-term value than interventions that are less self-determined.

Many faculty development programs fail to treat the faculty as autonomous adults. Consider the five interventions discussed earlier: workshops, consultations, grants, resource materials, and colleagues helping colleagues. All are likely to place the teacher in a dependent and subordinate relationship to a workshop leader, a consultant, a funding source, or a colleague. This is true of interventions such as those described in the literature; it is also true when interventions are catalogued from the experience of faculty development practitioners. Angelo (1989) offers the following list of practice-based approaches to instructional development: information/inspiration, rewards and recognition, specific skill training, clinical technical consultation, and coaching/mentorship. For each of these except the last, Angelo argues that faculty members are placed in a dependent relationship with another person. For the first two, the teacher is a member of an audience; for the third and the fourth, the teacher is a trainee or client. A partnership is likely only for coaching/mentorship, but even then the apprentice may become subordinate to the master.

Autonomy is a researchable issue. One potentially informative line of research would be to study interventions in which faculty members' autonomy is operationalized in different ways and then to attempt to determine which interventions are most effective for which kinds of faculty.

Research methods as well as programmatic activities must safeguard autonomy. In the 1981 review, we noted that few studies:

> engage faculty as collaborators. Instead, colleagues are treated as objects of training programs and subjects for research. . . . The next generation of research will, we hope, include fewer studies where faculty are assigned to treatments and more studies where participants collaboratively examine the dynamics of teaching and learning. (Levinson-Rose & Menges, 1981, p. 420)

The need remains for qualitative, collaborative research.

CONDITIONS FOSTERING INQUIRY

If inquiry is to become more likely, several conditions are necessary. (The first two conditions described below are derived in part from the theory of reasoned action; see Ajzen & Fishbein, 1980.)

Beliefs favorable to inquiry.   Our behavior is determined in part by beliefs and assumptions about the consequences of our actions. For example, I may believe that inquiring into my teach-ing will have the following consequences; higher quality teaching, higher salary, less time available for nonteaching activities, and so on. Some of these consequences I regard as more important than others, some as more positive than others, and some as more likely than others. The more important, more positive, and more likely I believe these consequences to be, the stronger will be my intention to engage in inquiry. If my beliefs about adopt-ing particular instructional practices were analyzed along these lines, they could be viewed as indicators of my intentions to adopt the practice.

Supportive environment and organization.   Two kinds of environ-mental and organizational support make inquiry more likely. The first is subjective; the second, objective.

The first, subjective kind of support relates to the perceived social norm regarding the behaviors in question. How do people who are important to me view my inquiries into teaching? How much do I wish to comply with their views? A list of these sig-nificant people might include certain colleagues, the department chair, the dean, students, my spouse, my research collaborator, and so on. My beliefs about their views and my desire to comply with these views affect my intention to engage in inquiry.

Environmental/organizational support also has an objective side in the form of external factors that help to maintain relevant behaviors. If inquiry requires gathering data, keeping a journal, attending meetings, and other activities, these behaviors are more likely to be sustained when external support is available. Organizational psychologists note that after training, people often lapse into earlier patterns of behavior. Even if I am committed to inquiry, new behaviors may not persist unless I have acquired strategies that prevent relapse and unless supports for the new behaviors are built into my continuing work environment (Marx, 1986).

An appropriate heuristic framework.   Inquiry is always about some problem or issue. If the topic of inquiry is embedded more deeply in a conceptual framework, the inquiry is likely to be more productive. The heuristic framework might be a model of instruc-tion, a model of student or faculty development, or a model of attributional style. Models need not be complex to be useful. A simple instructional model may be sufficient—for example, a model that incorporates contextual variables, teachers' beliefs, instructional goals, methods of delivering instruction, and procedures for evaluation and revision (Menges, 1990). In the next section I describe another potentially useful instructional model, one that focuses on feedback.

If the inquirer is a professional development specialist, a cognitive apprenticeship framework is likely to be useful. The six methods advocated by the learning sciences as instructive for cognitive apprenticeships—modeling, coaching, scaffolding/fading, articulation, reflection, and exploration—constitute an appropriate framework with which to inquire, for example, into the strengths and weaknesses of programs for first-year teaching assistants.

Finally, consider frameworks that are relevant to the kinds of knowledge needed by college teachers. A guiding framework for inquiries into this topic by professional development specialists can be taken from Shulman's (1986) discussion of three forms of teachers' knowledge: propositional knowledge, case knowledge, and strategic knowledge. Propositional knowledge includes research-based principles, maxims derived from practical experience, and normative statements about what is ethically and morally right. Case knowledge is contextualized and specific; it includes what Shulman terms prototypes, precedents, and parables (these parallel the three types of propositional knowledge). Strategic knowledge is relevant in situations where principles clash with one another or where no case applies. In those situations, one draws on strategic knowledge; that is, one makes judgments. Professional development specialists might inquire into the forms of knowledge that college teachers say they possess and into the effects of activities that introduce new and different forms of knowledge.

CONDUCTING INQUIRY

No set of rules exists for conducting inquiry. Case reports can be useful, such as those collected by Grimmett and Erickson (1988) for illustrating Donald Schön's approach to reflective practice (an approach already so well-known to teacher educators that I shall not detail it here).

The approaches described below are compatible with the case format. They could be the basis of cases describing implementation of inquiry as part of faculty development programs. These approaches suggest possible techniques and potentially useful tools for teacher educators who are inquiring into their own teaching. The approaches are meant to be discussed and adapted, not imitated literally.

Inquiry into personal theories.   Personal theories about teaching and learning are often implicit. Making implicit theories into coherent explicit theories can be exciting and intellectually challenging. Faculty members might commit themselves to a series of small-group meetings in which they inquire into their own personal theories. Each would discuss a belief about teaching or learning that recently has come into awareness, and in doing so would follow these steps: (a) articulating the belief as clearly as possible, (b) identifying a problematic teaching situation relevant to that belief, (c) reporting behavioral steps that were taken to resolve the problem, and (d) discussing with the group the extent of consistency between the belief and the behaviors.

Here is one description of how an inquiry group might proceed.

A teacher of history may assert her belief that only when students compare and contrast assigned readings, by discussing them in class, do they master the skills of complex reasoning about history. When she asks students to do this in class, however, she says that her questions are greeted with silence. Colleagues in the discussion group suggest that a videotape of one of her classes may be revealing. On the basis of the tape, she decides that she is not giving the students enough time to formulate their responses before she breaks the silence by answering her own questions. She resolves to pause longer after posing questions, and to give students some suggestions about managing comparison-contrast questions. As her theory becomes explicit, she extends it to include speculations about why students behave as they do, that is, they may need more time for higher order thinking. She may also be ready to explore formal cognitive theories and to select cognitive learning strategies . . . that can be blended with her personal theories. (Rando & Menges, 1991, pp. 11–12)

These faculty discussions are more likely to be productive when they are concrete rather than general, and when the group has access to classroom data, particularly from students or from videotapes.

Classroom research.   In 1986, K. Patricia Cross and Thomas Angelo began a project aimed at reducing the distance between educational researchers and teachers in higher education. In the Classroom Research Project they encouraged teachers to study their teaching and their students' learning under the assumption that teachers are more likely to apply new knowledge if that knowledge comes from their own investigations. In classroom research, "researcher and teacher are one and the same person, and the research-practice gap disappears" (Angelo, 1991, p. 8).

According to Cross, "Classroom research consists of any systematic inquiry designed and conducted for the purpose of increasing insight and understanding of the relationships between teaching and learning" (1990, p. 136). Classroom research usually begins with assessment techniques that help to monitor what students are learning and how well they are learning it. These assessments are not extensions of regular quizzes or tests, nor are they new teaching techniques. Rather they provide information that helps the teacher modify instruction in order to improve learning. A philosophy professor, for example, who wanted to help students think critically began to probe their concepts of critical thinking (as well as testing their critical thinking skills). She found that students' notions of critical thinking were quite narrow; that discovery led her to devise some new instructional approaches (Angelo, 1991).

Typical steps in classroom assessment are listed in Figure 3-2 and are grouped under the categories of planning the assessment, conducting the assessment, reviewing results, and follow-up. After several cycles through steps such as these, the teacher has

FIGURE 3-2   The Classroom Assessment Cycle

Plan the Assessment

1. Focus on one class, a class that presents teaching/learning problems or questions that are challenging, but tractable;
2. Identify and clarify teaching/learning goals for that class;
3. Adapt or develop simple techniques to assess one of those critical goals.

Conduct the Assessment

4. Teach to the "focus" goal;
5. Assess students' achievement of that goal by carrying out the planned project and collecting data.

Review the Results

6. Analyze data collected through the assessment project;
7. Interpret results and draw implications for future teaching and learning in that class, and plan an appropriate response to the feedback.

Follow Up

8. Tell students about the results and the planned response;
9. Evaluate effects of the project on students' learning;
10. Design a follow-up project, if appropriate, and start the cycle again.

Adapted from Angelo, 1989, p. 52. Copyright ©1989, New Forums Press. Used with permission.

accomplished what Cross and Angelo term *classroom research.* Because most teachers require some assistance in getting started with classroom assessment, the project developed a handbook of assessment techniques (Cross & Angelo, 1993). The 30 instruments in the handbook cover a number of topics: assessments of students' academic skills, self-awareness, intellectual development, reactions to teachers and teaching methods, and so on. Many inquiring teachers will find here at least one instrument useful for their projects. The teacher who is uncertain about a direction for inquiry will find possibilities worth considering.

Essays collected by Angelo (1991) constitute another resource for those who are curious about classroom research. Brief examples from a variety of disciplines show how assessment can improve complex as well as simple learning. Longer essays describe projects in classes of varying size and content and in different types of institutions. These essays were written by teachers who designed and conducted the projects. A list of assessment techniques appears in the book's appendix.

A feedback-seeking framework.   In contrast to classroom research, which is impelled by the need for specific information, the framework I call "feedback-seeking" steps back from immediate problems. The feed-back seeking framework helps one identify and clarify issues and problems before gathering information. (This framework is elaborated further in Menges, 1991b.)

The feedback-seeking framework is modeled on familiar feedback loops such as those in the household thermostat. A decrease in room temperature is sensed by the thermometer (input). The thermostat (comparator) checks the actual temperature against the setting (standard) and switches the furnace on. Heat from the furnace (output) raises room temperature and returns the system to equilibrium.

Suppose we translate this model into instructional terms. Information of various kinds constitutes input. The teacher, by reviewing standards, acts as comparator. The teacher's instructional behavior is the output. A teacher might experience discomfort, for example, because students' examination scores fall below her standard. She may deal with this discrepancy between input and standards by gathering additional kinds of data, including performance in courses that students took previously, and perhaps she will conclude that the students are not deficient after all; thus, equilibrium is restored. Again, she may deal with the discrepancy by reflecting on what she expects of students. Perhaps she will decide that her standards are too high, and will adjust those expectations to restore equilibrium. Then again, she may schedule review sessions in order to raise students' level of performance, thereby restoring equilibrium through her new instructional activities.

The feedback framework helps us to differentiate and name these three ways of restoring equilibrium. To adjust the nature and timing of available information is to restore equilibrium by modifying input. To adjust expectations, beliefs, and values is to restore equilibrium by modifying standards. To adjust instructional behaviors and methods is to restore equilibrium by modifying output. In each case the goal is to correct a discrepancy and to restore the system to a steady state.

Many college teachers do this naturally. They solicit information as feedback; reflect on their expectations, beliefs, and values; and experiment with different ways of teaching. Yet the information they obtain may be complete and biased, and it may be interpreted hastily or used inconsistently. A feedback-seeking framework can improve the quality of information and can lead to more systematic inquiry and experimentation.

Improving information (input).   To improve information available to teachers is to alter input. Perceptions occurring during class are no doubt the most frequent input. Teachers scan students' faces during class to determine how things are going, and they watch for signs of enthusiasm as students leave after class. Because perceptions during class are immediate and concrete, they have great impact.

Other information comes from students, most commonly through end-of-course questionnaires. Unfortunately, this information may be poorly timed, or it may be discarded because it was not gathered at the professor's behest. When faculty members choose items for the questionnaire, the information is more likely to be seen as credible. Other ways to improve information include open-ended as well as closed questions, comments gathered through interviews as well as through questionnaires, and reports in narrative as well as in statistical form.

Changes in students' learning may constitute the information (input) most relevant for improving teaching. Examinations, papers, laboratory reports, and other graded work are informative, as is information about study habits and scores on standardized tests. The major problems in using data on students' learning to improve teaching are that: (a) graded work represents intended learning outcomes only incompletely, (b) it is difficult to connect particular features of teaching with specific learning outcomes, and (c) some important influences on learning are beyond the teacher's control.

Reviewing standards (comparator).   Feedback models strike some observers as excessively mechanistic and reductionistic, and as poor reflections of the complexities of teaching and learning. Unlike human systems, mechanical systems have no intentionality. Standards for mechanical systems are set from outside, as in the case of a homeowner setting the thermostat. In human situations, however, standards can be set from within the system. For example, a teacher adjusts expectations while carrying on a kind of conversation between personal values and external information. In the feedback framework, the comparator reflects the intentionality of human behavior.

Questionnaires about teachers' and students' goals help in examining values and standards. The "Teaching Goals Inventory" (Cross & Angelo, 1990), a product of the Classroom Research Project, asks teachers to indicate the importance, to them, of a large number of possible course goals: mastering knowledge of subject matter, developing a creative openness to new ideas, preparing for more advanced education, collaborating and working productively with others, synthesizing and integrating information and ideas from different sources, and so on. It is enlightening to learn how one's own preferences compare with those of colleagues who teach other courses, particularly if the courses have similar goals.

In considering standards, some limitations of the single feedback loop become clear. Most instructional situations actually have multiple feedback loops that are arranged hierarchically. Because a particular course is affected by much more than its immediate circumstances, standards can be reviewed in relation to feedback loops at other levels. These include loops within the institution and loops connecting the institution with its external constituencies. For example, a teacher may raise standards for students' performance as part of an effort to increase selectivity of the institution. This adjustment of standards leads to dissonance because weeding out poor students causes considerable disruption. The system ultimately will regain equilibrium, but at a different level than before. Dissonance is not necessarily undesirable, but it is important that the imbalance be brief because systems out of balance are unstable and risk self-destruction.

Enhancing teaching repertoires (output).   To increase the variety and quality of instructional skills is to alter output. Output is the result of intentions about new and future behaviors. The intentions are derived from comparisons between input and standards.

A psychology teacher, for example, said the following about a problem with students in a large class who were doing field projects: "I couldn't possibly see them all tutorially. So I thought of putting them into small groups and asking them to explicitly talk to each other about their projects, to give explicit suggestions for other activities, recording techniques, or anything else" (Stevens, 1988, p. 69).

Pleased with that change, the teacher went further when the course was offered next by giving each group an agenda that would help guide discussion. The agenda dealt with substantive ideas as well as with communication patterns in the group. Still hoping for more contact with students, she decided to meet with each group in her office. In subsequent terms, she introduced further refinements. None of the changes required that she learn new or difficult skills.

Other teachers in that study engaged in a similar "pattern of continual adjustment." As Stevens (1988) says, they "tinkered" with their teaching. They tried small variations in an instructional approach, attended to its effects, and further modified their subsequent teaching. A professor of communications described the process in this way: "It's not like a pendulum, switching back and forth between techniques. It's more like a bedspring. Instead of swinging back and forth, you kind of circle around. You pick up something you were doing before but this time when you use it, you use it differently" (Stevens, 1988, p. 69).

Some faculty members undeniably need training in particular skills—training to lecture clearly, to conduct discussions wisely, and to assess learning accurately. When skill training is requested, it should be available. Many faculty members, however, already are skillful enough to change their teaching once they have identified clearly what they intend to do. For them, it may be more urgent to learn how to derive new intentions and how to maintain new behaviors. These two skills are not likely to take care of themselves; acquiring them may require training and support.

To refine the skill of identifying behavioral intentions, faculty members need occasions on which they share with one another their possible intentions and describe how they arrived at them. When that is done explicitly, the process of forming intentions becomes clear and replicable. Maintaining new behaviors over time is difficult in the harried world of teaching, but we might extrapolate from other areas of research about strategies that prevent relapse into unwanted behavioral patterns. These strategies include forceful reminders from a partner, making the teacher accountable to colleagues who monitor progress, and rehearsing what to do in circumstances where the risk of relapse is particularly high (Walton, 1989).

INQUIRY ACTIVITIES: ILLUSTRATIVE SCENARIOS

Inquiry can take a variety of forms while meeting the conditions set forth in this chapter—that participation be voluntary, that significant decisions about features of the activity be made by each faculty member, and that the activity be guided by a heuristic framework.

The scenarios below meet those conditions, and they integrate several topics discussed earlier in this chapter. Each activity applies knowledge about what promotes students' learning, each proceeds within a theoretical perspective drawn from recent scholarship, and each is guided by a heuristic framework.

Discussion in the multicultural classroom.   After attending a workshop about effective class discussions, a professor decided to document the patterns of participation in his upper-division course. He invited a colleague to visit the class and to note which students spoke and how often each participated. Subsequently he analyzed audiotapes of several class meetings in the same way.

Results showed that almost no one who sat in the rear half of the room spoke, that few nonwhites spoke unless called upon, and that African-American women did not participate at all. The professor suggested that cultural factors were to blame. Students from Asian backgrounds are likely to be reticent, he reasoned, and previous experiences of African Americans, especially females, may lead them to expect that their classroom contributions will be devalued.

When he mentioned these explanations to the colleagues who had led the workshop, she challenged what she called his deterministic beliefs. She contended that although students may behave in this way at the beginning of a course, their participation will change under the right circumstances. Feeling challenged by her comments, the teacher proceeded to read about sexism and racism in the classroom. He vowed to try the boldest method he could find to see if he could change participation in discussion. This method, it turned out, was the "poker chip strategy" described by Sadker and Sadker (1992). According to this strategy, each student in the class is given three poker chips. Whenever a student speaks, he or she must deposit a chip. No student may speak without depositing a chip, and all the chips must be spent by the end of the session.

The professor initially thought this was a terribly contrived gimmick, and the students groaned loudly when he explained it. In almost no time, however, they were behaving as if they had created this classroom game themselves. Participation became more equitable, and the teacher was pleased to find that the students' contributions were thoughtful and to the point. End-of-term evaluations, in comparison with evaluations from previous courses, showed that students were better satisfied with the opportunity for discussion and rated the course more highly on "rapport with the instructor."

Not least among the consequences of this experience were changes in the teacher's beliefs. When the workshop leader asked him about the class, the teacher surprised himself by describing positively how these previously silent women and minority students were participating eagerly and skillfully. His beliefs about students were revised substantially as a result of the poker chip strategy.

This scenario links a social perspective on learning with research knowledge about the importance of students' interpersonal participation. The inquiry was not planned originally to focus on beliefs and theories, but under the workshop leader's probing questions, in fact it tested the teacher's personal theories against classroom realities.

Classroom research to improve learning of concepts.   Classroom research can be conducted individually, in collaboration with colleagues, or with assistance from a teaching consultant. In this scenario a teacher's topic for classroom research grew out of her concern that students were failing to master the key concepts of an introductory course. Their examinations showed that they were acquiring little more than memorized information.

A teaching consultant suggested some readings about the cognitive perspective on learning, including Weinstein and Meyer (1991) and a survey about students' study practices, the Motivated Strategies for Learning Questionnaire (Pintrich, Smith,

Gracia, & McKeachie, 1991). The questionnaire responses were revealing. Few students endorsed the following items: "When I study for this course, I write brief summaries of the main ideas from the readings and the concepts from the lectures": "I try to apply ideas from course readings in other class activities such as lecture and discussion"; "I try to relate ideas in this subject to those in other courses whenever possible."

The instructor concluded that the students required help with elaboration strategies. They needed to solidify their learning in long-term memory and to connect elements from their readings with content from lectures, discussions, and other course materials.

To train students in elaboration strategies, she devised tasks based on the teaching tips manual for the Motivated Strategies for Learning Questionnaire (Johnson et al., 1991). At every third class meeting, for example, she allocated time for students to work in pairs. They took turns summarizing and explaining to each other particularly problematic passages chosen by the teacher from reading assignments. They were instructed to accomplish three things: to summarize accurately, to connect the key idea of the passage to something from the lecture, and to create an analogy linking the key idea to other course material and to material in other courses. A few student pairs reported on their discussions to the class. Another task required that students answer the following four questions within two hours of the end of the class: What was the main point of the lesson? What in the lesson did I find most interesting? What is one probable test question that will come out of the lesson? What one question do I most want to ask of my instructor? At the beginning of some classes, the instructor called on students to report their answers. In other classes she asked all students to turn in their answers and assured them that some of the "probable test questions" would appear on course examinations.

When this instructor uses these procedures, course examinations should reveal improved learning of complex concepts. Longer retention and deeper understanding should result from students' reviewing, rehearsing, and connecting materials, and from their increased awareness about likely test questions.

This scenario links the cognitive perspective on learning with research findings that learning is enhanced by the kinds of tasks assigned to students. It also incorporates many of the steps of classroom research (refer back to Figure 3-1, page 70).

Expert and apprentice.   Once inquiry into one's own teaching becomes an accepted part of workplace culture, faculty members will be willing to commit themselves to relatively long-term activities. The following scenario describes the second year of an inquiry group in which teachers have agreed to form expert–apprentice pairs and to work on particular teaching skills. (Some readers may prefer terms other than *expert* and *apprentice*, but I use them here to echo the cognitive apprenticeships that are part of the learning sciences perspective.)

Group members begin by discussing teachers' behaviors that are most critical for students' learning (for examples, see Cohen, 1981; Feldman, 1989; Murray, 1983). Using course evaluation data, each member chooses areas of expertise and areas for improvement. For example, one teacher felt dissatisfied with this ability to "motivate students by setting high standards," as the course evaluation item phrased it. He decided to try to improve his skills in that area, and he found a partner in the group as expert—that is, someone already accomplished in these skills.

After considerable discussion about what behaviors are relevant to "setting high standards," the partners agreed that course standards become evident on the first day of class. They further agreed to videotape the first class meeting. (Subsequently they taped other key classroom events related to standards including return of test papers and explanations of course projects.) From the tapes it became evident that the expert is upbeat and optimistic, as well as rigorous, when discussing course requirements. The apprentice, on the other hand, seemed intimidating, almost threatening. Students' questions were few, and discussion was inhibited; in contrast, considerably more humor and enthusiasm were evident in the expert's class.

Once targeted skills were identified and expert–apprentice relationships were formed, each pair followed the methods for moving toward expertise that were advocated by Collins, Brown, and Newman (1989); modeling, coaching, scaffolding, articulation, reflection, and exploration.

The professor in the tape of the first class provided an expert *model*. With this in mind, the apprentice practiced rephrasing for his partner the comments about course standards. The expert *coached* him about nonverbal as well as verbal communication. The apprentice planned how to introduce an upcoming test to the class and showed a practice tape to the group. Their comments provided further *scaffolding*. Responding to their reactions helped him *articulate* a framework of goals and strategies to guide his actions.

As the term proceeded, the apprentice had other opportunities to review taped behaviors and to *reflect* on how they compared with tapes of the expert in her class. Next term, he will extend his skills into new territory by *exploring* their applicability to other courses. He will inspect student's course evaluations to determine whether their perceptions have changed because of his new approach to standards.

This inquiry fits the feedback-seeking framework. The apprentice identified an aspect of teaching that was not working. Information was fed back to the teacher from students and from the expert. The new data helped to refine his skills until they matched his expectations more closely. Thus, the scenario links knowledge about teaching behaviors that promote learning with methods from the learning sciences perspective, all within a feedback-seeking framework.

SUMMARY

In the first part of this chapter I described a number of factors related to students' learning in postsecondary education. Substantial research shows that class size, students' interpersonal activity, systems of individualized instruction, academic tasks assigned to students, grading practices, and teachers' behaviors influence the quality and quantity of both students' satisfaction and learning of subject matter. These factors are most important, I argue, when the teacher deliberately uses them to improve students' contact with the subject matter (exposure), to enhance active involvement with the subject matter (practice), and to increase information to students about their learning (feedback).

In the second part of the chapter, I described and critiqued in terms of available research the interventions most commonly used with faculty members for improving teaching. Each of these interventions—workshops, consultations, grants, resource materials, and colleagues teaching colleagues—can enhance faculty members' performance, but existing research does not tell us precisely how to use these interventions most effectively with particular faculty members. Even less is known about ways to enhance the effectiveness of professional development specialists, members of support staff, and administrators.

One problem shared by these interventions is that most of them treat professors as dependent rather than as autonomous learners. An inquiry approach, in which activities are largely self-initiated, avoids that problem. In the third part of the chapter, I described several approaches to inquiry in the context of programs for professional development and improvement of teaching. The inquiry approach is most likely to succeed when faculty members' beliefs about engaging in inquiry are positive, when the organizational environment is supportive, and when the particular topic for inquiry is embedded in an appropriate heuristic framework. Three scenarios show how topics discussed in the chapter can be pursued as inquiry activities.

In schools and colleges of education, opportunities for professional development of faculty members are extensive; they are also challenging. This chapter raises many issues about content and method in such programs, as well as about program evaluation and refinement. I hope that the chapter will provoke discussion about efforts to improve teaching and learning among teacher educators and that it will stimulate discussion about improving the knowledge on which these efforts rest.

REFERENCES

Ajzen, I., & Fishbein, M. (1980). *Understanding attitudes and predicting social behavior.* Englewood Cliffs, NJ: Prentice-Hall.

Andrews, J. D. (1980). The verbal structure of teacher questions: Its impact on class discussion. *POD Quarterly, 2,* 129–163.

Angelo, T. A. (1989). Faculty development for learning: The promise of classroom research. *To improve the Academy, 8,* 37–60.

Angelo, T. A. (Ed.) (1991). *Classroom research: Early lessons from success.* San Francisco, CA: Jossey-Bass.

Angelo, T. A., & Cross, K. P. (1993). *Classroom assessment techniques: A handbook for college teachers* (2nd ed.). San Francisco, CA: Jossey-Bass.

Bennett, J. B., & Figuli, D. J. (1990). *Enhancing departmental leadership.* New York: Macmillan.

Billson, J. M., & Tiberius, R. G. (1991). Effective social arrangements for teaching and learning. In R. J. Menges & M. Svinicki (Eds.), *College teaching: From theory to practice* (pp. 87–105). San Francisco, CA: Jossey-Bass.

Blake, V. M., & Dinham, S. M. (1991). *Design and management of academic tasks in university teaching.* Paper presented at the Annual Meeting of the American Educational Research Association, Chicago, IL.

Boice, R. (1991). New faculty: Quick starters who succeed. In M. Theall & J. Franklin (Eds.), *Effective practices for improving teaching* (pp. 111–121). San Francisco, CA: Jossey-Bass.

Boyer, E. L. (1990). *Scholarship reconsidered: Priorities of the professoriate.* Princeton, NJ: Carnegie Foundation for the Advancement of Teaching.

Brown, J. S., Collins, A., & Duguid, P. (1989). Situated cognition and the culture of learning. *Educational Researcher, 18*(1), 32–42.

Centra, J. A. (1978). Types of faculty development programs. *Journal of Higher Education, 49,* 151–162.

Cohen, P. A. (1981). Student ratings of instruction and student achievement: A meta-analysis of multisection validity studies. *Review of Educational Research, 51,* 281–309.

Collins, A. (1991). The role of computer technology in restructuring schools. *Phi Delta Kappan, 73*(1), 28–36.

Collins, A., Brown, J. S., & Newman, S. E. (1989). Cognitive apprenticeship: Teaching the crafts of reading, writing, and mathematics. In L. B. Resnick (Ed.), *Knowing, learning, and instruction: Essays in honor of Robert Glaser* (pp. 453–494). Hillsdale, NJ: Erlbaum.

Committee on the Evaluation and Improvement of Teaching. (1991). *Final report to the Provost.* Evanston, IL: Northwestern University.

Creswell, J. W., Wheeler, D. W., Seagren, A. T., Egly, N. J., & Beyer, K. D. (1990). *The academic chairperson's handbook.* Lincoln, NE: University of Nebraska Press.

Crooks, T. J. (1988). The impact of classroom evaluation practices on students. *Review of Educational Research, 58,* 438–481.

Cross, K. P. (1990). Classroom research: Helping professors learn more about teaching and learning. In P. Seldin & Associates (Eds.) *How administrators can improve teaching* (pp. 122–142). San Francisco, CA: Jossey-Bass.

Cross, K. P., & Angelo, T. A. (1990). *Teaching goals inventory.* Berkeley, CA: Classroom Research Project.

Doyle, W. (1983). Academic work. *Review of Educational Research, 53,* 159–199.

Doyle, W. (1991). Classroom tasks: The core of learning from teaching. In M. S. Knapp & P. M. Shields (Eds.), *Better schooling for the children of poverty.* Berkeley, CA: McCutcheon.

Dunkin, M. J. (1986). Research on teaching in higher education. In M. C. Wittrock (Ed.), *Handbook of research on teaching* (3rd ed.) (pp. 754–777). New York: Macmillan.

Eble, K., & McKeachie, W. J. (1985). *Improving undergraduate education through faculty development.* San Francisco, CA: Jossey-Bass.

Eisen, J., & Hill, H. H. (1990). Creating workshops for new faculty. *Journal of Staff, Program, and Organizational Development, 8,* 223–234.

Ellner, C. L., Barnes, C. P., & Associates. (1983). *Studies of college teaching: Experimental results, theoretical interpretations, and new perspectives.* Lexington, MA: Heath.

Ellsworth, R., Duell, O. K., & Velotta, C. L. (1991). Length of wait-times used by college students given unlimited wait-time intervals. *Contemporary Educational Psychology, 16,* 265–271.

Erickson, G. (1986). A survey of faculty development practices. *To Improve the Academy, 5,* 182–196.

Feldman, K. A. (1989). The association between student ratings of specific instructional dimensions and student achievement: Refining and extending the synthesis of data from multisection validity studies. *Research in Higher Education, 30,* 583–645.

Fenstermacher, G. (1986). Philosophy of research on teaching: Three aspects. In M. Wittrock (Ed.), *Handbook of research on teaching* (3rd. ed.) (pp. 37–49). New York: Macmillan.

Forsyth, D. R., & McMillan, J. H. (1991). Practical proposals for motivating students. In R. J. Menges & M. Svinicki (Eds.), *College teaching: From theory to practice* (pp. 53–65). San Francisco, CA: Jossey-Bass.

Golin, S. (1990). Four arguments for peer collaboration and student interviewing: The master faculty program. *AAHE Bulletin, 43*(4), 9–10.

Grimmett, P. P., & Erickson, G. L. (Eds.). (1988). *Reflection in teacher education.* New York: Teachers College Press.

Hansen, D. W. (1983). Faculty development activities in Illinois Community College System. *Community/Junior College Quarterly, 7,* 207–230.

Jacobsen, R. H. (1989). *The impact of faculty incentive grants on teaching.* Paper presented at the meeting of the American Educational Research Association, San Francisco, CA.

Johnson, G. R. (1990). *Motivated strategies for learning.* Presentation at the Annual Meeting of the Professional and Organizational Development Network, Lake Tahoe, NV.

Johnson, G. R., Eison, J. A., Abbott, R., Meiss, G. T., Moran, K., Gorgan, J. A., Pasternak, T. L., Zaremba, E., & McKeachie, W. J. (1991). *Teaching tips for users of the Motivated Strategies for Learning Questionnaire (MSLQ).* Ann Arbor, MI: National Center for Research to Improve Postsecondary Teaching and Learning, School of Education, University of Michigan.

Katz, J., & Henry, M. (1988). *Turning professors into teachers.* New York: Macmillan.

Keller, F. S. (1968). "Good-bye teacher . . ." *Journal of Applied Behavior Analysis, 1,* 79–89.

Konrad, A. C. (1983). Faculty development practicers in Canadian universities. *The Canadian Journal of Higher Education, 13*(2), 13–25.

Kulik, J. A. (1987). Keller Plan: A personalized system of instruction. In M. J. Dunkin (Ed.), *International encyclopedia of teaching and teacher education* (pp. 306–311). New York: Pergamon.

Kulik, J. A., Jaksa, P., & Kulik, C-L. C. (1978). Research on component features of Keller's Personalized System of Instruction. *Journal of Personalized Instruction, 3,* 2–14.

Kulik, J. A., Kulik, C-L. C., & Cohen, P. A. (1979). A meta-analysis of outcome studies of Keller's Personalized System of Instruction. *American Psychologist, 34*, 307–318.

Levinson-Rose, J., & Menges, R. J. (1981). Improving college teaching: A critical review of research. *Review of Educational Research, 51*, 403–434.

Marx, R. D. (1986). Self-managed skill retention. *Training and Development Journal, 40*(1), 54–57.

McKeachie, W. J. (1990). Learning, thinking, and Thorndike. *Educational Psychologist, 25*, 127–141.

McKeachie, W. J., Pintrich, P. R., Lin, Y-G., Smith, D. A. F., & Sharma, R. (1990). *Teaching and learning in the college classroom: A review of the research literature* (2nd ed.). Ann Arbor, MI: National Center for Research to Improve Postsecondary Teaching and Learning.

McMillan, J. H., & Forsyth, D. F. (1991). What theories of motivation say about why learners learn. In R. J. Menges & M. Svinicki (Eds.), *College teaching: From theory to practice* (pp. 39–52). San Francisco, CA: Jossey-Bass.

Menges, R. J. (1990). Using evaluative information to improve teaching. In P. Seldin & Associates (Eds.), *How administrators can improve teaching* (pp. 104–121). San Francisco, CA: Jossey-Bass.

Menges, R. J. (1991a). *Promising areas in faculty/staff development.* Address at the Seventeenth International Conference on Improving University Teaching, Glasgow, July 2–5.

Menges, R. J. (1991b). The real world of teaching improvement: A faculty perspective. In M. Theall & J. Franklin (Eds.), *Effective practices for improving teaching* (pp. 21–37). San Francisco, CA: Jossey-Bass.

Menges, R. J. (1994). Improving your teaching. In W. J. McKeachie (Ed.), *Teaching tips: Strategies, research, and theory for college and university teachers* (9th ed.) (pp. 297–312). Lexington, MA: D. C. Heath.

Menges, R. J., & Brinko, K. T. (1986). *Effects of student evaluation feedback: A meta-analysis of higher education research.* Paper presented at the American Educational Research Association, San Francisco, CA (ERIC ED 270 408).

Menges, R. J., & Mathis, B. C. (1988). *Key resources on teaching, learning, curriculum, and faculty development.* San Francisco, CA: Jossey-Bass.

Menges, R. J., & Svinicki, M. (Eds.). (1991). *College teaching: From theory to practice.* San Francisco, CA: Jossey-Bass.

Moses, I. (1985). Academic development units and the improvement of teaching. *Higher Education, 14*, 75–100.

Murray, H. G. (1983). Low-inference classroom teaching behaviors and student ratings of college teaching effectiveness. *Journal of Educational Psychology, 75*, 138–149.

Partington, P. A. (1991). *Staff (faculty) development policy: Recent trends and their implications.* Address at the Seventeenth International Conference on Improving University Teaching, Glasgow, July 2–5.

Pascarella, E. T., & Terenzini, P. T. (1991). *How college affects students: Findings and insights from twenty years of research.* San Francisco, CA: Jossey-Bass.

Pintrich, P. R. (1989). The dynamic interplay of student motivation and cognition in the college classroom. In M. Maehr & C. Ames (Eds.), *Advances in motivation and achievement: Motivation enhancing environments* (pp. 117–160). New York: JAI Press.

Pintrich, P. R., Smith, D. A. F., Gracia, T., & McKeachie, W. J. (1991). *A manual for the use of the Motivated Strategies for Learning Questionnaire (MSLQ).* Ann Arbor, MI: National Center for Research to Improve Postsecondary Teaching and Learning, School of Education, University of Michigan.

Rando, W., & Menges, R. J. (1991). How practice is shaped by personal theories. In R. J. Menges & M. Svinicki (Eds.), *College teaching: From theory to practice* (pp. 7–14). San Francisco, CA: Jossey-Bass.

Richardson, R., & Moore, W. (1987). Faculty development and evaluation in Texas community colleges. *Community/Junior College Quarterly, 11,* 19–32.

Sadker, M., & Sadker, D. (1992). Ensuring equitable participation in college classes. In L. L. B. Border & N. V. N. Chism (Eds.), *Teaching for diversity* (pp. 49–56). San Francisco, CA: Jossey-Bass.

Sherman, T. M., Armistead, L. P., Fowler, F., Barksdale, M. A., & Reif, G. (1987). The quest for excellence in university teaching. *Journal of Higher Education, 58,* 66–84.

Shulman, L. S. (1986). Those who understand: Knowledge growth in teaching. *Educational Researcher, 15*(2), 4–14.

Smith, A. (1981). Staff development goals and practices in U.S. community colleges. *Community/Junior College Research Quarterly, 2,* 209–225.

Sprague, J., & Nyquist, J. D. (1991). A developmental perspective on the TA role. In J. D. Nyquist, R. D. Abbott, D. H. Wulff, & J. Sprague (Eds.), *Preparing the professoriate of tomorrow to teach* (pp. 295–312). Dubuque, IA: Kendall/Hunt.

Steiner, D. D., Dobbins, G. H., & Trahan, W. A. (1991). The trainer-trainee interaction: An attributional model of training. *Journal of Organizational Behavior, 12,* 271–286.

Stevens, E. (1988). Tinkering with teaching. *Review of Higher Education, 12,* 63–78.

Svinicki, M. (1991a). Practical implications of cognitive theories. In R. J. Menges & M. Svinicki (Eds.), *College teaching: From theory to practice* (pp. 27–37). San Francisco, CA: Jossey-Bass.

Svinicki, M. (1991b). Theories and metaphors we teach by. In R. J. Menges & M. Svinicki (Eds.), *College teaching: From theory to practice* (pp. 111–119). San Francisco, CA: Jossey-Bass.

Tiberius, R. G., & Billson, J. M. (1991). The social context of teaching and learning. In R. J. Menges & M. Svinicki (Eds.), *College teaching: From theory to practice* (pp. 67–86). San Francisco, CA: Jossey-Bass.

Tucker, A. (1984). *Chairing the academic department* (2nd ed.). New York: Macmillan.

Walton, J. M. (1989). Self-reinforcing behavior change. *Personnel Journal, 68*(10), 64–68.

Weimer, M., & Lenze, L. F. (1991). Instructional interventions: A review of the literature on efforts to improve instruction. In J. Smart (Ed.), *Higher education: Handbook of theory and research, Vol. VII* (pp. 294–333). New York: Agathon.

Weinstein, C. E., & Meyer, D. K. (1991). Cognitive learning strategies and college teaching. In R. J. Menges & M. Svinicki (Eds.), *College teaching: From theory to practice* (pp. 15–26). San Francisco, CA: Jossey-Bass.

4

THE ARTS AND SCIENCES AS PREPARATION FOR TEACHING*

G. WILLIAMSON McDIARMID

National Center for Research on Teacher Education
Michigan State University

For decades, elementary and secondary teachers and schools have been under siege from various critics. Typically, critics trace the problems they see in public school teaching back to teacher

*The author gratefully acknowledges the assistance of Lamar Fertig, Jaime Grinburg, Margaret Malenka, and Steve Smith in gathering and evaluating much of the material reviewed herein. Peter Vinten-Johansen provided thoughtful comments from an arts and science perspective. This research was supported in part by the National Center for Research on Teacher Learning (NCRTL), Michigan State University. The NCRTL is funded primarily by the Office of Education Research & Improvement, United States Department of Education (OERI/ED) with additional funding from the College of Education, Michigan State University (COE/MSU). The opinions expressed in this paper are those of the author and do not necessarily reflect the position, policy, or endorsement of the OERI/ED or the COE/MSU.

education, charging that education courses are intellectually vapid (e.g., see Kramer, 1991). Yet arts and science faculty, rather than their teacher education counterparts, traditionally have been responsible for teaching prospective teachers their subject matter. Teacher educators may not even regard the teaching of subject-matter content as their responsibility, assuming that prospective teachers learn the content they need in their arts and science courses (Floden, McDiarmid, & Wiemers, 1990). One needn't be an apologist for teacher education to suggest that it has been a visible and easy target for critics—many of whom, incidentally, call arts and science departments home. As Tobias (1990) noted, college science professors tend to call for reforms of precollegiate teaching but remain remarkably uncritical of their own efforts: "Reformers . . . are most comfortable dealing with problems that have their origins (and, hence, their solutions) elsewhere" (p. 8).

In its recently completed longitudinal four-year Teacher Education and Learning to Teach (TELT) study, researchers at the National Center for Research on Teacher Education (NCRTE) found what many people suspected and what other investigators (e.g., Cohen et al., 1990) also have found: elementary and high school teachers frequently lack connected, conceptual understandings of the subjects they are expected to teach (NCRTE, 1991). High school teachers major in the subject they teach, and in many institutions they must take the same required courses as all other majors. More important, the teachers in the TELT sample rarely reported encountering opportunities in college (either in arts and science or in teacher education), much less in elementary or high school, to develop the deep, connected understanding of subject matter that some advocate as vital if teachers are to help diverse learners to develop meaningful understandings (see Ball & McDiarmid, 1990).

That teachers frequently lack the kind of understanding of subject matter that they need is puzzling. Aren't they taught the knowledge they need? In some cases—such as in mathematics—the answer is no. Few institutions offer mathematics courses that include number theory, for instance. Consequently many teachers must rely on what they learned about numbers in elementary school. In other cases, however, teachers have attended courses—in mathematics, history, composition, or physics—which include topics or concepts that they are responsible for teaching. For instance, history majors planning to teach high school are generally required to take at least a survey course in

American history. So what's going on? What are undergraduates learning in their arts and science courses? How does what they learn prepare those who plan to teach for the increasingly diverse classrooms of today?

Many of the colleges and schools of education that constitute the Holmes Group are engaged or, perhaps more accurately, embroiled in transforming their traditional four-year baccalaureate degrees into five-year programs. All teachers in such programs will be required to major or specialize in an academic subject. This reform, in part, is a response to the criticism, heard for years from various quarters, that teachers lack adequate knowledge of their subject matter (Bestor, 1953/1985; Conant, 1963; Kramer, 1991; Rickover, 1960). Because they have traditionally regarded arts and science courses as teachers' primary sources for knowledge of subject matter, teacher educators and policy makers have lighted on more arts and science courses and fewer education courses as the remedy. Although this reform doubtless delights the many critics of education courses, the question remains: Will reforms requiring more arts and science courses result in prospective teachers' developing more of the knowledge and understandings they need for teaching? In particular, how will requiring arts and science majors of teachers prepare them to teach in ways that enable diverse students to develop the critical and meaningful understandings called for by various reform proposals (American Association for the Advancement of Science, 1989a; National Council of Teachers of Mathematics, 1989; National Research Council, 1989, 1991)?

In the following discussion, I review some of the evidence that has been gathered on teaching and learning in arts and science courses. To write about higher education is to risk overgeneralizing. Because more than 2,100 institutions grant baccalaureate degrees in the United States, few generalizations will hold true for the full array of colleges and universities (Boyer, 1987). When one undertakes to write about teaching and learning, the number and variety of courses offered in these diverse institutions compound further the dangers of overgeneralizing. Certainly many students, particularly during their junior and senior years, experience inspiring classes in which they develop deep insights and meaningful, connected knowledge. Many students who attend liberal arts colleges or participate in honors programs in large public universities—institutions and programs that pride themselves on their teaching—encounter teaching that is focused as much on ensuring that students understand as on covering the subject. Nonetheless, this is only one of the stories that can be told about teaching and learning in arts and science courses.

CRITIQUES OF UNDERGRADUATE TEACHING

Another story about teaching in higher education concerns a particular set of beliefs about teaching, learning, and knowledge that appear remarkably consistent over time. Edwin Slosson, a journalist who undertook a study of the "great American universities" in 1910, labeled the teaching that he observed in the more than 100 classes he attended largely a "waste of time and energy." He reported "no lack of industry, devotion, and enthusiasm on the part of the teachers, but the educational results are not commensurate with the opportunities afforded and the efforts expended" (quoted in Smith, 1990, p. 214). Slosson found the lectures he attended not merely dry as dust but weighted down by unnecessarily detailed information.

Nearly eighty years later, Boyer (1987) and his associates observed classes in a stratified sample of 29 institutions of higher learning. Presenting a picture of teaching and learning that differs little in substance or tone from Slosson's, Boyer notes that "with few exceptions," his research team observed university faculty presenting information that "students passively received." Typically these classes afforded "little opportunity for positions to be clarified or ideas challenged" (p. 150). Another researcher estimated that students listen to lectures about 80 percent of the time they are in class and attend to what the lecturer is saying about half of the time (Pollio, 1984). After reviewing observational studies of university teaching, Dunkin and Barnes (1986) concluded that most college courses, like classes at other levels, emphasize "lower-level and convergent types of cognitive operations" (p. 763). If these investigators and others are to be believed, the instruction that typifies many, if not most, undergraduate classes appears to have changed little over this century.

And what a century! Not only has the sheer volume of information expanded numbingly, but information—via electronic databases, on-line information services, CD-ROM, and other technologies—is more readily available to potentially more people than almost anyone could have foreseen even three or four decades ago. The ready availability of information in most fields through a variety of easily accessible sources raises questions about the efficacy of the lecture as primarily a source of information. In addition, a dramatic change has taken place in who attends college. In most, if not all, of the lecture halls he visited in 1910, Slosson observed almost exclusively young, male, white students bent over notebooks. Lecturers who were themselves predominantly male and white could presume shared values, experiences, and expectations. Such presumptions no longer pertain as student populations have grown more socially, racially, and culturally diverse, and the economic and technological environment has changed radically. Although the world has changed dramatically, college teaching apparently has not.

Perhaps college instruction has not changed because it is satisfactory. After all, some researchers have generated evidence that those who attend college do, in fact, score higher on tests of verbal and mathematical skills than those who do not—even after controlling for race, parents' education, father's occupation, gender, handicapped status, region of the country, high school mathematics courses, public or private school, and scores at time of high school graduation. (For a review of this research, see Pascarella & Terenzini, 1991.) After testing both freshmen and seniors on a variety of measures, including analyses of argument, tests of thematic analysis, and concept learning, Whitla (1977), for instance, reported that the seniors consistently did better.

Many critics, however, are not persuaded. Perkins (1986), for example, asked students, both when they began and when they completed college, a series of questions that required them to reason informally. He concluded that students' capacities for such reasoning did not appear to be enhanced by the experience of college. A number of recent treatments have excoriated college teaching in language and in a tone reserved previously for secondary and elementary teaching. A National Research Council study (1991) of undergraduate mathematics described much university teaching as "casual." Rigden and Tobias (1991) reported, on the basis of observations by faculty and graduate students from fields outside science who attended undergraduate science classes, that the "basic ideas and concepts that compose science . . . receive little direct or explicit attention in introductory classrooms" (p. 52). Boyer (1987), noting that on most campuses "teaching is often viewed as a routine function, tacked on, something almost anyone can do" (p. 23), recommended "a more inclusive view of what it means to be a scholar" (p. 24); such a view would recognize that knowledge is acquired through teaching as well as through research. Historian Page Smith (1990), in a scathing attack on universities in the United States, decried the "sorry state" of college teaching and overreliance on lecturing, noting that in more than 30 years in the university he can recall only five or six really good lecturers. Without dialogue in the classroom, Smith argues, no genuine education occurs.

In *Integrity in the College Curriculum*, the Project on Redefining the Meaning and Purpose of Baccalaureate Degrees (1985) bemoaned the "transformation of the professors from teachers concerned with the characters and minds of their students to professional scholars with Ph.D. degrees with an allegiance to academic discipline stronger than their commitment to teaching" (p. 6), although the authors do not reveal when this golden age of college teaching existed. Reacting to the passive role that it believes students play in most college courses, the Study Group on the Conditions of Excellence in American Higher Education (1984) called on college faculty to design curriculum and instruction that engage students more actively—a recommendation consistent with the findings of Astin (1985) and other researchers (see Pascarella & Terenzini, 1991).

In short, if these various reports are to be believed, all is not well in the college classroom. The experience of developing knowledge and understandings that are connected and meaningful may be less widespread than advocates of more arts and science courses for prospective teachers appear to assume. The authors of the Project on Redefining the Meaning and Purpose of Baccalaureate Degrees (1985) worry that the "decline and devaluation of the undergraduate degree," due in part to the frequently poor quality of undergraduate teaching, leaves graduates inadequately prepared for the business and corporate world. For those of us who are concerned with the education of teachers, a greater worry is that more prospective teachers are likely to be spending more time in arts and science classes. In these classes they are likely to encounter teaching which, according to a number of critics and investigators, is often mechanical and focused on disembodied detail, however well intended. What will prospective teachers learn in these courses? Will they have opportunities to develop the knowledge and understandings required to help all children learn?

A VIEW OF KNOWLEDGE FOR TEACHING

Before turning to the evidence on undergraduate learning in specific subjects, I wish to describe the kind of content knowledge that a number of people believe teachers need. After all, one's notion about what teachers need to know about their subjects is the basis from which one argues for what teachers should have the opportunity to learn. Regardless of their beliefs about what teachers need to know about the school subjects they teach, nearly everyone should be concerned about the evidence on teachers' knowledge of the subjects taught in schools. For those who believe that teachers need to know only what is conventionally included in the curriculum of schools in the United States—no more, no less—the evidence is that many undergraduates, including prospective teachers, do not know fundamental information and procedures in the subjects they must teach (Ball, 1988a, 1988b, 1989; Ball & Wilson, 1990; McDiarmid & Wilson, 1991; Ravitch, 1989; Rosaen, Roth, & Lanier, 1988).

Knowledge of the contents of the conventional school curriculum may be sufficient for teaching some subjects. As the demands of schooling change, however, teachers will need to know more than the facts, events, procedures, ideas, and so on, in the written school curriculum. Hirsch (1987) argues that in addition to knowing who Grant is, "we need to know . . . the broad social and historical significance of the American Civil War" (p. 59). Calls for reform in the teaching of mathematics consistently include recommendations for greater attention to mathematical reasoning and problem solving, quantitative sense and power, and the capacity and inclination to use mathematics to make sense of everyday situations (National Council of Teachers of Mathematics, 1989a, 1989b; National Research Council, 1989, 1991). The goal of a recent national initiative to reform science teaching is the scientifically literate citizen:

> who is aware that science, mathematics, and technology are interdependent human enterprises with strengths and limitations; understands key concepts and principles of science; is familiar with the natural world and recognizes both its diversity and unity; and uses scientific knowledge and scientific ways of thinking for individual and social purposes. (American Association for the Advancement of Science, 1989, p. 4)

These calls for reform posit a new kind of learning and knowing in the various subjects—deeper, more connected, and more meaningful to the learner than generally was the case in the past. To help increasingly diverse learners develop such knowledge, teachers will need knowledge that is likewise more connected, deeper, and more extensive than most teachers have had the opportunity to develop during their own schooling (National Council of Teachers of Mathematics, 1989b; Wilson & Sykes, 1989). Not only do they need such knowledge; as teachers, they also must be able to organize their knowledge in ways that enable them to construct compelling and accurate explanations (Leinhardt, 1987; Leinhardt & Smith, 1985).

Indeed, some observers argue that knowledge of subject matter and a general understanding of the field, although absolutely necessary, are not sufficient for teachers: Teachers also need to know about the subjects they teach (Anderson, 1991; Ball, 1991; Banks, 1971, 1991; Buchmann, 1984; Grossman, 1990; Scheffler, 1973; Shulman, 1986, 1987; Watts, 1972; Wilson, 1991). Knowing about a subject includes knowing how new knowledge is created or discovered and tested, major debates and disagreements in the field, the principal perspectives or "schools," how the field has developed, who has contributed to that development, and who has not done so and why not (Ball & McDiarmid, 1990; Kline, 1977; Schwab, 1964; Shulman, 1986, 1987; Watts, 1972).

Several arguments are made to support the idea that teachers must learn about the subjects they teach. The argument made above is that teachers need such knowledge in order to help their learners develop similar understandings (Buchmann, 1984; Scheffler, 1973). An understanding of the nature of a subject also enhances learners' capacity to learn more on their own. Not only do they know where to look for new ideas and information, they have standards for evaluating these when they find them. A teacher who understands how scientific knowledge evolves and what role the scientific community plays in testing new knowledge claims could help students make better sense of controversies, such as those over cold fusion research and genetic engineering, than could a teacher who lacks such understanding. Such a capacity to judge the validity of competing claims and to learn on one's own is critical to a democratic society and to a world in which knowledge in nearly every field is growing at a dizzying pace.

The obligation to engage diverse students in learning is yet another argument (McDiarmid, 1991a). By understanding who constructed the accounts of history that find their way into textbooks, curriculum guides, standardized tests, and so on, teachers can help students from groups whose roles in the past are frequently ignored, misrepresented, or underrepresented in these accounts to understand why and how this happens and what it demonstrates about the nature of history (Banks, 1971). After reading summaries of four competing interpretations of Reconstruction, 16 history majors in a required historiography course—half of whom plan to teach—reported that they had encountered only one of the interpretations in high school (McDiarmid, Wiemers, & Fertig, 1991). The single one they had encountered, moreover, casts African Americans in the postwar South as passive dupes of manipulative carpetbaggers. This view has been contested for more than 50 years (DuBois, 1935; Woodward, 1986) and has been revised by other historians beginning in the 1940s (Current, 1988; Foner, 1988), but apparently it has yet to be displaced in many high schools or in the wider culture. What does this interpretation, unchallenged, convey to African-American students about their heritage and themselves? What does it convey to other students about African Americans? Without a critical perspective on the knowledge that finds its way into the curriculum, teachers are unprepared to help students develop a similarly critical stance—a stance essential for all students, but particularly for those whose people have been excluded from the curriculum.

Knowing about the subject matter—for instance, that writing historical accounts involves interpreting as well as chronicling events—also helps teachers understand how ideas, theories, facts, events, and interpretations are connected to form a big picture of a subject. If they appreciate that experts in a field may disagree about the relative importance of various evidence or arguments, as well as the relationships among them, teachers are able to seek and make such connections in the various materials that they and their students use. Teachers then can help students develop an overarching picture of events or epochs that goes beyond the skeletal information usually provided in the published materials.

Although teachers rarely do so consciously and deliberately, as a matter of course they communicate to their students their understanding of the nature of the subject (Beers, 1988). The teacher's understanding of the subject is embodied in the social organization and interactions of the classroom, the kinds of instructional tasks pupils perform, the ways in which instructional representations, such as textbooks, are treated, and the kinds of discourse that the teacher encourages (Ball & McDiarmid, 1990; Doyle, 1986; McDiarmid, Ball, & Anderson, 1989; Wilson & Wineberg, 1988). Findings from observational studies of classrooms show why this situation is currently problematic:

Teachers tend to promote an uncritical view of validity claims (Young, 1987), thus leading students to develop assumptions that what is in books is "true," that scientific results are "correct," and that adults' claims must be well-founded.

For instance, teachers who view history as little more than a chronicle of past events, who are not aware of the contentious and interpretive nature of historical knowledge, are likely to take an uncritical position towards the textbooks they use. Recently a variety of critics of history textbooks (Axtell, 1987; FitzGerald, 1979; Gagnon, 1988; London, 1984; Sewall, 1987) pointed out the dangers of such a position. In both history and social studies, as in other subjects, elementary and secondary teachers "depend heavily on textbooks as their major source of course content" (Sewall, 1987, p. 62). With only one or two exceptions, these critics charge, the textbooks are bloodless "catalogues of factual material about the past" (p. 65) that portray history as "just one damned thing after another" (FitzGerald, 1979, p. 161). Without considerable knowledge of content and an understanding of the nature of history, teachers are at the mercy of such texts, unable to put textbook accounts into perspective or to offer alternative interpretations (Wilson & Sykes, 1989; Wilson, 1991). Comparable charges have been leveled at mathematics textbooks that typically "foster an algorithmic approach to the subject" (Ball & McDiarmid, 1990, p. 445). Small wonder that most pupils consistently rate these subjects among their least favorite and score low on tests of knowledge in these fields (National Research Council, 1989; Ravitch, 1989).

One final argument for teachers knowing the content of the subjects they are to teach as well as knowing about that content—its construction, its growth, its development over time—is the critical nature of the ties between knowledge of subject matter and the particular knowledge of subject matter needed for teaching that has been termed "pedagogical content knowledge" (Shulman, 1986, 1987). This phrase expresses the idea that teachers not only must know the subject matter for themselves, but they also must be capable of representing it in ways that are true to the discipline and that build bridges between the subject and learners from a variety of backgrounds. The empirical and conceptual work that has been done on pedagogical content knowledge is linked by a common theme: Teachers must attend to the interaction of pedagogy and content. Their capacity to attend to this interaction—to think through the implications of pedagogy for organizing and representing the subject and those of the subject for their role, for their students' roles, and for orchestrating their instruction—depends on their knowledge of the nature of knowing in the subjects they must teach (Ball, 1990; Ball & McDiarmid, 1990; Lampert, 1985; McDiarmid et al., 1989; Shulman, 1986, 1987; Wilson, in press; Wilson, Shulman, & Richert, 1987; Wilson & Sykes, 1989; Wilson & Wineberg, 1988; Wineberg & Wilson, 1991).

In sum, I find agreement among critics whose expectations for teachers' subject-matter knowledge range from the purely factual to knowledge about the nature of knowing in a field: As society's expectations for students' learning rise, many teachers' knowledge of the subjects they must teach will become increasingly inadequate to the task of helping pupils learn what they need to know. Arts and science courses continue to be a primary source of subject-matter knowledge for prospective teachers. The movement to five-year programs, alternate routes, and state-mandated restrictions on courses in education foreshadows an even greater role for arts and science courses in educating prospective teachers. Consequently, the knowledge and understanding that they develop in these courses must be a primary concern to those intent on improving the education of teachers.

STUDYING THE LEARNING OF SUBJECT MATTER IN THE ARTS AND SCIENCES: DIFFERENT KINDS OF KNOWLEDGE

For decades, researchers have been studying what students learn in college. In doing so, they have used a variety of instruments in an effort to measure the impact of college. Most frequently, the instrument of choice has been a standardized instrument such as the Scholastic Aptitude Test, the American College Test, or the Graduate Record Examination—paper-and-pencil, multiple-choice tests (Pascarella & Terenzini, 1991). The reason is obvious: Because these tests are standardized, students' performances can be compared regardless of treatment. This quality allows researchers to compare the effectiveness of different treatments. The disadvantages of such instruments are also obvious: They reveal little about why students answer the way they do, and they measure a limited range of knowledge. If investigators are studying a treatment in order to understand (say) how to improve the teaching of fractions, knowing that most of the students in the sample cannot choose a correct example to illustrate

1 3/4 divided by 1/2 tells them little that serves the purpose of instructional improvement. Researchers know only that the treatment under study does not seem to help students develop such knowledge.

These instruments do not even register other types of knowledge—for instance, students' understanding of what a fraction is and the different ways in which fractions can be interpreted and are used. Moreover, for those interested in the education of teachers, even the knowledge that a few prospective teachers can choose the correct answer for a calculation reveals little about whether they would be able to help learners figure out similar problems.

Pascarella and Terenzini (1991), who reviewed the research on undergraduate learning of subject matter, conclude that "the more a student studies in a particular area of knowledge . . . the more the student knows in terms of the knowledge and skills specific to that area" (p. 65). This conclusion relies almost exclusively on studies that measured learning on standardized tests. These studies may tell us whether students can choose the correct response from five alternatives presented, but they tell us little about the nature of students' learning. What sort of framework do students use to make sense of the discrete information and procedures presented on most standardized tests? How will this framework serve them in learning new information and ideas in the subject? These questions are crucial because of the role of prospective teachers in helping their students develop personally meaningful and accurate frameworks that will serve them well in future learning.

Another approach to studying what undergraduates learn is to examine students' understanding of concepts that are fundamental, in the eyes of those in the field, to a particular subject. In history, for instance, objectivity is a fundamental notion that has been debated for years (Novick, 1988). Objectivity has been so controversial for so long because historians, in writing history, cannot avoid it. What position will the historian adopt toward the evidence from and about the past and towards the actors on the stage of the past? This question is at the heart of Schama's (1991) provocative *Dead Certainties: (Unwarranted Speculations).* How do historians steer between the Scylla of presentism—in which past events and actions are judged by the moral standards of their own age—and the Charybdis of what Schama calls "unwarranted speculation" about the past and about the characters and happenings in the past? The latter possibility is particularly dangerous if the historian conceives of his or her task—as many do—as imaginatively recreating the past, projecting themselves into the past in order to understand the motives of those involved in a given set of events. Furthermore, as Novick (1988) details meticulously in his study of the "objectivity question" in American history, the standards for judging the validity and sufficiency of warrants change over time and across circumstances. What one generation may have accepted unquestioningly as warranted speculations may be regarded by the next as tenuous guesswork.

What has this issue to do with teaching and with studying learning among prospective teachers? Teachers depend on various accounts of the past, usually those included in textbooks. Without some understanding of how historians think about writing history, and of the various stances that historians might adopt, teachers have little perspective on the accounts they and their students encounter. Lacking an appreciation for the many mansions that constitute the house of history (Hexter, 1979) and for the socially constructed nature of historical accounts, prospective teachers are unlikely to be prepared or disposed to help students assume a critical position toward those accounts. Possible approaches are abundant: the putatively dispassionate analyses of "cliometricians" who borrow quantitative methods from the social sciences; the rich, explanatory narratives of such historians as Parkman, Hexter, Elton, Mattingly, and Tuchman; the panoramic accounts of Braudel and his epigones in the French *Annales* school, for whom enduring geographic, technical, and administrative structures are more genuinely history than are political narratives; and yet many other perspectives.

Moreover, without an understanding of the standards that historians apply in judging the adequacy of historical works, teachers are ill prepared to help their students learn how to view historical accounts critically. Recall the earlier example of the Reconstruction. The accounts that epigones of the so-called Dunning school wrote of Reconstruction were inadequate not because their portrayals of African Americans were so politically and morally unpalatable, but because they were untrue. Rather than a scholarly product, their point of view represented "a regional white consensus" (Woodward, 1986, p. 24). Their racist premises led them to view past events in a particular light, to slight some events and people and to magnify others beyond what historians who did not share their prejudices believed were justified, to paper over "the breaks and fissures and conflicts in Southern history with myths of solidarity and continuity" (Woodward, 1986, p. 27), and to reach conclusions not supported by all the available evidence (Foner, 1988). By the standards of both contemporary (DuBois, 1935; Lynch, 1913) and later historians (Foner, 1988; Woodward, 1986), the accounts of historians in the Dunning school are fatally flawed by their assumptions.

Standardized tests are ill suited to gauging the degree to which students perceive history as a debate about the meaning of events in the past, and of written history as constructions that must be judged by how well they account for what is known about the past. The investigator must see evidence of how students reason about the task not in general but in relation to specific moments in history. As Watts (1972) argues, historical knowledge is concrete; it evolves not from the concrete to the abstract, but from "a simple understanding of the concrete to a more sophisticated understanding of the concrete" (p. 54). Historians thrive on details, on the particularities and peculiarities of the past. What problems do historians encounter in writing accounts of the origins of the Civil War? How do these problems compare with those historians face in writing about the civil rights movement? When students are asked to discuss the problems of writing the history of a particular set of events in the past, we learn more than whether they know concepts such as reliability. They also reveal their notions of evidence, of the sufficiency of evidence, and of the role of the historian as a product of his or her time and circumstances (McDiarmid, Wiemers, & Fertig, 1991). These considerations are closely related to what teachers in a variety of disciplines work to help students learn: to resist the inclination to reach premature conclusions, and to suspend judgment until they have gathered and evaluated the available evidence.

THE TEACHING–LEARNING CONNECTION

Most existing research on undergraduate learning has limited applicability to the issues of concern to teacher educators. This limitation is not due merely to the kind of knowledge that is measured. Some researchers, in fact, have tried to measure change in what Pascarella and Terenzini (1991) call undergraduates' "cognitive skills and intellectual growth" (p. 114). These researchers, however, attend to changes in general dimensions of knowledge— formal operations reasoning, critical thinking, communications, reflective judgment, conceptual complexity (Pascarella & Terenzini, 1991)—that are believed to be applicable to a range of disciplines rather than to students' understanding of ideas, information, procedures, methods, and controversies that are specific to a subject.

To determine what and how undergraduates learn from their arts and science classes, we must look not only at what they seem to learn but at their opportunities to learn. Why do many prospective teachers fail to learn critical knowledge in and about a subject matter? To what degree is this failure due to the nature of their opportunities to learn? to the sheer complexity and difficulty of some of the ideas and concepts themselves? to the students' capacity or readiness to handle particular information and ideas? to other factors?

To address these questions, investigators must gather information on learning opportunities in arts and science courses. Again, there is a substantial body of research that exists on teaching in arts and science courses. (A number of reviews of this literature exist, including Dunkin & Barnes, 1986; Kulik & Kulik, 1979; McKeachie, Pintrich, Lin, & Smith, 1986; Pascarella & Terenzini, 1991.) Much of this research follows the lead of similar studies of teaching at the precollegiate level. That is, it focuses on teaching behaviors or teaching formats—lecture versus discussion versus individual instruction. For example, some researchers (Hines, Cruickshank, & Kennedy, 1985) found that gains in students' achievement are correlated with certain teaching behaviors such as using relevant examples, reviewing materials, asking questions, step-by-step teaching, allowing students time to think after explanations, and explaining the object of the lesson.

Pascarella and Terenzini (1991) report on studies that examine the effects of various instructional approaches (such as the approach that Karplus, 1974, calls the "inquiry or learning cycle") on general dimensions of cognitive development—for example, the transition from concrete to formal reasoning, the development of critical thinking (McMillan, 1987), and postformal reasoning. Some of the most potentially useful investigations in this area were conducted around an innovative freshman-year curriculum at the University of Nebraska—Accent on Developing Abstract Processes of Thought (ADAPT)—which used the inquiry or learning cycle approach (Tomlinson-Kreasey & Eisert, 1978). The researchers report that faculty in six different disciplines adopted the innovative approach. Because these researchers provided scant descriptions of the classes themselves and because they measured students' learning with instruments designed to register generic knowledge and attitudes, the reader learns little about students' actual experiences in ADAPT courses, much less what sense the students made of these experiences.

Winter, McClelland, and Stewart (1981) sought to discover whether students who attended a liberal arts institution demonstrated changes in several dimensions of cognition, particularly critical thinking, in comparison to students attending a state teachers' college and a community college. To measure changes in critical thinking, they developed an interview instrument, the Test of Thematic Analysis, which was designed to avoid favoring majors in a particular discipline. Students were given 30 minutes to write a comparison of two groups of brief stories. The researchers report that the liberal arts experience contributed to growth in critical thinking; however, they provide few details of the students' learning experience. Exactly which aspects of the liberal arts academic experience contribute to critical thinking is not clear.

In short, much of the existing research on teaching and learning in arts and science courses is not particularly helpful in considering the kind of subject-matter knowledge that prospective teachers develop in relation to specific learning opportunities. Most of this work used standardized tests to measure gains in subject-matter knowledge. Such tests are not designed to measure the changes in some of the kinds of knowledge that one may argue are critical to a genuine understanding of a subject and to teaching. Researchers, moreover, provide few details about the kinds of learning opportunities students encounter. In the mode of similar work on precollegiate teaching, much of the research that does focus on teaching examines generic teaching behaviors—the type and frequency of the teacher's questions, whether the teacher reviews the previous lessons, how the teacher treats students' ideas, and so on. The findings of such research might be useful to faculty in changing particular behaviors, such as accepting and using students' ideas. Less clear is how this work contributes to helping teachers of undergraduates understand what is difficult about teaching and learning—and learning about—such matters as differential calculus, the mechanics of moving bodies, the narrator's use of anachronistic allusions in *Middle Passage* (Johnson, 1990), or crafting and supporting a thesis about a historical event. What does it mean to accept and use students' ideas in mechanics when these ideas, from a physicist's point of view, are simply wrong?

INVESTIGATIONS OF STUDENTS'
UNDERSTANDING OF SUBJECT MATTER AND THE
TEACHING OF SUBJECT MATTER IN THE ARTS
AND SCIENCES

Investigations of students' understandings of subject matter and the teaching of subject matter do exist. Typically they do not find their way into reviews, even a review as extensive and thorough as that by Pascarella and Terenzini (1991). Moreover, they are often the product of investigators who are experts in subject matter—mathematicians, physicists, English scholars—rather than researchers who study higher education or adult learning. Frequently they undertake to find out what their students do and do not understand about the subject matter, and why. To find out, these investigators typically collect various kinds of information on students' understanding: interview data, students' writing, and observations of students engaged in activities designed to reveal their understanding. The samples are small because of the kinds of questions the researchers wish to address and the kind of data needed to do so.

The advance of this type of inquiry has been uneven. In both physics and mathematics, a core of scholars has been investigating and reporting on students' learning and understanding for several years. Composition is another subject in which scholars have explored students' understanding in relation to the opportunities to learn. Graves (1981), a pioneering and influential scholar in the field, is a proponent of case-study inquiries into the teaching of writing. Attention to the development of students as writers has had some spill-over effect into literature, particularly among faculty who view literature and writing as two sides of the same intellectual and pedagogical coin. In other areas, such as history, I have been unable to find reports of systematic inquiry into undergraduate learning (beyond my own work).

PHYSICS

For years, faculty who teach undergraduate physics courses have been puzzled and frustrated by particular patterns in the persistent misunderstandings that students manifest about mechanics. In one study, a significant number of college physics students—about four out of five—predicted that the heavier of two objects of the same size and shape would fall faster (Champagne, Gunstone, & Klopfer, 1985). Even in their second course in mechanics and after exposure to numerous counterexamples, students persist in believing that motion requires a constant force acting in the direction of the movement. Many students continue to believe that if an object such as a pendulum is to remain in motion, it must be acted on by a constant force propelling it in the direction of its motion (McDermott, 1984). Ninety percent of engineering majors who had yet to take a course in mechanics and 70 percent of those who had finished the course believed that two forces act on a coin that has reached the midpoint in its trajectory after being tossed into the air. In addition to the force of gravity, these students believed that the force exerted by the hand that tossed the coin continued to act on the coin in flight (Clement, 1982).

To find out why students' beliefs withstood their physics instructors' best efforts, faculty began to interview their students. They discovered that the students tended to draw on their own experience of the physical world in developing an implicit theory about bodies in motion. That is, the common-sense understanding of the relationship between force, motion, and direction that the students had built up over years of experience overrode the principled explanations they encountered in their formal coursework.

Students are not alone in their beliefs. Aristotle relied on his experience of the world, which apparently was much like that of the physics students described above, and similarly assumed that motion implies a force in the direction in which an object is moving. His view appears to have been virtually unchallenged until Newton's time, largely because Aristotle "merely formulated the most commonplace experiences in the matter of motion as universal scientific propositions." Newtonian physics, on the other hand, "makes assertions which not only are never confirmed by everyday experience, but whose direct experimental verification is fundamentally impossible" (Dijksterhuis, 1969, p. 30). McDermott (1984) describes research on students' understanding of force and motion conducted by Laurence Viennot at the University of Paris, which led him to evolve a model of students' understanding of mechanics.

In this vein, Viennot (1979) believes that students may simultaneously hold both Newtonian and non-Newtonian ideas of force. The conception on which they rely to make sense of a given situation depends on the circumstances in which they confront representations of force. When students confronted representations of motion, velocity, and acceleration that instructors designed to challenge their common-sense conceptions, they could compare their implicit theories with physicists' under-standings of motion and force (McDermott, 1984; Trowbridge & McDermott, 1981). Arons (1990), Champagne, Gunstone, and Klopfer (1985), and Rosenquist and McDermott (1987) describe examples of physics instruction that draw on studies of students' conceptions. These examples are designed to confront students' common-sense ideas as well as providing evidence that such approaches apparently succeed with many students.

The research of Viennot, Champagne, McDermott, Arons, and others raises several issues. First of all, it reveals the shortcom-ings of much "teaching-as-usual" in college physics. As Arons (1990) notes:

> Deficiencies in assimilation and understanding of the concepts remain concealed from us physics teachers partly because of our own wishful thinking regarding the lucidity of our presentations and partly because conventional homework problems and test questions do not reveal the true state of student thinking and com-prehension. It is tempting to believe that adequate performance on conventional end-of-the-chapter problems indicates understanding, but, in fact, it does not. (p. 38)

These studies also underline the potential of pedagogy tailored to confront students' habitual ways of thinking about the world, and to challenge and apparently change their beliefs—in this case, about mechanics. A number of scholars (Ball, 1988b, 1989; Bird, 1991; King & Ladson-Billings, 1990; McDiarmid, 1990) have described their attempts to challenge prospective teachers' beliefs about teaching. The creation of nonevaluative opportuni-ties for students to explain their understandings of such funda-mental concepts as force, motion, learning, teaching, and stu-dent diversity is common to these experiences in two quite distinct subjects. Also common to physics and pedagogy are instructors who used information about their students' initial understandings to design experiences that would lead their stu-dents to reflect critically on the adequacy of these understand-ings.

Tobias (1990) was interested principally in learning why more successful undergraduates do not major in science. Accordingly, she enlisted seven postgraduates—all of whom had been science avoiders in college but had succeeded in other fields—to audit introductory courses in physics, chemistry, and mathematics. These surrogate undergraduates not only did all the work in the course, but also kept notes on their experience, the instructor, and their classmates. The auditors complained most frequently that their instructors failed to provide them with "road maps" of the subject matter, some indication of where they were and where they were going. One auditor wrote: "I never really knew where we were heading or how much, in the real scheme of things, we had already covered. Each topic the professor discusses feels like it's being pulled out of a hat" (Tobias, 1990, p. 38). The same auditor, as well as the others, bemoaned what Tobias terms the "tyranny of techniques":

> They hungered—all of them—for information about how the various methods they were learning had come to be, why physicists and chemists understand nature the way they do, and what were the connections between what they were learning and the larger world. (p. 81)

In addition, the auditors, as humanities scholars, were unprepared for what they perceived as the lack of community that resulted (as Tobias and the auditors believed) from large classes and competition among students.

Asked to comment on an auditor's observation that his course was dull, a chemistry instructor wrote, "It is dull. It is dull to learn, and it is dull to teach. Unfortunately, it is the basic nuts and bolts stuff that must be mastered before anything useful can be accomplished" (p. 55). Instructors in a variety of fields and across many decades have defended the dreariness of their courses in similar terms. Sixty years ago Howard Mumford Jones rationalized the pedantry of his American literature courses in these words:

> No conscientious teacher . . . but realizes with regret that his days and nights are practically given over to the teaching of obvious and necessary information and technique; and though he would gladly push on to higher matters, practically he is unable to do so. (quoted in Graff, 1987, p. 142)

Underlying the comment made by the chemistry instructor in Tobias's study is the view that the structure of knowledge in chemistry is hierarchical. Although this point helps explain why this instructor—and probably many others both in chemistry and in other disciplines—organize their content as they do, the comment also raises questions about such perceptions; only subject-matter specialists can discuss such questions fruitfully. Do other views of chemical knowledge exist? If so, do they imply other ways of organizing the content? If there is only one structure of knowledge in chemistry, does it follow that information, ideas, and procedures must be taught hierarchically? Does this approach to chemistry and the teaching of chemistry systematically limit access to categories of learners such as women? The data that Tobias presents do not suggest that the faculty who taught the courses in this study were provoked to such considerations by the auditors' comments.

All of Tobias's auditors succeeded in the courses they took, but all were intellectually frustrated, not by the subject but by the way the subject was taught. This was true even when the auditor was profoundly interested in the subject. If the way science is taught repels people as it repelled the auditors in this study—who possess sophisticated habits of mind, considerable resources for integrating new knowledge with old, and the capacity to make sense of arcane material on their own—one can imagine the effect on most undergraduates.

MATHEMATICS

In mathematics, research on students' understanding has revealed that many may lack understanding of fundamental ideas despite their apparent success in university mathematics courses. A number of recent studies (Clement, 1982; Clement, Lochhead, & Monk, 1981; Maestre, Gerace, & Lochhead, 1983; Maestre & Lochhead, 1983) have demonstrated the inability of undergraduates majoring in science and engineering to represent correctly a simple algebraic relationship between two variables, namely, the famous "student–professor" problem: "Write an equation using the variables S and P to represent the following statement: There are six times as many students as professors at this university. Use S for the number of students and P for the number of professors" (Maestre & Lochhead, 1983). Typically, students who offer an incorrect equation reverse the variables as follows: $6S = P$. Clement and his colleagues (1981) report that more than one-third of the engineering students they tested and nearly six of ten nonscience majors could not offer an appropriate representation. Through interviews with the students and by varying the form of the problem, the researchers discovered that the reversal is not merely a matter of carelessness but is systematic. Many students, even when they have mastered the mechanics of the subject, apparently fail to develop an under-standing of the underlying meanings.

Ball (1988a) reports that mathematics majors planning to teach produced more correct answers for division involving fractions, zero, and algebraic equations than did elementary education majors. Even so, the mathematics majors frequently struggled in "making sense of division with fractions, connecting mathematics to the real world, and coming up with explanations that go beyond restatement of the rules" (p. 39). Schoenfeld (1985) reports on the efforts made by his undergraduates—most of whom had previously done well in college calculus as well as in high school geometry—to solve fairly simple geometric problems. Although the students, working as a group, could solve the problems, they struggled to explain why the solutions worked: "My class spent a week (at the college level) uncovering the reasons for two constructions that they had been able to produce from memory in less than two minutes" (p. 376).

In both physics and mathematics, evidence is mounting that all students, not only those intending to be teachers, can meet instructors' expectations for satisfactory work without developing a conceptual understanding of the subject matter—the lack of which, I believe, seriously inhibits teachers' capacities to help pupils learn in meaningful ways. No doubt, this is unsurprising: Many of us, I imagine, have had the experience of cramming for an examination and doing well, and yet realizing that we really did not understand many of the facts and procedures with which we stuffed our memory.

WRITING AND LITERATURE

As mentioned above, a number of small-scale studies have resulted from the reorientation of many composition instructors to writing as a process and to students as working writers. Typical of this work is Coleman's (1984) ethnographic study of five students in her introductory undergraduate writing course. Coleman used both learning logs and peer response groups to help her students develop their ideas about writing and to document the evolution of their thinking and writing. Ritchie (1989) followed the development of two students in an introductory composition course taught as a writers' workshop, in which she was a participant-observer. Drawing on interviews and observations of the students and on the evolution of their written work,

Ritchie identified four aspects of their experience that she believed were critical to the growth in their writing ability: their personal histories, the assumptions about writing and learning to write that they brought from their prior education, the nonauthoritative role that the instructor assumed, and the students' responses to one another's writing.

Miller (1983) has examined how three student teachers thought of themselves as writers and of the writing process. When they started to teach, the student teachers found that the lack of an integrated writing experience in their own pasts limited and undermined their desire to teach writing and literature in a more integrated way. "Because they, themselves, had only experienced writing as a segmented and grammar-bound process, they were unable to fully implement the theoretical constructs which they had studied in their preparatory courses with confidence or even enthusiasm" (p. 13).

To learn how English majors who planned to teach differed from those who did not, Clift (1987) interviewed three students from each group. She asked them about English as a subject of inquiry, about their experiences in learning English, about teaching English, and about learners in the English classroom. She found that the two groups responded similarly to questions about organizing concepts related to English, but differed in their views about learners and about who has the authority to interpret literature. For instance, the English majors who did not plan to teach seemed more inclined to believe that the professor's view of literature is most important. They tended to think that part of the student's task is to figure out how the instructor interprets a text, and to style their papers accordingly: "Like I use the historical approach in X's and I would use the psychological approach in Y's class" (p. 232). These students preferred the approach they had experienced in university English classes; they believed that time devoted to discussion should be limited. On the other hand, the English majors who intended to teach seemed to be more inclined to try to involve learners in interpreting literature through identifying with the characters.

Certain issues are suggested by small-scale studies of the learning of composition and literature such as these. The studies that focused on academic majors who plan to teach highlight the role of the undergraduates' prior experience with learning the subject. This experience strongly influences their capacity to adopt unfamiliar pedagogical roles and approaches. In general, these studies emphasize the salience of the ideas and the under-standings undergraduates bring with them to the kinds of under-standings they develop in college.

HISTORY

Our search for studies of teaching and learning history at the university level produced little. Nicholls (1984) and Simmonds (1989), both members of history faculties at British universities, collected data on the undergraduate history curriculum and the teaching of undergraduate history in the United States. Nicholls surveyed eight of his compatriots who taught at American col-leges and universities under the Fulbright program. Summariz-ing his respondents' views, he wrote,

> History courses were perceived as being organized around a lecture program and an accompanying text, with these two vehicles assuming excessive weight in the overall scheme of things, while the information thus imparted was later "retrieved" by some "objec-tive" test to measure just how much of it the excessively grade-con-scious student had ingested. (Nicholls, 1984, p. 65)

Simmonds visited 23 institutions—from small private liberal arts colleges to large state research universities—to observe classes and to interview faculty and department chairs. Many of the classes he observed conformed to the image reported in Nicholls (1984): "Teaching methods often seemed purely didactic" (p. 66). Simmonds was quick to point out that the sheer num-bers of students in these classes appeared to preclude any gen-uine discussion. Historical knowledge itself, he further reported, was presented as undisputed, at least in lower division courses. Finally, Simmonds (1989) commented that coursework for a major in history was a patchwork at many institutions: "overall there is no concern that students take courses which progress towards a final piece of work, or courses that interrelate to devel-op a coherent pattern of study" (p. 313).

O'Brien (1984) described an intriguing American history sur-vey course that he taught, which involved community college stu-dents in making their own sense of historical "moments" while he provided data and guidance. He failed, however, to present sufficient information on students' learning to allow the reader to assess his approach. Others, such as Cannon (1984), on the basis of their own experience, urge particular approaches to pedagogy and curriculum. Typically, however, these works contain little or no information on how the author came to believe what he or she believes about teaching, much less data that would allow the reader to determine the efficacy of the recommended approach.

McDiarmid and his colleagues (McDiarmid, 1991b; McDiarmid, Wiemers, & Fertig, 1991) examined a required historiography course taken by both prospective teachers and nonteachers. They selected this course to study because it was billed as a "history workshop"; thus, it represented learning opportunities not usually present in lecture courses. In addition to observing all meetings of the course and tape recording the instructor's conferences with individual students, the researchers interviewed the instructor and the students before and after the class and collected copies of the students' written work with the instructor's comments.

McDiarmid found that the instructor's pedagogical goals grew from his knowledge of both the students and history. For instance, the structured writing assignment in the course required the students to identify an author's thesis and the evidence supporting the thesis. Subsequently, the students had to craft theses of their own about an event that professional historians had not attempted to explain (McDiarmid, 1991b). Making convincing arguments about the past, the instructor believes, lies at the heart of writing history. He also realizes that most of his students come with little or no experience in constructing sound arguments; consequently, they need a series of activities structured to help them.

In addition to describing and analyzing the learning opportunities in the workshop, McDiarmid and his colleagues described the students' knowledge and understanding during and after the course. They analyzed data on students' experiences with learning history, their knowledge of specific facts about events typically taught in high school (the Civil War and the civil rights movement), their understanding of how historical accounts are constructed, their dispositions toward conflicting accounts of the same events, and their views of teaching and learning history. Although these researchers have reported only preliminary results, several themes run through their work.

For instance, most of the central ideas about history to which the students are exposed—such as the notion of objectivity and the idea that history is a social and historical construction—are the subject of intensive and protracted debate among professional historians. That students continue to struggle with such "big" ideas, even after an experience that they view positively and that appears to the observer to offer numerous chances to learn, is not surprising. Moreover, while in the long-term process of struggling with more sophisticated and more critical notions of historical knowledge students may be ill prepared to consider the implications of these ideas, which are still unformed in many cases, for teaching and learning. Hence, when asked how they would teach secondary students the origins of the American Civil War, they fall back on what they remember of their own experiences in high school. They seem to believe either that they are incapable of creating opportunities to learn that they experienced in the historiography workshop or that most high school students are incapable of learning from such experiences.

In sum, a growing body of literature in several disciplinary areas—particularly physics, mathematics, and composition—focuses on the learning of the knowledge in these disciplines. In some cases, it examines students' learning in relation to specific opportunities. Two operations—collecting information on students' subject-matter knowledge and on their understanding from a variety of sources, and attending to learning in response to particular opportunities—tend to distinguish these investigations from those that focus on narrow definitions of learning, generic cognitive skills, and teaching as a set of generic techniques. Yet because of the case study or small-sample nature of this research as well as its subject-specific focus, results from this work cannot be generalized broadly.

Nonetheless, this research is suggestive. In a variety of fields, much of it reveals the salience of the understandings that students bring to their encounters with subject matter in the college classroom. Such understandings can frustrate or facilitate university teachers' efforts to bring about understandings of ideas, processes, and phenomena thought to be fundamental in their fields (Duckworth, 1987). Further, this research highlights the difficulty of many of these fundamental understandings. University faculty, accustomed as they are to thinking within the ideas and concepts of their field, may underestimate the difficulty of many of these ideas and concepts for undergraduates. The pedagogical problem of helping students to grasp difficult ideas seems to be compounded by the belief among many faculty that they must cover certain topics or fail in their responsibility to prepare the student for subsequent courses in the field. Rather than devoting more time to certain ideas, faculty feel they must hurry on, fearful that they will not finish the syllabus. Finally, the research focusing on the teaching of particular subjects emphasizes the problems with a pedagogy that concerns itself with representing the subject matter faithfully, while largely ignoring both what learners bring with them and possible alternative ways of organizing the content that may be both true to the field and more accessible to more students.

CONCLUSION: IMPLICATIONS FOR FACULTY DEVELOPMENT

The evidence on undergraduate learning in arts and science courses seems to be mixed. Some research appears to show that students may learn certain factual knowledge of subject matter and certain generic cognitive skills from their undergraduate education. On the other hand, closer examinations of students' learning in specific subjects raise questions about the kinds of knowledge students develop, particularly about their understanding of fundamental concepts in arts and science courses. Such concepts include mechanics in physics, algebraic and geometric relationships, the nature of historical accounts, the purpose and the process of writing, and the interpretation of literary texts.

The sheer difficulty of these and many of the other ideas and procedures that students encounter means many students do misunderstand or understand incompletely. Not understanding, for many students, presents no major impediment to their doing quite well in most careers. Marketing managers may succeed brilliantly even though they believe that a constant force acting in the direction of the motion of a pendulum is required to keep it moving, that seven divided by zero is zero rather than being undefined, or that during Reconstruction unscrupulous carpetbaggers and ignorant blacks wreaked havoc on the prostrate South. On the other hand, appreciating the nuances and implications of these and other ideas, their compatibility with related concepts, and their robustness in the face of close examination is essential, one may argue, to a critical perspective on knowledge in any field. Such a critical stance toward historical knowledge, for example, may be essential to full, contributing membership in the variety of communities that make up a democracy.

Although I grant for a moment that most undergraduates would not be hindered appreciably by an inaccurate or incomplete understanding of various subjects, the same may not be said of teachers responsible for teaching those subjects. Much of the current reform effort consists of educating learners both to know more about the subjects taught in school and to take a more critical view of knowledge. To help diverse students achieve these goals, teachers themselves need deeper, more connected, and more critical knowledge and understanding.

In view of the current policy drift toward more arts and science courses and fewer education courses, what are the prospects that teachers will develop such knowledge during their undergraduate years? On the basis of the evidence on arts and science teaching and learning, the prospects seem to be slim at best. In fact, just when policy makers and teacher educators have decided to increase prospective teachers' exposure to arts and science courses as formal preparation for teaching, institutions of higher education are in the grip of another fiscal crisis, which is exacerbating some of the conditions that contribute to the ineffectiveness of much college teaching. Class sizes are increasing, survey courses—the money cows of many departments—are likely to become more common, and faculty are subjected to increasing pressure to teach more. Increasingly at some institutions, part-time instructors are hired to teach introductory and service courses—a situation that Booth (1988) describes with some passion:

> The great public fears us or despises us because we hire a vast army of underpaid flunkies to teach the so-called service courses, so that we can gladly teach, in our advanced courses, those precious souls who survive the gauntlet. Give us lovers and we will love them, but do not expect us to study courtship. (p. 23)

In sum, the current reform trend may produce more teachers who log more seat-time in arts and science courses. But will they know more about the subjects they must teach? Will what they learn about those subjects sustain them in helping diverse students to learn? According to the evidence on students' learning in the arts and sciences, it ain't necessarily so.

What does all of this imply for faculty development? One response would be to communicate promising teaching approaches to faculty. A raft of advice on improving college teaching is—and has been—available. (See, for instance, Chickering & Gamson, 1987; Elbe, 1972, 1980, 1988; Gullette, 1982; Levinson-Rose & Menges, 1981; McKeachie, 1986; Menges &

Svinicki, 1991; Runkel, Harrison, & Runkel, 1969; Weaver, 1989; Weimer, 1987.) Many of the recommendations are similar: attend more to students' ideas and thinking and lecture less; provide students with opportunities to understand the relationship between particular ideas and the big picture of the discipline, between their own experience and the world in which they live; represent ideas and concepts in a variety of ways to reach students who come with a variety of experiences and understandings; enable students to cooperate rather than to compete in addressing issues and problems; design ways to investigate the subject that involve students in active inquiry; and so on.

Yet the issue may be less one of technique, less a lack of knowledge about good practice, than a matter of values. If arts and science faculty believe that all their students can learn and that their job is to figure out how to help them learn, they seek out ways to improve their practice. (See for instance, American Association for the Advancement of Science, 1990; Booth, 1988; Elbow, 1986; McDiarmid, 1991b.) Unless universities, disciplinary communities, and the public at large come to place a greater value on teaching and to think of learning differently, the best advice on teaching will continue to go largely unheeded.

Arts and science faculty work within a variety of cultures, which, like all cultures, value some activities over others. In the first place, they are members of disciplinary departments. These departments, in turn, are part of larger disciplinary communities that extend across institutions and national borders. Physicists, English professors, mathematicians, and historians each have their standards for judging the activities and products of the members of their culture. Generally, the members of the disciplinary communities value, above all else, contributions to knowledge in their field. Also valued is the cultivation of new, contributing members of the community—that is, graduate students. In most disciplines teaching undergraduates is far down the list of valued activities.

The institutions that employ arts and science faculty also constitute cultures. Over time, as noted above, the faculty and administration in some institutions have cultivated undergraduate teaching as a valued activity. These institutions appear to be primarily liberal arts colleges that emphasize grantsmanship and research less than do larger, research-oriented universities. In institutions of the latter type, administrators pay lip service to the importance of teaching. In such institutions, promotion and tenure decisions hinge not on the quality of candidates' teaching or of their students' learning, but on their research and publications.

Despite invectives such as Boyer's (1990) against the fact that universities value research and publications above teaching and service, we see scant evidence of change in the activities and products that institutions or disciplinary communities value and reward. Even if individual institutions attempted to reconfigure the value and reward structure as reformers such as Boyer urge, faculty still would be part of larger disciplinary cultures in which (as noted) the development of new knowledge and members, not teaching undergraduates, is paramount. In addition, universities operate within the broader Western culture. In this culture, teaching and learning have taken on particular meanings and are associated with particular images (Cohen, 1988; Cuban, 1984). In such a context, university teaching is largely synonymous with lecturing, with the transmission of large volumes of information; reciprocally, learning is understood as the mastery, retention, and reproduction of information. Other ideas and images coexist with these but are held less widely.

Within and even outside the university faculty members generally have not been expected to be responsible for finding out whether their students genuinely seem to be coming to understand key ideas and, if they are not, changing their teaching; or for providing students with opportunities to integrate new ideas and information with their prior experiences and understandings; or for helping students see the relationship between an idea and the larger issues or knowledge structures in the field. Certainly some faculty members define their responsibilities along these lines, but those who do not do so usually are not penalized. On the contrary, many faculty who have thrived in their institutions and been rewarded handsomely have done so although they pay little attention to their responsibilities as teachers.

The current fiscal crisis in higher education seems likely to reinforce rather than to challenge existing values. As state support of public universities declines, faculty are likely to find themselves pressured to compete for more research money. Also, in a time of budget cuts, faculty who bring in money will be even more valuable in the eyes of those who shape the reward structure of universities.

One way to persuade arts and science faculty to attend more closely to their students' ideas and understandings about the subject would be to find ways for these teachers to work with faculty from teacher education. Arts and science faculty bring to such work both their grounding in their subject matter and, in some cases, considerable experience in teaching the subject. Teacher education faculty, on the other hand, bring knowledge of and deep interest in pedagogy and, in some cases, knowledge of the difficulties that particular subjects pose for students. At various institutions, arts and science faculty and education faculty have cooperated to help undergraduates to think about the pedagogical implications of a subject matter even as they are studying it. At Millersville University in Pennsylvania, for instance, teacher education faculty attend certain arts and science courses and, together with the instructor, offer one-credit "pedagogy seminars" that examine the transformation of subject matter into representations that students can comprehend (Project 30, 1991). Kleinfeld (1992), in another recent example, reports that she invited a colleague from the English department to teach *Hamlet* to her prospective teachers, who were examining a case of a secondary teacher teaching the play.

Yet examples of such cooperation are relatively scarce. (For descriptions of collaborative efforts between liberal arts and teacher education, see Project 30, 1991.) This situation is due in part to another issue of values: Many arts and science faculty have little regard for teacher education faculty and their programs. In many cases, this lack of regard stems from the belief among arts and science faculty that, in Gertude Stein's words, "there is no *there* there." That is, teacher education is not a genuine discipline; it can claim no body of knowledge, and teacher education courses lack substance. This perception appears to be related to the view that many university faculty seem to take of teaching: straightforward and unproblematic, teaching is largely a matter of telling and then checking to see that students can reproduce what has been told and read. Students who fail to learn don't have what it takes, or else haven't worked hard enough. (Without denying that students have greater and lesser capacities for particular subjects or that genuine understanding requires concerted, sustained effort, we can argue that teachers at least share the responsibility when students do not learn.) From this perspective on teaching and learning, what's to study? What's to know?

In the eyes of many university faculty, teacher educators are tainted further by their association with schools and teachers, neither of which commands much regard or respect in the academy. Consequently, arts and science faculty are unlikely to respond to opportunities to work with teacher educators, much less to seek them out.

Recommending that university administrators devise ways and allocate funds to encourage arts and science faculty and education faculty to work, perhaps even teach, together does not address the underlying cultural issues. Current reward structures do not engender the kinds of cooperation that could lead to changes in the ways teaching and learning are viewed and valued at universities. Yet without such change, prospective teachers seem unlikely to experience the teaching, learning, and understanding that prepare them to help others learn in connected and meaningful ways.

REFERENCES

American Association for the Advancement of Science. (1989). *Science for all Americans: A project 2061 report on literacy goals in science, mathematics, and technology*. Washington, DC: American Association for the Advancement of Science.

American Association for the Advancement of Science. (1990). *The liberal art of science: Agenda for action*. Washington, DC: American Association for the Advancement of Science.

Anderson, C. W. (1991). Policy implications of research on science teaching and teachers' knowledge. In M. M. Kennedy (Ed.), *Teaching academic subjects to diverse learners* (pp. 5–30). New York: Teachers College.

Arons, A. B. (1990). *A guide to introductory physics teaching*. New York: Wiley.

Astin, A. (1985). *Achieving educational excellence: A critical assessment of priorities and practices in higher education*. San Francisco: Jossey-Bass.

Axtell, J. (1987). Europeans, Indians, and the age of discovery in American history textbooks. *American Historical Review, 92*, 621–632.

Ball, D. L. (1988a). *Knowledge and reasoning in mathematical pedagogy: Examining what prospective teachers bring to teacher education*. Unpublished doctoral dissertation, Michigan State University.

Ball, D. L. (1988b). Unlearning to teach mathematics. *For the Learning of Mathematics, 8*(1), 40–48.

Ball, D. L. (1989). *Breaking with experience in learning to teach mathematics: The role of the preservice methods course* (Issue Paper 88–1). E. Lansing, MI: Michigan State University, National Center for Research on Teacher Education.

Ball, D. L. (1990). The mathematical understandings that prospective teachers bring to teacher education. *The Elementary School Journal, 90*, 449–466.

Ball, D. L. (1991). Teaching mathematics for understanding: What do teachers need to know about subject matter? In M. M. Kennedy

(Ed.), *Teaching academic subjects to diverse learners* (pp. 63–83). New York: Teachers College.

Ball, D. L., & McDiarmid, G. W. (1990). The subject matter preparation of teachers. In R. Houston (Ed.), *Handbook of research on teacher education* (pp. 437–449). New York: Macmillan.

Ball, D. L., & Wilson, S. W. (1990). *Knowing the subject and learning to teach it; Examining assumptions about becoming a mathematics teacher* (Research Report No. 90–7). E. Lansing, MI: Michigan State University, National Center for Research on Teacher Education.

Banks, J. (1971). Relevant social studies for Black pupils. In J. Banks & W. Joyce (Eds.), *Teaching social studies to culturally different children* (pp. 202–209). Reading, MA: Addison-Wesley.

Banks, J. (1991). Social science knowledge and citizenship education. In M. M. Kennedy (Ed.), *Teaching academic subjects to diverse learners* (pp. 117–128). New York: Teachers College.

Beers, S. (1988). Epistemological assumptions and college teaching: Interactions in the college classroom. *Journal of Research and Development in Education, 21*(4), 87–94.

Bestor, A. (1953/1985). *Educational wastelands: The retreat from learning in our public schools* (Second ed.). Urbana, IL: University of Illinois.

Bird, T. (1991). *Making conversations about teaching and learning in an introductory teacher education course* (Craft Paper 91–2). E. Lansing, MI: Michigan State University, National Center for Research on Teacher Education.

Booth, W. C. (1988). *The vocation of a teacher: Rhetorical occasions, 1967–1988.* Chicago: University of Chicago.

Boyer, E. (1987). *College: The undergraduate experience in America.* New York: Harper & Row.

Boyer, E. (1990). *Scholarship reconsidered: Priorities of the professoriate.* Princeton, NJ: The Carnegie Foundation for the Advancement of Teaching.

Buchmann, M. (1984). The priority of knowledge and understanding in teaching. In L. G. Katz & J. D. Raths (Eds.), *Advances in teacher education, Vol. 1* (pp. 29–50). Norwood, NJ: Ablex.

Cannon, J. (1984). *Teaching history at university.* London: The Historical Association.

Champagne, A. B., Gunstone, R. F., & Klopfer, L. E. (1985). Effecting changes in cognitive structures among physics students. In L.H.T. West & A. L. Pines (Eds.), *Cognitive structure and conceptual change* (pp. 163–187). New York: Academic Press.

Chickering, A. W., & Gamson, Z. F. (1987). Seven principles for good practice in undergraduate education. *American Association for Higher Education Bulletin, 39*(7), 3–7.

Clement, J. (1982). Students' preconceptions in introductory mechanics. *American Journal of Physics, 50,* 66–71.

Clement, J., Lochhead, J., & Monk, G. S. (1981). Translation difficulties in learning mathematics. *American Mathematical Monthly, 8,* 286–290.

Clift, R. T. (1987). English teacher or English major: Epistemological differences in the teaching of English. *English Education, 19,* 229–236.

Cohen, D. K. (1988). *Teaching Practice: Plus ca change . . .* (Issue paper 88–3). E. Lansing, MI: Michigan State University, National Center for Research on Teacher Education.

Cohen, D. K., Peterson, P. L., Wilson, S., Ball, D., Putnam, R., Prawat, R., Heaton, R., Remillard, J., & Wiemers, N. (1990). *Effects of state-level reform of elementary school mathematics curriculum on classroom practice* (Research Report No. 90–14). E. Lansing, MI: Michigan State University, National Center for Research on Teacher Education.

Coleman, E. (1984). *An ethnographic description of the development of basic writers' revision skills.* In ERIC Document Reproduction Service No. ED 283 151.

Conant, J. (1963). *The education of American teachers.* New York: McGraw-Hill.

Cuban, L. (1984). *How teachers taught: Constancy and change in American classrooms, 1890–1980.* New York: Longman.

Current, R. (1988). *Those terrible carpetbaggers: A reinterpretation.* New York: Oxford University Press.

Dijksterhuis, E. J. (1969). *The mechanization of the world picture.* London: Oxford University Press.

Doyle, W. (1986). Content representation in teachers' definitions of academic work. *Journal of Curriculum Studies, 18,* 365–379.

DuBois, W. E. B. (1935). *Black reconstruction in America.* New York: Harcourt Brace.

Duckworth, E. (1987). *"The having of wonderful ideas" and other essays on teaching and learning.* New York: Teachers College.

Dunkin, M. J., & Barnes, J. (1986). Research on teaching in higher education. In M. C. Wittrock (Ed.), *Handbook of research on teaching (3rd ed.)* (pp. 754–777). New York, NY: Macmillan.

Elbe, K. E. (1972). *Professors as teachers.* San Francisco: Jossey-Bass.

Elbe, K. E. (Ed.) (1980). *Improving teaching styles.* San Francisco: Jossey-Bass.

Elbe, K. E. (1988). *The craft of teaching (2nd ed.).* San Francisco: Jossey-Bass.

Elbow, P. (1986). *Embracing contraries: Explorations in learning and teaching.* New York: Oxford University.

FitzGerald, F. (1979). *America revisited.* Boston: Atlantic-Little, Brown.

Floden, R. E., McDiarmid, G. W., & Wiemers, N. (1990). *Learning about mathematics in elementary methods courses.* (Research report 90–1). E. Lansing, MI: Michigan State University, National Center for Research on Teacher Education.

Foner, E. (1988). *Reconstruction: America's unfinished revolution, 1863–1877.* New York: Harper & Row.

Gagnon, P. (1988, November). Why study history? *Atlantic Monthly*, 43–66.

Graff, G. (1987). *Professing literature: An institutional history*. Chicago, IL: University of Chicago.

Graves, D. H. (1981). Writing research for the eighties: What is needed. *Language Arts, 58*(2).

Grossman, P. L. (1990). *The making of a teacher: Teacher knowledge & teacher education*. New York: Teachers College.

Gullette, M. M. (Ed.) (1982). *The art and craft of teaching*. Cambridge, MA: Harvard-Danforth Center for Teaching and Learning, Harvard University.

Hexter, J. H. (1979). *On historians: Reappraisals of the masters of modern history*. Cambridge, MA: Harvard.

Hines, C., Cruickshank, D., & Kennedy, J. (1985). Teacher clarity and its relationship to student achievement and satisfaction. *American Educational Research Journal, 22*, 87–99.

Hirsch, E. D., Jr. (1987). *Cultural literacy; What every American needs to know*. New York: Vintage Books.

Johnson, C. (1990). *Middle passage*. New York: Plume.

Karplus, R. (1974). *Science curriculum improvement study: Teacher's handbook*. Berkeley, CA: Lawrence Hall of Science.

King, J. E., & Ladson-Billings, G. (1990). *Dysconscious racism and multicultural illiteracy: The distortion of the American mind*. Paper presented at the annual meeting of the American Educational Research Association, Boston, MA.

Kleinfeld, J. S. (1992). *Can cases carry pedagogical content knowledge? Yes, but we've got signs of a "Matthew effect."* Paper presented at the annual meeting of the American Educational Research Association, San Francisco, CA.

Kline, M. (1977). *Why the professor can't teach: Mathematics and the dilemma of university education*. New York: St. Martin's Press.

Kramer, R. (1991). *Ed school follies*. New York: The Free Press.

Kulik, J., & Kulik, C. (1979). College teaching. In P. L. Peterson & H. J. Walberg (Eds.), *Research on teaching: Concepts, findings, and implications* (pp. 70–93). Berkeley, CA: McCutchan.

Lampert, M. (1985). How do teachers manage to teach? Perspectives on problems of practice. *Harvard Educational Review, 55*, 178–194.

Leinhardt, G. (1987). Development of an expert explanation: An analysis of a sequence of subtraction lessons. *Cognition and Instruction, 4*, 225–282.

Leinhardt, G., & Smith, D. (1985). Expertise in mathematics instruction: Subject matter knowledge. *Journal of Educational Psychology, 77*, 247–271.

Levinson-Rose, J., & Menges, R. (1981). Improving college teaching: A critical review of research. *Review of Educational Research, 51*, 403–434.

London, H. (1984). *Why are they lying to our children?* New York: Stein & Day.

Lynch, J. R. (1913). *The facts of reconstruction.* New York: Harcourt Brace.

Maestre, J. P., Gerace, W. J., & Lochhead, J. (1983). The interdependence of language and translational math skills among bilingual Hispanic engineering students. *Journal of Research in Science Teaching, 19,* 339–410.

Maestre, J. P., & Lochhead, J. (1983). The variable-reversal error among five culture groups. In J. C. Bergeron. & N. Herscovics (Ed.), *The fifth annual meeting of the North American Chapter of the International Group for the Psychology of Mathematics Education* (pp. 180–189). Montreal, Canada: North American Chapter of the International Group for the Psychology of Mathematics Education.

McDermott, L. (1984). Research on conceptual understanding in mechanics. *Physics Today, 37,* 24–32.

McDiarmid, G. W. (1990). Challenging prospective teachers' beliefs during an early field experience: A quixotic undertaking? *Journal of Teacher Education, 41*(3), 12–20.

McDiarmid, G. W. (1991a). What teachers need to know about cultural diversity: Restoring subject matter to the picture. In M. M. Kennedy (Ed.), *Teaching academic subjects to diverse learners* (pp. 257–270). New York: Teachers College.

McDiarmid, G. W. (1991b). *A case of historical pedagogy: How an instructor's view of history and learning are incorporated in an undergraduate history workshop.* Paper presented at the annual meeting of the American Educational Research Association, Chicago.

McDiarmid, G. W., Ball, D. L., & Anderson, C. W. (1989). Why staying one chapter ahead doesn't really work: Subject-specific pedagogy. In M. C. Reynolds (Ed.), *Knowledge base for the beginning teacher* (pp. 193–205). New York: Pergamon.

McDiarmid, G. W., Wiemers, N. J., & Fertig, L. (1991). *Bounded by their pasts: Exploring the relationship between understandings of history and the views of teaching and learning of history among majors in a historiography seminar.* Paper presented at the annual meeting of the American Educational Research Association, Chicago, IL.

McDiarmid, G. W., & Wilson, S. W. (1991). An exploration of the subject matter knowledge of alternate route teachers: Can we assume they know their subject? *Journal of Teacher Education, 42,* 93–103.

McKeachie, W. J. (1986). *Teaching tips: A guidebook for the beginning college teacher (8th ed.).* Lexington, MA: D. C. Heath.

McKeachie, W., Pintrich, P., Lin, Y., & Smith, D. (1986). *Teaching and learning in the college classroom: A review of the research literature.* Ann Arbor, MI: National Center for Research to Improve Postsecondary Teaching and Learning.

McMillan, J. (1987). Enhancing college students critical thinking: A review of studies. *Journal of Teacher Education, 26,* 3–29.

Menges, R. J., & Svinicki, M. D. (1991). *College teaching: From theory to practice.* San Francisco, CA: Jossey-Bass.

Miller, J. L. (1983). A search for congruence: Influence of past and present in future teacher's concepts about teaching writing. *English Education, 15*(1), 5–16.

National Council of Teachers of Mathematics. (1989a). *Curriculum and evaluation standards for school mathematics.* Reston, VA: National Council of Teachers of Mathematics.

National Council of Teachers of Mathematics. (1989b). *Professional standards for teaching mathematics: Working draft.* Reston, VA: National Council of Teachers of Mathematics.

National Research Council. (1989). *Everybody counts: A report to the nation on the future of mathematics education.* Washington, DC: National Academy Press.

National Research Council. (1991). *Moving beyond the myths: Revitalizing undergraduate mathematics.* Washington, DC: National Academy Press.

NCRTE. (1991). *Teacher education and learning to teach study: Final report.* Lansing, MI: Michigan State University, National Center for Research on Teacher Education.

Nicholls, D. (1984). College level history in the United States. *The History Teacher, 18*(1), 57–67.

Novick, P. (1988). *That noble dream: The "objectivity question" and the American historical profession.* Cambridge, UK: Cambridge University Press.

O'Brien, W. A. (1984). *Modernization and the changing nature of community in colonial America: A "moment" in the United States history survey course at J. Sargeant Reynolds Community College, Richmond, Virginia.* Paper presented at the annual meeting of the Community College Humanities Association, Charleston, SC.

Pascarella, E. T., & Terenzini, P. (1991). *How college affects students.* San Francisco: Jossey-Bass.

Perkins, D. (1986). *Knowledge as design.* Hillsdale, NJ: Erlbaum.

Pollio, H. (1984). *What students think about and do in college lecture classes* (Teaching-Learning Issues No. No. 53). University of Tennessee.

Project on Redefining the Meaning and Purpose of Baccalaureate Degrees. (1985). *Integrity in the college curriculum.* Washington, DC: Association of American Colleges.

Project 30. (1991). *Year two report: Institutional accomplishments.* Newark, DE: University of Delaware.

Ravitch, D. (1989). The plight of history in American schools. In P. Gagnon & The Bradley Commission on History in Schools (Eds.), *Historical literacy* (pp. 51–68). New York: Macmillan.

Rickover, H. G. (1960). *Education and freedom.* New York: E. P. Dutton.

Rigden, J. S., & Tobias, S. (1991). Too often, college-level science is dull as well as difficult. *The Chronicle of Higher Education, 37*(28), 52.

Ritchie, J. S. (1989). Beginning writers: Diverse voices and individual identity. *College Composition and Communication, 40*(2), 152–174.

Rosaen, C. R., Roth, K. J., & Lanier, P. E. (1988). *Learning to teach sub-*

ject matter: Cases in English, mathematics, and science. Paper presented at the midwest regional meeting of the Holmes Group, Chicago, IL.

Rosenquist, M. L., & McDermott, L. E. (1987). A conceptual approach to teaching kinematics. *American Journal of Physics, 55,* 407.

Runkel, P., Harrison, R., & Runkel, M. (Eds.) (1969). *The changing college classroom.* San Francisco: Jossey-Bass.

Schama, S. (1991). *Dead certainties: (Unwarranted speculations).* New York: Knopf.

Scheffler, I. (1973). *Reason and teaching.* New York: Bobbs-Merrill.

Schoenfeld, A. (1985). Metacognitive and epistemological issues in mathematical understanding. In E. A. Silver (Ed.), *Teaching and learning mathematical problem-solving: Multiple research perspectives* (pp. 361–379). Hillsdale, NJ: Erlbaum.

Schwab, J. J. (1964). The structures of the disciplines: Meanings and significances. In G. W. Ford & L. Pugno (Eds.), *The structure of knowledge and the curriculum.* Chicago: Rand McNally.

Sewall, G. T. (1987). *American history textbooks: An assessment of quality.* New York: Columbia University, Teachers College, Educational Excellence Network.

Shulman, L. S. (1986). Those who understand: Knowledge growth in teaching. *Educational Researcher, 15*(5), 4–14.

Shulman, L. S. (1987). Knowledge and teaching: Foundations of the new reform. *Harvard Educational Review, 57,* 1–23.

Simmonds, J. C. (1989). History curriculum and curriculum change in colleges and universities of the United States: A study of twenty-three history departments in 1988. *The History Teacher, 22*(3), 293–316.

Smith, P. (1990). *Killing the spirit: Higher education in America.* New York: Viking Penguin.

Study Group on the Conditions of Excellence in American Higher Education. (1984). *Involvement in learning: Realizing the potential of American higher education.* Washington, DC: National Institute of Education.

Tobias, S. (1990). *They're not dumb, they're different: Stalking the second tier.* Tucson, AZ: Research Corporation.

Tomlinson-Kreasey, C., & Eisert, D. (1978). Second year evaluation of the ADAPT program. In R. Fuller (Ed.), *Multidisciplinary Piagetian-based programs for college freshmen: ADAPT.* Lincoln, NE: University of Nebraska.

Trowbridge, D. E., & McDermott, L. C. (1981). Investigations of student understanding of the concept of acceleration on one dimension. *American Journal of Physics, 49,* 242.

Viennot, L. P. H. (1979). *Le raisonnement spontane en dynamique elementaire* [Spontaneous Reasoning in Elementary Dynamic]. Paris: Hermann.

Watts, D. G. (1972). *The learning of history.* London: Routledge & Kegan Paul.

Weaver, F. S. (Ed.). (1989). *Promoting inquiry in undergraduate learning.* San Francisco, CA: Jossey-Bass.

Weimer, M. G. (Ed.) (1987). *Teaching large classes well.* San Francisco: Jossey-Bass.

Whitla, D. K. (1977). *Value added: Measuring the outcomes of undergraduate education.* Cambridge, MA: Harvard College.

Wilson, S. W. (1991). Parades of facts, stories of the past: What do novice history teachers need to know. In M. M. Kennedy (Ed.), *Teaching academic subject matter to diverse learners* (pp. 99–116). New York: Teachers College.

Wilson, S. M. (in press). Mastodons, maps, and Michigan: Exploring uncharted territory while teaching elementary school social studies. *Elementary School Journal.*

Wilson, S. M., Shulman, L. S., & Richert, A. E. (1987). "150 different ways" of knowing: Representations of knowledge in teaching. In J. Calderhead (Ed.), *Exploring teachers' thinking* (pp. 104–124). London: Cassell.

Wilson, S. M., & Sykes, G., (1989). Toward better teacher preparation and certification. In P. Gagnon & The Bradley Commission on History in Schools (Eds.), *Historical literacy: The case for history in American education* (pp. 268–286). New York: Macmillan.

Wilson, S. M., & Wineberg, S. S. (1988). Peering at history from different lenses: The role of disciplinary perspectives in the teaching of American history. *Teachers College Record, 89,* 525–539.

Wineberg, S. S., & Wilson, S. M. (1991). Subject matter knowledge in the teaching of history. In J. Brophy (Ed.), *Advances in research on teaching, Volume 2* (pp. 305–347). Norwood, NJ: Ablex.

Winter, D., McClelland, D., & Stewart, A. (1981). *A new case for the liberal arts: Assessing institutional goals and student development.* San Francisco: Jossey-Bass.

Woodward, C. V. (1986). *Thinking back.* Baton Rouge, LA: Louisiana State University.

Young, R. E. (1987). Epistemologies. In M. J. Dunkin (Ed.), *The international encyclopedia of teaching and teacher education* (pp. 493–496). Oxford, UK: Pergamon.

5

INSTRUCTIONAL METHODS AND CONCEPTUAL ORIENTATIONS IN THE DESIGN OF TEACHER EDUCATION PROGRAMS: THE EXAMPLE OF SIMULATIONS, HYPERMEDIA, AND CASES*

KATHERINE K. MERSETH

Harvard Graduate School of Education

*The author wishes to acknowledge the valuable contributions of Catherine Lacey, Program Officer at the Spencer Foundation, Chicago, to this work. In addition, the author would like to thank James Cooper, Judith Sandholtz, and Sharon Feiman-Nemser for their comments on an earlier draft.

Teacher education programs grapple with fundamental uncer-
tainties: *What* do teachers need to know, and what should they
be able to do? *How* should teachers learn to teach? Many people
would say that we have come closer to assessing what teachers
need to know because the study of the relationship between
teachers' actions and students' outcomes has advanced significantly in the last 15 years (Berliner, 1985; Berliner & Rosenshine, 1976; Brophy & Good, 1986; Gage, 1978). This research,
building on the experimental methods of psychology, suggests
that there is a "science of education" that can be codified and
systematically communicated to students of education.

Yet, even as this determination of surer knowledge in teaching
progresses, insights into the complexity of teaching grow as well.
Research that focuses on classroom ecology and teachers' thinking, influenced by cognitive science and ethnographic methodologies, stresses the multidimensional and contextualized nature
of teaching (Clark & Lampert, 1986; Clark & Peterson, 1986;
Clark & Yinger, 1977; Doyle, 1990; Shulman, 1987). In this view,
novices construct knowledge about teaching by experiencing and
exploring the kinds of problems that practitioners actually face
(Cutler, 1992).

Most likely, persons learning to teach need to know both that
specific principles and techniques have been found to be effective in classroom instruction and that "thinking like a teacher"
means creating one's own knowledge in the face of uncertain and
ambiguous situations. Teacher educators might well agree that
future teachers would benefit by understanding both the science
and the complexity of teaching.

Lurking beneath this agreement, however, are a number of
deep differences. Teachers and teacher educators espouse various conceptional orientations toward teaching. Is teaching an
academic, practical, or technical endeavor? Is it a combination of
these and/or other orientations? Further differences exist with
regard to instructional activities within programs. Which activities—lectures, discussions, field-based observations, microteaching, simulations, case methods, interactive technologies, or computer networking—will best develop a deep understanding and
knowledge of teaching and of teaching specific subject matter as
the previous chapter underscored? Also how do decisions about
method relate to conceptual orientations?

An analogy might serve to illustrate the crisscrossing aspects
of the dilemma facing teacher educators. To create strong and
vibrant cloth, a weaver chooses and fixes threads vertically on a

loom at just the right tension. These stretched threads, the warp, provide the backdrop and make room for the movable threads of the woof to play horizontally across them, elaborating the pattern imagined by the weaver in the fabric. Analogously, to create strong and cohesive teacher education programs, designers would select and articulate the conceptual orientations of teaching that would form the backbone of a program. The warp of the orientations would provide firm threads, across which the woof of thoughtfully chosen instructional activities could be played to develop in students rich patterns of understanding of how to teach and learn. Also, as in weaving, certain intersections of conceptual orientation with instructional method are brighter than others.

THE PROBLEM

The ability to articulate a conceptual orientation and the degree to which it is believed and practiced by teacher education faculty members are central to effective teacher education programs (Zeichner & Liston, 1990; Zimpher & Howey, 1987). Understanding the purposes and objectives of any teacher education program includes a clear articulation of conceptions of teaching "critical to any understanding of the various purposes of teacher education is an explication of the different conceptions of teaching that underlie these programs" (Zimpher & Howey, 1987, p. 102). Explicit conceptual orientations provide a way to organize and orient teacher education programs. By outlining an interpretation of teaching, they offer a thoughtful response to the question "What do teachers need to know and what should they be able to do?" Clearly stated and commonly held conceptions of teaching, however, often are missing in the design of teacher education programs, leaving the warp slack instead of taut.

Unfortunately, this lack of articulation spills over into the rationale for the design and implementation of instructional methods in programs, leaving only a loose or sometimes nonexistent connection between aims and implementation (Feiman-Nemser, 1990; Howey & Zimpher, 1989; Zeichner, 1991; Zimpher & Howey, 1987). Instructional activities form the woof—the elaboration—that addresses the question "How shall the teachers be educated?"

One would hope to find a carefully reasoned and clear rationale for specific educative activities in a particular teacher education program. Instead some teacher educators use case methods, simulations, or other instructional practices without reference to their epistemological foundations or theories about learning to teach. They use these innovations because they are "hot" in the literature, because money is available to implement them, or because they fit conveniently in a given course or component of a program. Confusion and a lack of consistency, both in practice and in the literature, are the result. Willis Copeland (1982) describes this phenomenon:

> Most [activities] are not based on well-understood, tested, and refined models or principles, but at best they grow from a variety of assumptions about what good teaching is and how it can be trained. Often, these experiences reflect nothing more than the feelings and intuitions of independent teacher educators concerning what constitutes worthwhile or appropriate activities. (p. 1008)

To exacerbate the situation, many activities lack empirical data that document their impact on new teachers after they leave the university and move to the classroom. Clarity about outcomes and long-range changes in teachers' behavior is rarely available.

Certainly there are notable exceptions to this rather dismal picture of programmatic confusion. Scholars have provided rich and instructive descriptions of distinctive or exemplary programs (Barnes, 1987; Howey & Zimpher, 1989; Zeichner, 1991). These programs represent efforts to redesign entire programs, to offer thematic alternatives, or to create "small islands of coherence among a variety of typically unfocused programs" (Zeichner, 1991, p. 22). Such programs involve careful and conscious reflection and articulation of the orientations and underlying assumptions about learning and teaching, embodied in specific program activities.

THE AIM OF THIS CHAPTER

The aim of this chapter is to examine closely the relationship between commonly used conceptual orientations about teaching and instructional activities in the design of teacher education programs. By doing so, it seeks to stimulate conversation about three sets of instructional activities and their strengths and weaknesses in reinforcing five different conceptual orientations to teaching. The chapter concludes by examining some implications for faculty development.

The first set of instructional activities includes microteaching and examples of technologically enhanced simulations. A second set of instructional activities focuses on hypermedia as a particular example of innovative practice. The third examines cases and case methods of instruction. I included these three sets of activities because of the popularity and promise that each seems to hold for teacher education and because of the assumptions about teaching that they embody. The conceptual orientations represent past and current discussions in the teacher education literature; they include academic, practical, personal/developmental, technical, and social/critical interpretations of teaching.

In this chapter I seek to illuminate the fit between selected instructional methods in teacher education and certain conceptual orientations. In some instances, a close congruence exists between a particular orientation and the instructional method. Microteaching and a technical orientation to teacher education, for example, are quite consistent in philosophy and objective. Other examples, such as cases and hypermedia, contain merit for the practical and academic orientations. I argue here that in the presence of epistemological and philosophical agreements between the underlying assumptions of program orientation and the pedagogical materials and activities, the result will be greater coherence in the design of teacher education programs.

By examining the assumptions about learning, teaching, and learning to teach as evident in the orientations and the instructional methods, this chapter underscores a key point made by Feiman-Nemser (1990):

> An orientation refers to a set of ideas about the goals of teacher preparation and the means for achieving them. Ideally, a conceptual orientation includes a view of teaching and learning and a theory about learning to teach. Such ideas *should* give direction to the practical activities of teacher preparation such as program planning, course development, instruction, supervision, and evaluation. (p. 220, emphasis added)

This chapter also provides information about selected instructional approaches through a review of the literature and current practices. This review will enable teacher education faculty members to explore these activities and possibly integrate them into their courses and programs.

In this chapter I do not report on the effectiveness of each innovation or experience made available to students learning to teach. For some of these innovations, related empirical work examines the impact on outcomes for students or other measures of effectiveness, but often this is not the case. The task of documenting the impact of these activities and innovations remains as important work for teacher educators.

CONCEPTUAL ORIENTATIONS

A number of scholars have delineated differing orientations and views about the conceptual foundations of teaching and teacher education (Feiman-Nemser, 1990; Kennedy, 1987, 1990; Morine-Dershimer, 1991; Zeichner, 1983, 1991; Zeichner & Liston, 1990; Zimpher & Howey, 1987). Drawing from this rich discussion, this chapter explores five conceptual orientations: academic, personal/developmental, technical, practical, and social/critical. To illustrate the meaning of these five perspectives, I offer a brief discussion of each, including its epistemological assumptions and the role for teacher educators.

THE ACADEMIC ORIENTATION

The academic orientation emphasizes the acquisition of knowledge and the development of understanding of subject matter in teaching and is most commonly found in secondary teacher education programs. Knowledge of subject matter is central to the teacher's development. Often this knowledge is assumed to be acquired through an undergraduate major or advanced coursework in the field that the secondary teacher will teach.

Because the acquisition of academic knowledge often occurs outside the teacher education program in a liberal arts program or another part of the university, teacher educators historically abdicated responsibility for prospective teachers' knowledge of subject matter or content (Feiman-Nemser, 1990). In the last five years, however, this disengagement from subject matter has begun to change.

Many teacher educators now recognize their responsibility for the development of a closely related form of academic knowledge. Pedagogical content knowledge emphasizes the ways in which teachers transform and represent knowledge for students (Shulman, 1986, 1987; Wilson, Shulman, & Richert, 1987). With this recognition, teacher educators are engaged increasingly with subject matter and with the influence of its structure on teaching and learning.

The teacher's role in this orientation is that of a transmitter of knowledge, an individual firmly grounded in the subject matter to be taught who is facile in developing multiple representations of the material for different learning outcomes. Teacher education programs that emphasized the academic orientation included the MAT programs in place from the 1950s to early 1970s. More recently, the Academic Learning Program at Michigan State, as well as some alternative certification programs, have stressed this conception (Feiman-Nemser, 1990; Morine-Dershimer, 1991).

THE PERSONAL ORIENTATION

The personal orientation places the teacher's personal development at the center of the process of learning to teach. This orientation also gives great emphasis to understanding students and allowing them to determine their own learning objectives. The teacher in this tradition is self-reliant, and a sensitive guide and reflector of students' interest in the classroom. Here, "teaching is less a matter of prescribing and molding and more a matter of encouraging and assisting. The teacher is a facilitator who creates conditions conducive to learning. To do this, teachers must know their students as individuals" (Feiman-Nemser, 1990, p. 225).

A number of scholars, including Howey and Zimpher (1986), Morine-Dershimer (1991), Zeichner and Liston (1990), and Zimpher and Howey (1987), emphasize the developmental aspect of this orientation in their formulations. This orientation also focuses on the intrapersonal changes that occur in the process of becoming a teacher (Fuller & Bown, 1975). The teacher educator in the personal orientation functions as a counselor who fosters inquiry and self-knowledge in the prospective teacher. Through this process, the neophyte develops personalized theories and teaching methods that encourage meaningful learning. Also, the prospective teacher develops skills in observing and understanding students in order to facilitate student-centered activities.

Examples of programs that have stressed this orientation included the Personalized Teacher Education Program at the University of Texas and the advisement program at Bank Street College (Feiman-Nemser, 1990). In addition, individual faculty members rather than entire programs stress this philosophical orientation. For example, Eleanor Duckworth of Harvard University offers a course titled "Teaching and Learning," which encourages prospective teachers to explore and design their own learning (Duckworth, 1987). This course is available to all teacher education students in the university and models the way a teacher with a personal orientation would act in the classroom.

THE TECHNICAL ORIENTATION

Perhaps the most easily identified tradition in teacher education programs is the technical orientation. In this approach, the underlying belief is that knowledge about teaching and learning can be codified and presented in an organized fashion to people who are learning to teach. This orientation places faith in the scientific study of teaching. It suggests that particular situations of instruction can be generalized to principles and theories, and assumes that

> Even though particular situations are new, they are nonetheless examples of larger categories of situations and that there is a generally accepted best way to handle any given category of situation. Therefore, the role of professional educators is to provide students with knowledge of the generally accepted principles for handling each category. (Kennedy, 1990, p. 813)

In this orientation, learning to teach is fostered through the acquisition of specific knowledge and skills, often through skill-based modules, microteaching experiences, or simulations. Many of the teaching skills imparted by these programs are the result of research focusing on effective teaching (see Brophy & Good, 1986; Evertson, Hawley, & Zlotnick, 1984; Gage, 1978). Educating teachers in this perspective emphasizes behaviorism and the explicit quantification of skills and outcomes.

A teacher trained in the technical tradition will exhibit carefully honed skills in such areas as classroom management, lesson planning, lesson presentation, and forms of questioning. Sometimes this orientation emphasizes direct instruction as desirable; students are taught to include specific components, such as anticipatory sets and guided practice, in every lesson (Hunter, 1986).

Examples of this orientation existed in the competency-based programs (CBTE) that were popular nearly two decades ago and whose influence continues today. The renewed attention to competency-based programs exists because of the legislative and public interest in accountability and assessment of teachers' performance. Two programs that have employed a number of technically oriented activities include programs at the University of

Maryland (McCaleb, Borko, & Arends, in press) and the University of Toledo (Howey & Zimpher, 1989).

THE PRACTICAL ORIENTATION

The practical orientation, a fourth perspective on teaching and teacher education, looks to experience rather than to scientific principles for its knowledge about teaching. This orientation stresses the practical wisdom or "knowledge-in-action" exercised by the teacher in negotiating a wide array of variables in situations characterized by value conflict and ambiguity (Jackson, 1968; Lampert & Clark, 1990; Lortie, 1975; Schön, 1983; Shulman, 1986). It embraces Floden and Clark's (1988) succinct statement: "Teaching is evidently and inevitably uncertain" (p. 505).

Research on practical knowledge suggests that in exercising professional judgment, teachers operate not from a codified set of principles or theories but rather from "case" knowledge (Doyle, 1986; Shulman, 1986). Teachers seem to address complex problems by "crisscrossing" the landscape of their experience to draw on the knowledge gained in many past situations, with all their inherent differences (see Spiro & Jehng, 1990).

In this orientation, learning to teach does not involve the accumulation of knowledge about facts and procedures. Rather it entails engagement in apprenticeship experiences, case-based activities, or problem-solving contexts rich enough to help the prospective teacher to "think like a teacher" (Feiman-Nemser, 1990). This orientation shares Dewey's (1904) conviction that "the professional school does its best for its students when it gives them typical and intensive, rather than extensive and detailed, practice" (p. 11). Teacher educators need to "prepare students to think on their feet, giving them both reasoning skills and strategies for analyzing and interpreting new situations" (Kennedy, 1990, p. 813). In daily practice, the teacher is the decision maker and problem solver in situations in which decisions are inevitably conditional and problems are managed, not solved (Lampert, 1985).

Examples of programs embodying aspects of the practical orientation are the Teachers for Rural Alaska Program at the University of Alaska, Fairbanks (Feiman-Nemser, 1990) and Project START (Student Teachers as Researching Teachers) at the University of Pennsylvania (Cochran-Smith, 1991). At Fairbanks, case-based activities provide students with opportunities to think through the complexities of teaching in a multicultural setting.

In Project START, student teachers, master cooperating teachers, and university faculty members work together as teacher-researchers in a year-long process of inquiry in order to learn how to think for themselves about teaching and learning issues and problems.

THE SOCIAL/CRITICAL ORIENTATION

Finally, the social/critical orientation to teaching and teacher education emphasizes the teacher as a political actor as well as an educator. Supporters of this perspective believe that much of what goes on in school between teachers and students reflects and reinforces the conditions of society. Noting the presence of social inequities, they believe that teachers should help change them. Therefore, the teacher should promote democratic values in the classroom; teaching becomes social transformation.

Liston and Zeichner (1988) have written extensively about this perspective and use the term "social reconstructivism" to describe it. In their interpretation, the teacher's attention is focused both inward, at his or her own practice, and outward, at the context in which the practice is situated. The role of the teacher educator in this orientation is to raise prospective teachers' consciousness of societal conditions and to increase their influence and interaction with schooling. Teachers should come to recognize the "fundamentally political character of all schooling" (Zeichner, 1991, p. 19). They are encouraged to reflect and act on important moral and philosophical questions of education.

Examples of programs stressing this orientation include the student teaching component at the University of Wisconsin—Madison (Gore & Zeichner, 1991; Zeichner and Liston, 1987) and at Catholic University (Ciriello, Valli, & Taylor, 1992). Components of the Teachers for Rural Alaska Program at the University of Alaska, Fairbanks (Kleinfeld, 1989, 1990) also utilize this orientation.

A WORD OF CAUTION

Although the preceding section offers some insights into commonly held conceptual orientations of teacher education, an important caution is in order before we proceed. Separate examination of each orientation makes them appear to be independent of one other, but this is not necessarily the case. Orientations are not inherently mutually exclusive; more than one can and frequently does exist within the same teacher education program. For example, the influence of the academic, technical, and practical orientations may be present in the same teacher education program in different courses, instructors, and activities.

Yet in order to examine the three sets of instructional activities and their relationship to these representative orientations in teacher education, the reader must view each orientation temporarily as independent of the others. The purpose of this artificial separation is to clarify the analyses and discussions of the pedagogies. Although this exercise is clearly hypothetical, it should help to highlight teacher educators' understandings of the particular interaction between orientations and instructional activities.

Again, what do different orientations offer teacher educators? They offer the fixed threads of the warp, the structure of "why" on which to thread the thinking about the "how" of educating teachers. They provide a frame of reference to help guide the deliberations about teacher education activities. They help make explicit the potential impact of a variety of practices on the coherence and strength of overall programs. In the following sections I explore these assertions.

INSTRUCTIONAL ACTIVITIES

Recent contributions to the teacher education literature raise interest in the use of diverse instructional practices and activities in teacher education (Ball, Lampert, & Rosenberg, 1991; Goldman & Barron, 1990; Merseth, 1991a, 1991b; Strang, Landrum, & Ulmer, 1991; Zeichner, 1991). In this work, various activities and practices in teacher education are asserted to develop a variety of skills, forms of knowledge, and "habits of the mind" (Shulman, 1989) in prospective teachers. The representative instructional activities explored here are simulation activities (including technologically based activities), hypermedia-enhanced activities, and cases and case methods. The rationale for the selection of these activities, as mentioned earlier, is that each seems to hold promise for teacher education. In addition, these collections offer interesting contrasts in their underlying interpretations of teaching and in their assumptions about the conditions under which prospective teachers learn.

The first set of activities includes microteaching and simulations. I grouped these activities because they have a common objective: to reduce the representation of teaching from a complex, confusing environment to a simpler environment, relying on a set of clearly identified teaching behaviors. For example, one of the original developers of microteaching in the early 1960s claimed, "Much of the complex act of teaching can be broken down into simpler more easily trainable skills and techniques" (Cooper, 1967, p. 119). These activities seek to develop clearly identified skills and behaviors, and seem likely to yield good results as the field of teacher education continues to develop a well-defined, codified knowledge about teaching.

The development of hypermedia environments represents the second set of activities. This emerging educational technology capitalizes on recent advances in videodisc technology and in computer programming to create environments that represent the "real world" of practice, with all of its simultaneity, multidimensionality, and immediacy (Doyle, 1986). Researchers argue that thoughtful hypermedia designs have great potential for introducing the complexities of practice to novices (Ball et al., 1991; Bransford, Goin, Hasselbring, Kinzer, Sherwood, & Williams, 1986; Goldman, Barron, & Witherspoon, 1991; Risko, in press). Because a wide array of data in many media (for example, video, audio, graphic, text) can be stored, retrieved rapidly, and linked flexibly, educators can create environments with easily accessible representations of classrooms.

The third set of activities consists of cases and case-based instruction. Recent contributions to the teacher education literature have created interest in the potential of these materials and approaches for enhancing teacher education ("Case Methodology," 1990; "Case Methods," 1991; Merseth, 1991a, 1991b; Sykes & Bird, 1991). This literature asserts that cases develop a variety of skills, forms of knowledge, and ways of thinking. Although empirical research to substantiate these claims is still in its earliest stages (cf., Kleinfeld, 1991; Welty, Silverman, & Lyon, 1991), the prospects for contribution to teacher education appear bright. Morine-Dershimer (1991) suggests that the case method "has a strong possibility of success" (p. 14); Merseth (1991b) states that case instruction based on actual classroom experience "could play an important part" (p. 7) in designing teacher education programs.

To explore the interaction between instructional activities and certain conceptual orientations in the design of teacher education programs, this section examines the three sets of instructional activities and their relationship to particular conceptual orientations.

SIMULATIONS

Simulations are activities whereby "elements of real situations are presented to learners to provide them with an awareness and an opportunity to learn and practice responses" (Cruickshank & Metcalf, 1990, p. 486). Three qualities typically define simulations: an emphasis on repeated practice using feedback from past experience; the ability to manipulate and control predetermined variables and characteristics of the experience; and selectivity with respect to the representation of the context.

Students participating in simulations actually take on the role of teacher. Through feedback, reinforcement, and repeated practice, they have multiple opportunities to experience the simulated situation. Simulations assume that important behavioral learning occurs through repeated practice. Also, they offer teacher educators a form of control through the use of "planned variation," so that learning experiences may be tailored individually in order to optimize learning.

Simulations selectively limit certain characteristics or variables of a context in order to focus and control the learner's attention. Copeland (1982) observes:

> If all characteristics of the real world were contained in the activity, that activity would not be a simulation but a slice of reality. Situational characteristics may be omitted because they are considered unimportant and the expense of including them is not justified, or because their inclusion would pose a danger to the trainee or lend an excess of unpredictability to the activity. (p. 1014)

These characteristics distinguish simulations from other instructional practices, such as hypermedia and case-based instruction. Case-based instruction, for example, tries to represent reality as fully as possible in order to "bring a chunk of reality" (Lawrence, 1953) into the classroom. Also, feedback in case discussions provides fewer opportunities for repeated practice because case discussions provide no opportunities for replicated practice with feedback.

Simulations appear in multiple forms and with tremendous variety (Megarry, 1981). The literature often interchanges terms, thus producing some confusion as techniques and approaches evolve. One author may categorize the development of a simulated classroom as an example of protocol materials (Megarry, 1981); another may describe the same material as an elaborate attempt at simulation (Copeland, 1982).

Two important examples of simulation are microteaching and computer-assisted simulations. Microteaching, which is appropriately called teaching in "miniature" (Turney, Clift, Dunkin, & Traill, 1973, p. vii), usually includes activities in which teachers practice a clearly delineated teaching skill in a prepared lesson of 5 to 20 minutes to a group of students (who are often peers). Teachers frequently study a model of the specific skill, through either videotapes or printed materials, before the execution of the lesson. The lesson is videotaped and used for discussion and review by the group and instructor. After the review, the teacher has additional opportunities to reteach the lesson while incorporating the feedback of the group and the instructor (Allen, 1967; Borg, Kelley, Langer, & Gall, 1970; Cruickshank, 1984). Microteaching is teaching that is scaled down in class size, content, skill, and time.

The literature on microteaching evidences fairly wide consensus about its definition, aims, and purposes (Copeland, 1982; Cruickshank, 1984; Cruickshank & Metcalf, 1990). Skills that microteaching emphasizes include questioning skills, reinforcement techniques, presentation skills, nonverbal responses, and the development of student-initiated questions. No particular set of skills is believed to be the best, however. In fact, "the selection and development of technical skills of teaching depend upon the objectives of the teacher education program" (Cooper, 1967, p. 121).

Microteaching seeks to reduce teaching into separate components, isolating principles or skills found by researchers to be effective (Berliner, 1985). It attempts to provide practice in these skills in a controlled environment. This approach has a natural ally in the computer, which can assist tirelessly in replicating the component parts of teaching in order to foster competencies in prospective teachers (Copeland, 1982, 1989). Computer-driven programs, which exhibit the characteristics of simulations, confront a trainee with problem situations involving skills predefined by the teacher educator, require the selection of alternative responses, and give immediate feedback regarding the adequacy of the trainee's performance. After attending to the feedback, students replicate the exercise, gaining mastery of discrete teaching skills through repeated practice.

The work of Harold Strang and his colleagues at the Curry School of Education at the University of Virginia presents an example of computer-based simulation (Strang, Badt, & Kauffman, 1987; Strang, Landrum & Lynch, 1989; Strang, Landrum,

& Ulmer, 1991; Strang & Loper, 1983). Convinced that students of teaching have too little opportunity to apply all that they are learning about effective teaching, the Curry group developed several interactive computer simulations between 1981 and 1986, in which preservice teachers could simulate teaching a group of computer-generated pupils.

In these simulations, teacher educators create custom-simulated classroom experiences for their students by presetting certain parameters. These parameters include lesson content; the frequency with which common types of student misbehavior will occur; certain attributes such as readiness, enthusiasm, and propensity to misbehave of 12 software-generated pupils in the class; the type of postteaching feedback; and the training path that will guide the student automatically through a sequence of lessons and feedback (Strang et al., 1991). During a simulation exercise, the screen displays the lesson content that the student is to teach. He or she then begins to "dialogue" with the pupils via keyboard entries of options displayed on screen menus. As the student articulates various interventions with different pupils, he or she receives feedback via pupils' response about the efficacy of the instructional choices and management interventions. After the lesson, the student receives feedback about the chain of events and obtains other information about the previously identified variables.

Microteaching and computer-assisted simulations are a particularly compelling example of activities that are consistent with a technical orientation to teaching. In fact, microteaching often is called "technical-skill training" (Cruickshank & Metcalf, 1990, p. 480). Both types of simulations exemplify the belief inherent in the technical orientation, namely that complexities of teaching can be reduced accurately and representatively through the scientific study of teaching to smaller, more manageable, more comprehensible behaviors and activities. While microteaching advocates admit that teaching is complex, they observe that in microteaching, "the trainees are exposed to variables in classroom teaching without being overwhelmed by the complexity of the situation" (Cooper & Stroud, 1967, p. 8).

According to the technical orientation, learning to teach is fostered through the acquisition of specific knowledge and skills. Microteaching and computer-aided simulations, with their focus on specific skills and on repeated practice following feedback, offer an exquisite example of activities resting on this assumption. These activities stress the positive impact of practice on the learning of desired behaviors that have been identified through research (Brophy & Good, 1986; Evertson et al., 1984; Gage, 1978). Strang et al. (1989), for example, argue that students can practice the simulation at any time of day or night. The practice is consistent and patient. Teacher education students can practice the same exercise repeatedly with computer-simulated pupils, who will exhibit the same behaviors tirelessly and can do so without suffering effects.

Whether by simulating probable events in classroom interaction, as in certain computer-assisted simulations, or by simulating segments of classroom instruction, as in microteaching, teacher educators using these pedagogical activities seek to create environments that represent selected aspects of the teacher's real world, real time, and real practice (Berliner, 1985; Copeland, 1982, 1989; Strang et al., 1991). Thus, the dominant emphasis of simulations is on developing important behavioral skills in prospective teachers through controlled practice and feedback. This objective aligns simulations most coherently and most consistently with the technical orientation of learning to teach.

HYPERMEDIA ENVIRONMENTS

A second set of instructional activities grows from the development of hypermedia environments representing classrooms. These environments offer radically new ways to support inquiry into teaching and learning in teacher education. Recent advances in videodisc and computer technologies give users access to multiple representations including video, audio, graphics, text, and animation of activities in real classrooms in random ways. The random access capability of videodisc technology overcomes the linear problems associated with rewinding and replaying videotape because it allows video segments to be retrieved almost instantly for analysis, illustration, or contrast. In addition, advanced programming technologies permit access to information through a variety of media; hence the term *hypermedia*. As a result, teacher educators and their students have the advantage of experiencing and exploring multiple viewpoints on specific teaching and learning contexts via any number of paths—paths determined by their own questions and frames of inquiry, rather than by the computer program.

Well-articulated examples are offered by two groups of researchers currently involved in the development of hypermedia environments for use in teacher education. Lampert and Ball

(1990) videotaped a year of their own innovative teaching of elementary mathematics in the third and the fifth grade, and collected a variety of perspectives on that teaching in video, audio, and text form. They included their own perspectives as teachers and researchers, their students' perspectives, and those of others, such as learning theorists and subject-area specialists. Many other kinds of graphic and textual data, including chalkboard work, papers, quizzes, and achievement tests, provide further information for study.

The hypermedia design piloted by Ball and colleagues (Ball, Lampert, & Rosenberg, 1991) gives the students in their teacher education classes both the data and the tools to experience and explore multiple perspectives on teaching and learning:

> What we envision is the use of learning modules in teacher education settings that will be built around videotaped lessons taught by the authors, in which teacher educators will be able to present to their students a replay of a real time lesson and then conduct an analysis of that lesson in a seminar discussion format. Using this technology, they will be able to access incidents in the lesson for consideration quickly and in direct response to student's concerns and inquiries. (Lampert & Ball, 1990, p. 6)

Another example of hypermedia use in teacher education is under development in a variety of methods courses at Vanderbilt's Peabody College of Education. Goldman and her colleagues (Goldman, Williams, Bassler, Sherwood, Barron, & Witherspoon, 1990) have developed hypermedia designs to provide structured experiences in analyzing various aspects of elementary mathematics lessons. Their work includes a program that explores a lesson, such as teaching subtraction, from a variety of perspectives, including that of a mathematician, a sociolinguist, and the individual teaching the lesson. Other programs contrast expert with novice approaches in teaching mathematics and science lessons, and examine the use of manipulative materials. Also at Vanderbilt, Risko and her colleagues (Risko, Yount, & Towell, 1992) have a set of hypermedia materials that explore the teaching of children with reading difficulties. These materials allow teacher educators to present rich sources of information simultaneously, thus helping their students to integrate items usually taught separately (Goldman & Barron, 1990; Risko, 1992).

Proponents of hypermedia in teacher education (Bransford et al., 1986; Goldman & Barron, 1990; Lampert & Ball, 1990; Risko et al., 1992) see two significant advantages in hypermedia for instruction in the "ill-structured" domains of teaching and learning. First, the nonlinear capability of hypermedia design distinguishes it from more traditional methods of instruction, such as lecturing, which rely on a more orderly and more linear presentation of subject matter:

> Linearity of media is not a problem when the subject matter being taught is well structured and fairly simple. However, as content increases in complexity and ill-structuredness, increasingly greater amounts of important information are lost with linear approaches and the unidimensionality [*sic*] of organization that typically accompanies them. (Spiro & Jehng, 1990, p. 163)

Also, the ability of hypermedia systems to revisit scenes or perspectives quickly and easily makes it possible to hold and consider many perspectives on an event simultaneously.

Second, "that which is learned" through exposure to hypermedia activities is individualized because it is constructed by the users in much the same way as practical knowledge is constructed in the classroom by teachers. Hypermedia quickly and effortlessly accesses and links perspectives in multiple ways. This capacity enables novices to build their own knowledge about teaching. In contrast, in other uses of computers in teacher education, "that which is to be learned" is already "known" by the computer, and the program guides the learner along linear, rule-bound paths (however exhaustive) to learn what it already "knows" (Nix, 1990).

Proponents of hypermedia design in educating teachers believe that classroom teaching is characterized by multidimensionality and that teachers' knowledge is idiosyncratic, highly contextualized, and constantly being constructed (Ball et al., 1991; Lampert & Ball, 1990). Through its design, hypermedia embodies the multisource nature of learning, as described by a solid body of research in cognitive psychology. "The more meaningful, the more deeply or elaboratively processed, the more situated in context, and the more rooted in cultural, background, metacognitive, and personal knowledge an event is, the more readily it is understood, learned, and remembered" (Iran-Nejad, McKeachie, & Berliner, 1990, p. 511).

Hypermedia designs seem to be eminently suited to support the practical orientation in teacher education because they seek to foster a "knowing how to use knowledge" (Bransford et al., 1986; Goldman & Barron, 1990; Lampert & Ball, 1990; Risko, 1992). In its design, hypermedia attempts to foster in novices the ability to do what researchers (Carter, Sabers, Cushing, Pinnegar, & Berliner, 1987; Sabers, Cushing, & Berliner, 1991) say experts do well—namely, to discern and use effectively that information that is salient and relevant in the wide array of data available at any moment of practice. The nature of hypermedia experiences encourages the development of problem-solving heuristics: first identifying and framing problems, and then using all the knowledge at hand to reframe, invent, and transactionally explore responses to the situation (Schön, 1983).

Specifically, three characteristics of hypermedia design reinforce the epistemological assumptions of the practical orientation to teaching and learning.

First, hypermedia creates a context complicated enough for novices to experience, without being overwhelmed by the problems inherent in practice (Lampert & Ball, 1990; Spiro & Jehng, 1990). Through hypermedia, students can begin to see teaching as complicated and can begin to dislodge the simplistic or reductive views of teaching (Ball et al., 1991; Risko et al., 1992). The ability of hypermedia to represent teaching as complex and ambiguous, yet not overwhelming, is a key element in its ability to enhance a practical orientation to teaching.

In addition, rather than drawing on and delivering theory and research that "necessarily reduce[s] the complexity of the learning process in order to focus on its regularities" (Lampert & Ball, 1990, p. 2), hypermedia deliberately turns teacher education on its head by expanding the complexities. Moreover, hypermedia design makes it possible to revisit scenes or minicases several times as the novice's understanding grows; each visit brings forth additional aspects of the complexity it contains (Bransford et al., 1986; Goldman et al., 1991; Lampert & Ball, 1990; Spiro & Jehng, 1990). This capability strengthens the capabilities that characterize practitioners at work: "Human beings function well in the soft, slimy swamp of the real world because they have a natural talent for simplifying complex real-world problems by coordinating and integrating the influences of the multiple sources that simultaneously bear on these problems" (Iran-Nejad et al., 1990, p. 510).

Second, the random-access capability of hypermedia design facilitates access to information relevant to problematic situations (Bransford et al., 1986; Spiro & Jehng, 1990). This ease encourages the novice to develop a problem-solving heuristic that explores the many sources of data relevant to a particular situation of practice. The development of a "way of thinking" aids novices who are just learning to assess learning situations. Students develop their skills of problem identification and problem management in ambiguous situations of practice (Carter, Cushing, Sabers, Stein, & Berliner, 1988). Hypermedia provides an opportunity to "learn from experience."

Third, in hypermedia design, students not only change their thinking as they gain experience in analyzing hypermedia cases, they also become *aware* of the change in their thinking (Bransford, Kinzer, Risko, Rowe, & Vye, 1989; Cognition and Technology Group, 1990; Spiro & Jehng, 1990). New conditions and new contexts trigger different types of knowledge; students notice more and notice themselves noticing more. This metacognitive awareness empowers; students become more confident.

In addition to its particularly good fit with the practical orientation, hypermedia also holds promise for use from other perspectives, such as the academic orientation. Growth in pedagogical content knowledge, an explicit goal of the academic orientation, is also an explicit goal of the hypermedia programs at Michigan State University and Vanderbilt (Ball et al., 1991; Goldman & Barron, 1990; Risko, in press). Both programs seek to create environments in which methods of instruction can be examined for "the ways of representing and formulating the subject" that an expert teacher uses in making a subject comprehensible to others (Shulman, 1986, p. 9). As preservice teachers analyze lessons for this specialized knowledge-in-practice, they grow in their abilities to use and evaluate the effectiveness of this knowledge. Also, the technology encourages extended conversations about the nature and process of "principled discourse" in a field (Ball et al., 1991; Bereiter, 1991; Lampert & Ball, 1990).

The ability of hypermedia to encourage examination of concepts applied across cases also suggests a potential for promoting the knowledge advocated by the social/critical orientation in teacher education. Lampert and Ball (1990) suggest that surveying instances in a year's worth of teaching, for example, could facilitate analysis of hegemonic methodologies, of gender, race, and class inequities. Use of hypermedia designs for the practice of specific skills, however, as promoted by the technical orientation in teacher education, would not be the most promising application. In contrast to the technical orientation, hypermedia design embodies the belief that learning is best accomplished when humans acquire knowledge by integrating information simultaneously from multiple sources. Hypermedia does not seek to build knowledge by isolating specific skills to be learned (Bransford et al., 1986; Spiro & Jehng, 1990). As a result, hypermedia designs have greater potential for examining the way in which general principles are conditioned by a particular case.

CASES

Teacher educators are participating in a growing dialogue about a third type of instructional activity—cases and case methods of instruction—to enhance the education of teachers (see Doyle, 1990; Kleinfeld, 1991; Merseth, 1991a; Sykes, 1989; Sykes & Bird, 1991). The tone of these conversations is positive and optimistic. Though little empirical data exist to support this optimism, many teacher educators believe cases and case methods are an important instructional innovation (Merseth, 1991b; Morine-Dershimer, 1991; Shulman, 1986, 1992). For example, Sykes and Bird (1991) assert

> The case idea can help teacher education . . . because it helps to balance the stance of the actor in the situation with the stance of the observer on the scene, provides means to represent situational complexity, provides a form for grappling with the interaction of possibilities for action, and by encouraging joint consideration of relevant arguments, helps to control abstractive illusion. (p. 48)

Teacher educators hold divergent views about the definition, purpose, and use of cases and their related pedagogy. For example, Shulman (1986) proposes a three-part typology: prototypes that exemplify theoretical principles, precedents that capture and convey principles of practice, and parables that explore norms and values. Broudy (1990) calls for "paradigmatic cases" representing a set of generic problems in teaching; he suggests that these cases would become the core of all teacher education curricula. In another interpretation, Doyle (1990) builds on Shulman's definitions but calls for "theoretically specified" cases. Such cases would encourage the development of teachers' knowledge structures. Spanning these views, D. Cohen (personal communication, April 1990) regards cases not as exemplars (as does Broudy), but as stimulants to deliberative analysis:

> Good cases could nourish deliberations about teaching, which I think of as including analyses that are oriented to decisions and analyses aimed more broadly at understanding. A good case would

offer grist for both sorts of mills. Hence, cases would get entangled with theory in many ways.

Certainly the definition of cases has a significant influence on their use and ultimate impact.

Not only do definitions differ in the discourse among teacher educators; the actual form of cases varies as well. Cases may be in written or video form; they may be constructed explicitly for pedagogical use or borrowed from other fields. Most typically they are based on real-life experiences, providing a means to explore the situational complexity of teaching. Their creators may include "participant observers" who played a role in the described event; at-distance, disciplined researchers whose understanding of the situation is secondhand; or others, such as film directors and popular writers, with little or no intention of providing material for teacher education.

A common language about cases and case-based instruction is now developing as educators offer accounts of their work (Carter & Unklesbay, 1990; Florio-Ruane & Clark, 1990; Kleinfeld, 1991; Merseth, 1990, 1991b; Richert, 1991a; Wilson, 1989a). This array of interpretations and applications means that case-based instruction, as an instructional method, has a versatility not often available to teacher educators. Morine-Dershimer (1991) views this flexibility as a strength: "Because of the potential flexibility of the case method in addressing the values and concerns of all five of the various orientations to teacher education, I believe it has a strong possibility of success as an innovation" (pp. 13–14).

Case-based instruction seems to be best suited to the practical orientation of teaching, and currently is used most widely in a form that supports that orientation. In the practical orientation, teachers are viewed as professionals using judgment, analysis, and strategic action to untie the "knots" of teaching (Wagner, 1984). Here, teaching is viewed as messy, complex, and ambiguous; uncertainty, rather than certainty, prevails. The popularity of case-based instruction in this tradition may be due to the use and availability of cases in other professional fields, where the processes of problem solving and analysis also are found (see Carter & Unklesbay, 1990; Christensen, 1987; Schön, 1987). Also, educators may be comforted by the widely cited (but not empirically supported) advantages of cases in the more prestigious fields of law and business (Christensen, 1981; Kowalski, Weaver, & Henson, 1990; McNair, 1954; Towl, 1969).

Kennedy (1987) helps guide teacher educators from the generalities of professional education in other fields to the specific needs of teacher education. She suggests that teachers need the ability to analyze a situation critically, to generate multiple interpretations of that situation, and to formulate deliberate action plans. Other teacher educators stress the complexity of teaching and the need to develop action plans and strategies that depend not only on prior knowledge, but also on the current context (Clark & Lampert, 1986; Merseth 1991a). As Clark and Lampert state, "Teachers work in situations where they are expected to accomplish complex and even conflicting goals. Under these circumstances, *a priori* knowledge identified by researchers about the relationship among particular decisions or actions and their outcomes is of limited worth" (1986, p. 28).

In this view, teachers survey their own experiences to find knowledge relevant to the current problem.

Like hypermedia environments, cases and case-based instruction create relatively complex representations of practice for discussion and study in teacher education classrooms. The representations, however, are less overwhelming than the actual classroom experience. Their form enables prospective teachers and teacher educators to examine events and explore them more deeply, much like peeling layers of an onion. Learners can hold a relatively complex event still, like an artifact, and examine it in many ways.

Case-based instruction also encourages the development of multiple perspectives and interpretations of a situation (Lang, 1986; Lyons, 1989; Merseth, 1992). Moreover, students identify and bring to bear on a case discussion their past experience as well as more personal feelings, dispositions, and values. This characteristic supports a deeper integration of self into the developing teacher role and creates a learning environment similar to the hypermedia environment. Students of teaching can construct their own knowledge through this instructional approach.

A number of teacher educators are actively involved in the use of cases in this tradition (Kleinfeld, 1988; Merseth, 1990; Silverman, Welty, & Lyon, 1992). Rather than focusing on specific skills, as would be common in the technical orientation, these educators seek to develop a way of thinking—a heuristic, actually—that teachers can use in the problematic and ambiguous world of teaching. Merseth (1992) emphasizes this objective by constructing and using cases that "develop the power to analyze a situation, to formulate action plans, and to evaluate those actions with respect to specific context variables" (pp. 13–14). This use of cases emphasizes the complexities and the ambiguities of teaching, presenting "not one well-defined issue but many ill-defined issues, intertwined like the fibers of a thick rope" (Kleinfeld, 1988, p. 9).

Experience with cases for enhancing an academic orientation to teaching and to learning to teach is more limited than in the practical orientation, although early efforts seem promising. The identification of subject-specific pedagogical knowledge or pedagogical content knowledge (Shulman, 1986), an interest in the nature of the discourse in the subject, and a concern about the role played by the subject in society (Ball, 1989; Cornbleth, 1989; Lakatos, 1979) offer teacher educators unprecedented opportunities to explore use of cases in this orientation.

A number of scholars offer accounts of their work with cases in this orientation (Barnett, 1991; Kleinfeld, personal communication, July 1991; Wilson, 1989a, 1989b). Barnett is exploring the use of cases to develop pedagogical content knowledge in mathematics, where the purpose of using cases is to "foster pedagogical thinking and reasoning skills that are broadly applicable in math teaching" (Barnett, 1991, p. 2). In the field of English, Kleinfeld (personal communication, July 1991) is exploring the ability of case methods to develop skills in identifying central pedagogical issues in teaching *Hamlet* and to transfer these skills to other literary classics. Also, researchers at Michigan State University are exploring case use in training history teachers (Wilson, 1989a, 1989b).

Cases also enhance the development of the personal orientation to teaching through teachers' writing of personal cases. A number of teacher educators ask teachers to write cases about their own experience (Richert, 1991a, 1991b; Shulman & Colbert, 1988). This activity causes prospective teachers to confront their personal experiences and beliefs; some researchers suggest that this approach encourages reflective practice and the development of a professional identity (Kleinfeld, 1988; Richert, 1991a, 1991b). Writing cases for personal reflection and self-study magnifies the centrality of the teacher in the educational process. This use of cases emphasizes the importance of individual learning and development, and is consistent with the personal orientation to teaching.

Specific work with cases to enhance the social/critical orientation to teaching remains primarily hypothetical (Harrington & Garrison, 1991). In discussing this potential, Shulman (1990) suggests, "If we can learn to make [cases] more vivid and inter-active, we can derive all of the virtues of their situatedness and their connectedness, and have the opportunity to add the *moral to the intellectual* in the teaching of pedagogy" (p. 309, emphasis added).

Depending on how they are written or presented, cases can offer students of teaching an opportunity to consider the influ-ence of the larger context in which the particular case is situat-ed (Florio-Ruane & Clark, 1990; Merseth, 1992) or can help to prepare new teachers for the emotional trauma of working in a seemingly unjust world.

In order to present these socially and culturally complex situ-ations, the cases are often longer—sometimes approaching 50 pages—than is typical in other case use. In fact, some scholars suggest that literary texts may be more effective than prepared cases in presenting the normative and moral dimensions of teaching because they situate dilemmas in the larger context of character and culture (Florio-Ruane, as cited in Sykes & Bird, 1991, p. 26). Examples such as Vivian Paley's *White Teacher* or excerpts from movies such as *Stand and Deliver*, although not intended to be used as teaching cases, may well convey the com-plexities of teaching and the influence of culture and society on education.

Few examples of case use support the technical orientation to teaching, in part because cases as traditionally constructed in professional fields are too complex to represent the controlled environments necessary for learning specific skills. In addition, unlike simulations, cases do not offer an opportunity to control the learning experience to enhance the development of clearly identified technical skills. A central assumption of the technical orientation—that teaching can be reduced to principles, theories, and precedents (Berliner & Rosenshine, 1976; Brophy & Good, 1986; Gage, 1978)—runs counter to the espoused purpose of case instruction. In fact, the notion that there is a "right" solu-tion to many teaching problems is anathema in traditional case-based instruction.

Empirical evidence on the effects of case-based instruction is relatively limited. More studies have explored the use of cases in the practical orientation than in any other orientation (Argyris, 1980; Fisher, 1978; Masoner, 1988). More recent work in this type of case suggests that students become more open to multi-ple interpretations and alternatives for action, more aware of the process of analysis, and more sophisticated in their ability to spot and interpret problematic teaching situations (Kleinfeld, 1991; Lyons, 1989; Richert, 1991b; Welty, Silverman, & Lyon, 1991). Also research investigating cases that emphasize social/ critical issues in the development of novice teachers' normative perspectives is in an early stage (Kleinfeld, 1991). All such research must consider both the effects of specifically designed cases in certain orientations and their most effective form.

FACULTY DEVELOPMENT ACTIVITIES

Although promise and hopefulness seem to characterize much of the foregoing discussion of instructional activities and orientations, no improvements in teacher education will be possible without enlightened and skillful faculty members who have adequate resources. The effective use of computer-enhanced simulations, hypermedia materials, or case-based instruction will necessitate a number of fundamental changes among teacher educators.

First, the use of these materials will require some teacher educators to adopt a new perspective on learning to teach and will necessitate a concomitant rethinking of the teacher education curriculum. All of the instructional innovations of simulations, hypermedia, and cases discussed in this chapter are based on the assumption that an exclusive emphasis on the traditional knowledge delivery system of teacher education, entailing lectures and theoretical expositions about teaching, shortchanges those who are learning to teach. These innovations seek to enable learners to participate more directly in their own learning, either by asking their own questions in hypermedia environments, by making their own observations in case discussions, or by indicating their intended actions in simulations. This encouragement of individual participation and of the construction of personal knowledge by persons learning to teach will define a new teaching environment for many teacher educators.

The use of these materials also will require a rethinking and redesign of the traditional teacher education curriculum (DeBloois, 1988; Howey & Zimpher, 1989; Lampert & Ball, 1990; Sykes & Bird, 1991). None of the educational researchers who work with these innovations advocate using them as the sole source of instruction. Thus, issues such as how and when the innovations are introduced and how they are combined with other learning experiences await careful consideration and thoughtful experimentation (Ball et al., 1991; Lyons, 1989; Sykes, 1989).

Second, faculty members will need to gain new skills with regard to their role as leaders in technologically enhanced classrooms and discussion-method teaching. The instructor's primary concern will no longer be content; these new approaches require an equal consideration of process. Instructors in these innovations must determine not only what they will teach, but how. In addition, both hypermedia and case-based instruction seek to transform the traditional delivery of knowledge in teacher education. Rather than delivering theory to reduce the complexity of the learning process to its regularities (Lampert & Ball, 1990), these innovations increase the complexities. As a result, predictable and measurable learning is less certain, and a new role is created for the teacher educator.

What will be needed to develop these new skills? Faculty members must work in environments that are supportive and that encourage innovation. One characteristic of such workplaces is that they offer multiple opportunities to share personal experiences in the classroom through such activities as organized faculty discussion groups or videotaping. Other undertakings, including concentrated workshops and formal peer mentoring programs for faculty members, will increase the likelihood that faculty will grow and learn from their personal experiences (Light, 1990; Merseth, 1991a; 1991c). Also, faculty members' writing about their experiences should be encouraged and valued in the research community (Kleinfeld, 1988; Lyons, 1989; Sykes, 1989).

Faculty members will benefit from ample time to experiment with these innovations, to assess their impact, and to reflect on the results. Changing course designs and introducing new instructional approaches should be regarded as a slow, iterative process. Thus, administrators must exhibit patience and perseverance, providing faculty members with ample support throughout the process of change.

Finally, the implementation of these instructional innovations will demand vast quantities of material. Developers of simulations, hypermedia, and cases openly discuss the tremendous problems of gathering, categorizing, editing, and producing materials (Cruickshank & Metcalf, 1990; Lampert & Ball, 1990; Merseth, 1991a; Risko, personal communication, September 1991). Both technological sophistication and training in production processes are required to bring simulations, hypermedia environments, and cases into full use. Further, such development procedures are expensive; thus, an additional constraint is created. The current scarcity of materials and the lack of an organized distribution system severely limit the promise for these innovations in reforming teacher education.

CONCLUSION

What activities, instructional methods, and program designs will build coherent teacher education programs and best serve the teachers of the 21st century? To design effective programs, teacher educators must answer the fundamental and interrelated questions "What do teachers need to know?" and "How shall teachers be educated?" In answer to the first question, recent progress in the development of codified knowledge in teaching, as well as advances in research on teachers' cognition, suggests that teachers need a combination of scientific and principled knowledge as well as procedural knowledge. Without agreeing upon which type of knowledge deserves emphasis, most teacher educators agree that both offer important answers to the question of what teachers need to know.

The answer to the second question is more complicated because it has many parts. Certainly teacher educators must make structural and organizational decisions about items such as program length, location, and control. Should a program have a four-year, a five-year, or an alternative form? Debates abound on this issue, and often produce more heat than light. What about the locus of control? Should teachers be educated in the university, at a professional development center, or in some creative combination of laboratory, school site, and higher education classroom? And by whom?

These structural questions are important in determining how teachers will be educated, as are the questions about the use of instructional activities and pedagogical designs. As this chapter illustrates, thoughtful consideration and careful reflection about the relationship between instructional activities and conceptual orientations can add coherence to the design of teacher education programs. The consideration of conceptual orientations brings some order to the difficult question of how teachers shall be educated. Well-articulated conceptual orientations offer a firm foundation for instructional activities. More coherent teacher education programs will result from careful consideration of these challenging questions.

REFERENCES

Allen, D. (1967). Preface. In D. Allen (Ed.), *Micro-teaching: A description* (pp. 2–3). Palo Alto, CA: Stanford University.

Argyris, C. (1980). Some limitations of the case method: Experiences in a management development program. *Academy of Management Review, 5*(2), 291–298.

Ball, D. L. (1989). Teaching mathematics for understanding: What do teachers need to know about subject matter? *In Competing visions of teacher knowledge: Proceedings from an NCRTE seminar for education policymakers: February 24–26, 1989: Vol. 1.* Academic subjects (Conference Series 89–1, pp. 79–100). East Lansing: Michigan State University, National Center for Research on Teacher Education.

Ball, D. L., Lampert, M., & Rosenberg, M. L. (1991). *Using hypermedia to investigate and construct knowledge about mathematics teaching and learning.* Paper presented at the 1991 Annual Meeting of the American Educational Research Association, Chicago, IL.

Barnes, H. (1987). The conceptual basis for thematic teacher education. *Journal of Teacher Education, 38*(4), 13–18.

Barnett, C. (1991). *Case methods: A promising vehicle for expanding the pedagogical knowledge base in mathematics.* Paper presented at the 1991 Annual Meeting of the American Educational Research Association, Chicago, IL.

Bereiter, C. (1991). Implications of connectionism for thinking about rules. *Educational Researcher, 20*(3), 10–16.

Berliner, D. C. (1985). Laboratory setting and the study of teacher education. *Journal of Teacher Education, 36*(6), 2–8.

Berliner, D. C., & Rosenshine, B. (1976). *The acquisition of knowledge in the classroom.* San Francisco, CA: Far West Laboratory for Educational Research and Development.

Borg, W., Kelley, M., Langer, P., & Gall, M. (1970). *The mini-course: A microteaching approach to teacher education.* San Francisco, CA: Far West Laboratory for Educational Research and Development.

Bransford, J. D., Goin, L. I., Hasselbring, T. S., Kinzer, C. K., Sherwood, R. D., & Williams, S. M. (1986). Learning with technology: Theoretical and empirical perspectives. *Peabody Journal of Education, 64*(1), 5–26.

Bransford, J. D., Kinzer, C., Risko, V., Rowe, D., & Vye, N. (1989). Designing invitations to thinking: Some initial thoughts. In S. McCormick & J. Zutell (Eds.), *Cognitive and social perspectives for literacy research and instruction* (pp. 35–54). Chicago, IL: National Reading Conference.

Brophy, J., & Good, T. (1986). Teacher behaviors and student achievement. In M. C. Wittrock (Ed.), *Handbook of research on teaching* (3rd ed.). New York: MacMillan.

Broudy, H. (1990). Case studies—Why and how. *Teachers College Record, 91*, 449–459.

Carter, K., Cushing, K., Sabers, D., Stein, P., & Berliner, D. (1988). Expert-novice differences in perceiving and processing visual classroom information. *Journal of Teacher Education, 39*(3), 25–31.

Carter, K., Sabers, D., Cushing, K., Pinnegar, S., & Berliner, D. C. (1987). Processing and using information about students: A study of expert, novice, and postulant teachers. *Teaching and Teacher Education, 3*(2), 147–157.

Carter, K., & Unklesbay, R. (1990). Cases in teaching and law. *Journal of Curriculum Studies, 21*(6), 527–536.

Case methodology in the study and practice of teacher education [Special Issue]. (1990). *Teacher Education Quarterly, 17*(1).

Case methods [Special Issue]. (1991). *Journal of Teacher Education, 42*(4).

Christensen, C. R. (1981). *Teaching by the case method*. Boston, MA: Harvard Business School Case Services, Harvard Business School.

Christensen, C. R. (1987). *Teaching and the case method*. Boston, MA: Harvard Business School Publishing Division.

Ciriello, M., Valli, L., & Taylor, N. (1992). Problem solving is not enough: Reflective teacher education at the Catholic University of America (pp. 99–115). In L. Valli (Ed.) *Reflective teacher education: Cases and Critiques*. Albany, NY: SUNY Press.

Clark, C., & Lampert, M. (1986). The study of teacher thinking: Implications for teacher education. *Journal of Teacher Education, 37*(5), 27–31.

Clark, C., & Peterson, P. (1986). Teachers' cognitions. In M. C. Wittrock (Ed.), *Handbook of research on teaching* (3rd ed., pp. 225–296). New York: Macmillan.

Clark, C., & Yinger, R. (1977). Research on teacher thinking. *Curriculum Inquiry, 7*(4), 279–394.

Cochran-Smith, M. (1991). Learning to teach against the grain. *Harvard Educational Review, 61*, 179–310.

Cognition and Technology Group at Vanderbilt. (1990). Anchored instruction and its relationship to situated cognition. *Educational Researcher, 19*(6), 2–10.

Cooper, J. (1967). Developing specific teaching skills through micro-teaching. In D. Allen (Ed.), *Micro-teaching: A description* (pp. 119–125). Palo Alto, CA: Stanford University.

Cooper, J., & Stroud, T. (1967). The Stanford summer micro-teaching clinic, 1966. In D. Allen (Ed.), *Micro-teaching: A description* (pp. 8–32). Palo Alto, CA: Stanford University.

Copeland, W. D. (1982). Laboratory experiences in teacher education. In H. E. Mitzel, J. H. Best, & W. Rabinowitz (Eds.), *Encyclopedia of educational research, Volume 2* (5th Edition, pp. 1008–1019). New York: The Free Press, Macmillan.

Copeland, W. D. (1989, July-August). Technology-mediated laboratory experiences and the development of clinical reasoning in novice teachers. *Journal of Teacher Education,* 10–18.

Cornbleth, C. (1989). Knowledge for teaching history. In *Competing visions of teacher knowledge: Proceedings from an NCRTE seminar for education policymakers: February 24–26, 1989: Vol. 1.* Academic subjects (Conference Series 89–1, pp. 173–182). East Lansing: Michigan State University, National Center for Research on Teacher Education.

Cruickshank, D. (1984). *Models for the preparation of America's teachers.* Bloomington, IN: Phi Delta Kappa Educational Foundation.

Cruickshank, D., & Metcalf, K. (1990). Training within teacher preparation. In W. R. Houston (Ed.), *Handbook of research on teacher education* (pp. 469–497). New York: Longman.

Cutler, A. B. (1992). *A network of novices: Exploring the first year of teaching.* Unpublished doctoral dissertation, Harvard Graduate School of Education, Cambridge, MA.

DeBloois, M. L. (1988). *Use and effectiveness of videodisc training: A status report.* Falls Church, VA: Future Systems Incorporated.

Dewey, J. (1904). The relation of theory to practice in education. In C. A. Murry (Ed.), *The third yearbook of the National Society for the Scientific Study of Education: Part I: The relation of theory to practice in the education of teachers* (pp. 9–30). Chicago, IL: University of Chicago Press.

Doyle, W. (1986). Classroom organization and management. In M. C. Wittrock (Ed.), *Handbook of research on teaching* (3rd ed. pp. 392–425). New York: Macmillan.

Doyle, W. (1990). Case methods in the education of teachers. *Teacher Education Quarterly, 17*(1), 7–15.

Duckworth, E. (1987). *The having of wonderful ideas.* New York: Teachers College Press.

Evertson, C., Hawley, W., & Zlotnick, M. (1984). *The characteristics of effective teacher education programs: A review of research.* Nashville, TN: Vanderbilt University, Peabody College.

Feiman-Nemser, S. (1990). Teacher preparation: Structural and conceptual alternatives. In W. R. Houston (Ed.), *Handbook of research on teacher education* (pp. 212–233). New York: Longman.

Fisher, C. (1978). Being there vicariously by case studies. In O. Milton (Ed.), *On college teaching* (pp. 258–285). San Francisco, CA: Jossey-Bass.

Floden, R., & Clark, C. (1988). Preparing teachers for uncertainty. *Teachers College Record, 89,* 505–524.

Florio-Ruane, S., & Clark, C. (1990). Using case studies to enrich field experiences. *Teacher Education Quarterly, 17*(1), 17–29.

Fuller, F. F., & Bown, O. (1975). Becoming a teacher. In K. Ryan (Ed.), *Teacher education* (74th yearbook of the National Society for the Study of Education, pp. 25–52). Chicago, IL: University of Chicago Press.

Gage, N. L. (1978). *The scientific basis of the art of teaching.* New York: Teachers College Press.

Goldman, E., & Barron, L. (1990). Using hypermedia to improve the preparation of elementary teachers. *Journal of Teacher Education, 41*(3), 21–31.

Goldman, E., Barron, L., & Witherspoon, M. L. (1991). Hypermedia cases in teacher education: A context for understanding research on the teaching and learning of mathematics. *Action in Teacher Education, 13*(1), 28–36.

Goldman, E., Williams, H. L., Bassler, O. C., Sherwood, R. D., Barron, L. C., & Witherspoon, M. L. (1990). *Bridging the gap between theory and practice in the teaching of elementary school mathematics.* Paper presented at the 1990 Annual Meeting of the American Educational Research Association, Boston, MA. (ERIC Document Reproduction Service No. ED 325 365).

Gore, J. M., & Zeichner, K. M. (1991). Action research and reflective teaching in preservice teacher education: A case study from the United States. *Teaching & Teacher Education, 7*(2), 119–136.

Harrington, H., & Garrison, J. (1991). *Cases as shared inquiry.* Unpublished manuscript. University of Michigan. Ann Arbor, MI.

Howey, K., & Zimpher, N. (1986). New curriculum directions in the education of teachers. *Journal of Teacher Education, 30*(4), 93–102.

Howey, K., & Zimpher, N. (1989). *Profiles of preservice teacher education.* Albany, NY: SUNY Press.

Hunter, M. (1986). Comments on the Napa County, California, follow-through project. *Elementary School Journal, 87,* 173–180.

Iran-Nejad, A., McKeachie, W. J., & Berliner, D. C. (1990). The multi-source nature of learning: An introduction. *Review of Educational Research, 60,* 509–515.

Jackson, P. (1968). *Life in classrooms.* New York: Holt, Rinehart and Winston.

Kennedy, M. (1987). Inexact sciences: Professional education and the development of expertise. In E. Rothkopf (Ed.), *Review of Research in Education* (Vol. 14, pp. 133–167). Washington, DC: American Educational Research Association.

Kennedy, M. (1990). Choosing a goal for professional education. In W. R. Houston (Ed.), *Handbook of research on teacher education* (pp. 813–825). New York: Macmillan.

Kleinfeld, J. (1988). *Learning to think like a teacher: The study of cases.* Fairbanks, AK: Center for Cross-Cultural Studies, Rural College, University of Alaska Fairbanks.

Kleinfeld, J. (1989). *Teaching "taboo topics:" The special virtues of the case method.* Unpublished manuscript. Fairbanks, AK: University of Alaska Fairbanks.

Kleinfeld, J. (1990). The special virtues of the case method in preparing teachers for minority schools. *Teacher Education Quarterly, 17*(1), 43–52.

Kleinfeld, J. (1991). *Changes in problem solving abilities of students taught through case methods.* Paper presented at the 1991 Annual Meeting of the American Educational Research Association, Chicago, IL.

Kowalski, T. J., Weaver, R. A., & Henson, K. T. (1990). *Case studies in teaching.* New York: Longman.

Lakatos, I. (1979). *Proofs and refutations: The logic of mathematical discovery.* New York: Cambridge University Press.

Lampert, M., & Ball, D. L. (1990). *Using hypermedia technology to support a new pedagogy of teacher education.* (Issue Paper 90–5). East Lansing, MI: Michigan State University, National Center for Research on Teacher Education. (ERIC Document Reproduction Service No. ED 323 209).

Lampert, M. (1985). How do teachers manage to teach? Perspectives on problems in practice. *Harvard Educational Review, 55*(2), 178–194.

Lampert, M., & Clark, C. M. (1990). Expert knowledge and expert thinking in teaching: A response to Floden & Klinzing. *Educational Researcher, 19*(5), 21–23.

Lang, C. (1986). *Case method teaching in the community college.* Boston, MA: Education Development Center.

Lawrence, P. (1953). The preparation of case material. In K. Andrews (Ed.), *The case method of teaching human relations* (pp. 215–224). Cambridge, MA: Harvard University Press.

Light, R. J. (1990). *The Harvard Assessment Seminars: Explorations with students and faculty about teaching, learning, and student life: First report.* Cambridge, MA: Harvard University Graduate School of Education and Kennedy School of Government.

Liston, D., & Zeichner, K. (1988). Reflective teacher education and moral deliberation. *Journal of Teacher Education, 38*(6), 2–8.

Lortie, D. (1975). *Schoolteacher.* Chicago, IL: University of Chicago Press.

Lyons, N. (1989). Teaching by the case method: One teacher's beginnings. *On Teaching and Learning, 3,* 28–35.

Masoner, M. (1988). *An audit of the case study method.* New York: Praeger.

McCaleb, J., Borko, H., & Arends, R. (1992). Reflection, research and repertoire in the masters certification program at the University of Maryland (pp. 40–64). In L. Valli (Ed.), *Reflective teacher education: Cases and critiques.* Albany, NY: SUNY Press.

McNair, M. P. (Ed.), (1954). *The case method at the Harvard Business School.* New York: McGraw-Hill.

Megarry, J. (1981). Simulations, games and the professional education of teachers. *Journal of Education for Teaching, 7*(1), 25–39.

Merseth, K. (1990). Case studies and teacher education. *Teacher Education Quarterly, 17*(1), 53–62.

Merseth, K. (1991a). *The case for cases in teacher education.* Washington, DC: American Association of Colleges for Teacher Education and the American Association for Higher Education.

Merseth, K. (1991b). What the case method offers the teaching profession. *Harvard Education Letter, 7*(4), 6–7.

Merseth, K. (1991c). The early history of case-based instruction: Insights for teacher education today. *Journal of Teacher Education, 42*(4), 243–249.

Merseth, K. (1992). Cases for decision making in teacher education. In J. Shulman (Ed.), *Using case methods in teacher education.* New York: Teachers College Press.

Morine-Dershimer, G. (1991). *Case methods in teacher education: Where do they fit?* Invited address. Harrisonburg, WV: James Madison University.

Nix, D. (1990). Should computers know what you can do with them? In D. Nix & R. Spiro (Eds.), *Cognition, education, multimedia* (pp. 143–162). Hillside, NJ: Erlbaum.

Paley, V. G. (1979). *White teacher.* Cambridge, MA: Harvard University Press.

Richert, A. (1991a). Case methods and teacher education: Using cases to teach teacher reflection. In R. Tabachnick & K. Zeichner (Eds.), *Inquiry-oriented teacher education* (pp. 130–150). London: Falmer.

Richert, A. (1991b). *Considering case methods to enhance teacher learning.* A paper presented at the 1991 Annual Meeting of the American Educational Research Association, Chicago, IL.

Risko, V. J. (1992). Videodisc-based case methodology: A design for enhancing preservice teachers' problem-solving abilities. In B. Hayes & K. Camperell (Eds.), *Literacy: International, national, state, and local (Vol. 11),* pp. 121–36. Utah State University: American Reading Forum.

Risko, V. J., Yount, D., & Towell, J. (1992). Video-based CASE analysis to enhance teacher preparation. In N. Padak & T. Rasinski (Eds.), *Reading enhances knowledge* (pp. 87–103). Provo, UT: College Reading Association.

Sabers, D. S., Cushing, K. S., & Berliner, D. C. (1991). Differences among teachers in a task characterized by simultaneity, multidimensionality, and immediacy. *American Educational Research Journal, 28*(1), 89–116.

Schön, D. (1983). *The reflective practitioner: How professionals think in action.* New York: Basic Books.

Schön, D. (1987). *Educating the reflective practitioner.* San Francisco, CA: Jossey-Bass.

Shulman, J., & Colbert, J. (1988). *The intern teacher casebook.* Eugene, OR: ERIC Clearinghouse on Educational Management, Educational Research and Development; Washington, DC: ERIC Clearinghouse on Teacher Education.

Shulman, L. (1986). Those who understand: Knowledge growth in teaching. *Educational Researcher, 15*(2), 4–14.

Shulman, L. (1987). Knowledge and teaching: Foundations of the new reform. *Harvard Educational Review, 57,* 1–22.

Shulman, L. (Speaker). (1989). *A case for cases.* (Cassette recording). Oakland, CA: American Association of Higher Education.

Shulman, L. (1990). Reconnecting foundations to the substance of teacher education. *Teachers College Record, 91*(3), 300–310.

Shulman, L. (1992). Toward a pedagogy of cases. In J. Shulman (Ed.), *Using case methods in teacher education.* New York: Teachers College Press.

Silverman, R., Welty, W., & Lyon, S. (1992). *Case studies for teacher problem solving.* New York: McGraw Hill.

Spiro, R., & Jehng, J. (1990). Cognitive flexibility and hypertext: Theory and technology for the nonlinear and multidimensional traversal of complex subject matter. In D. Nix & R. Spiro (Eds.), *Cognition, education, multimedia* (pp. 163–205). Hillside, NJ: Erlbaum.

Stand and Deliver. (1987). Produced by Tom Musca. Directed by Ramon Menendez. Screenplay by Ramon Menendez and Tom Musca.

Strang, H. R., Badt, K. S., & Kauffman, J. M. (1987). Microcomputer-based simulations for training fundamental teaching skills. *Journal of Teacher Education, 28*(1), 20–26.

Strang, H. R., Landrum, M. S., & Lynch, K. A. (1989). Talking with the computer: A simulation for training basic teaching skills. *Teaching & Teacher Education, 5*(2), 143–153.

Strang, H. R., Landrum, M. S., & Ulmer, C. (1991). A self-administered simulation for training basic classroom skills. *Computers in the Schools, 8*(1/2/3), 229–243.

Strang, H. R., & Loper, A. B. (1983). Microcomputer-based simulation in training elementary teachers. *Educational Technology, 23*(10), 30–31.

Sykes, G. (1989). Learning to teach with cases. *Colloquy, 2*(2), 7–13.

Sykes, G., & Bird, T. (1991). *Teacher education and the case idea.* Draft (6/30/91) of unpublished manuscript. Michigan State University, Lansing.

Towl, A. (1969). *To study administration by cases.* Boston, MA: Harvard Business School.

Turney, C., Clift, J., Dunkin, M., & Traill, R. (1973). *Microteaching: Research, theory and practice.* Sydney Australia: Sydney University Press.

Wagner, A. (1984). Conflicts in consciousness: Imperative cognitions can lead to knots in thinking. In R. Halkes & J. Olson (Eds.), *Teacher thinking: A new perspective on persisting problems in education* (pp. 163–175). Lisse, The Netherlands: Swets & Zeitlinger.

Welty, W., Silverman, R., & Lyon, S. (1991). *Student outcomes from teaching with cases.* A paper presented at the 1991 Annual Meeting of the American Educational Research Association, Chicago, IL.

Wilson, S. (1989a). *A case concerning content: Using case studies to teach subject matter.* East Lansing, MI: National Center for Research on Teacher Education.

Wilson, S. (1989b). Parades of facts, stories of the past: What do novice history teachers need to know? In *Competing visions of teacher knowledge: Proceedings from an NCRTE seminar for education policymakers: February 24–26, 1989: Vol. 1.* Academic subjects (Conference Series 89-1, pp. 137–158). East Lansing, MI: Michigan State University, National Center for Research on Teacher Education.

Wilson, S., Shulman, L., & Richert, A. (1987). 150 different ways of knowing: Representations of knowledge in teaching. In J. Calderhead (Ed.), *Exploring teachers' thinking* (pp. 104–124). London: Cassell.

Zeichner, K. (1983). Alternative paradigms of teacher education. *Journal of Teacher Education, 34*(3), 3–9.

Zeichner, K. (1991). *Conceptions of reflective teaching in contemporary U.S. teacher education program reforms.* A paper presented at the 1991 Annual Meeting of the American Educational Research Association, Chicago, IL.

Zeichner, K., & Liston, D. (1987). Teaching student teachers to reflect. *Harvard Educational Review, 57,* 23–48.

Zeichner, K., & Liston, D. (1990). Traditions of reform in U.S. teacher education. *Journal of Teacher Education, 41*(2), 3–20.

Zimpher, N., & Howey, K. (1987). Adapting supervisory practice to different orientations of teaching competence. *Journal of Curriculum and Supervision, 2*(2), 101–127.

6

PREPARING CLINICAL FACULTY MEMBERS: RESEARCH ON TEACHERS' REASONING

VICTOR M. RENTEL

The Ohio State University

I have no riches but my thoughts . . . .
Sara Teasdale, *Love Songs*

An extensive and still growing body of scholarship describing the structure of pedagogical knowledge and pedagogical reasoning has evolved over the past 15 years. Numerous reviews of this literature have produced various constructs describing teachers' thought and decision processes (Borko & Shavelson, 1990; Clark, 1988; Clark & Peterson, 1986; Kagan, 1988, 1990; Peterson, 1988; Shavelson & Stern, 1981; Yinger, 1986), broad descriptions of teacher belief systems (Eisenhart, Shrum, Harding, & Cuthbert, 1988; Elbaz, 1983), and models of teacher cognition (Borko & Shavelson, 1990; Kagan, 1990; Shulman, 1987). Other reviews have examined teachers' reasoning from a philosophical standpoint (Fenstermacher, 1986; Green, 1971; Morine-Dershimer,

1987, 1988; Rentel, 1988; Rentel & Pinnell, 1987; Shulman, 1987), arguing that reasoning permeates teaching. The kind of reasoning involved is not formal conditional reasoning, but instead is what Gauthier (1963) and Jarvis (1964) defined as practical reasoning. Practical reasoning is based on abstract pragmatic rules of inference related to particular contexts, relationships, and inferential goals (Nisbett, Fong, Lehman, & Cheng, 1987; Rentel, 1988).

Informal reasoning is another way of characterizing practical reasoning (Paul, 1990; Voss, Perkins, & Segal 1991). Voss et al. (1991) defined informal reasoning as "modes of thinking not restricted to rules of logic and mathematics, but to include inferential processes such as argumentation" (p. xii). They contend that informal reasoning involves such skills as drawing inferences, justifying beliefs, and explaining observations. They argue further that informal reasoning is mainly inductive, or at least conducted in nondeductive contexts. It is the form of reasoning and argumentation that permeates everyday life (Johnson & Blair, 1985, 1991). Johnson and Blair (1991) suggest, however, that the term informal is misleading because "informal" may imply a degree of casualness where none exists. Further, "informal" often is given no more exacting definition than "not formal." Moreover, this kind of definition implies a status for formal reasoning that, is overstated, at least in consistency of use. In fact, several modern philosophers (Harman, 1986; MacIntyre, 1981; Rorty, 1979) reject the notion that only formal logic can provide the principles and rigor necessary for sound reasoning.

Johnson and Blair (1991) go on to argue as follows:

> It seems to us that the crucial feature that makes informal reasoning what it is is the way in which it is conducted: that is, in natural language and without recourse to formal procedures or other formal mechanisms. Informal reasoning is open ended rather than algorithmic. Better still, it is reasoning for which the ideal of an algorithm would be out of place, an intruder. (p. 134)

Informal reasoning and practical reasoning refer to very similar, if not identical, concepts. Because the phrase *practical reasoning* has been used in education for roughly 20 years (Fenstermacher, 1986; Green, 1971, 1976; Morine-Dershimer, 1987, 1988), the older and more familiar *practical reasoning* will be employed here. Practical reasoning will be taken to mean the kinds of everyday reasoning and argumentation that teachers employ in their preparation, planning, decisions, and reflections about teaching.

Toulmin, Rieke, and Janik (1984) argue that most, if not all, fields and disciplines have evolved their own characteristic forms of practical reasoning and argumentation. They claim that science, law, business, and the arts have created traditions and forums for practical reasoning suited to the goals and purposes of argumentation in each of these fields. In business, for example, arguments are shaped by the need to determine a course of action that limits risks, maximizes profits, and minimizes losses. Reasoning in law, on the other hand, is influenced by the need to establish which set of facts provides, in a court of law, the best grounds for a verdict of guilt or innocence.

Several bodies of literature exist in medicine. These include, for example, a literature describing the clinical reasoning of medical students and medical clinicians (Balla, 1980; Christensen & Elstein, 1991; Elstein, Shulman, & Sprafka, 1978), a literature dealing with differences between expert and novice medical clinicians (Feltovich, Johnson, Miller, & Swanson, 1984; Feltovich & Patel, 1984; Lesgold, 1984; Lesgold et al., 1988; Patel & Groen, 1986), and recently, comparisons of experts with computerized expert systems (Johnson, 1983; Leland, 1991) and with expert causal flow charts (Patel & Groen, 1986). Descriptive studies of medical experts and novices show that during initial development, medical clinicians' reasoning conforms to standard textbook interpretations. Eventually, however, their experiences demonstrate that these standard rules of interpretation can be wrong; thus, novice clinicians are led to search for more sophisticated ways of interpreting information. This search then forces them to focus on deeper principles and on a fuller understanding of the bases for these interpretive rules. When they combine these deeper understandings with contextual considerations, medical clinicians achieve a much fuller expertise (Clancey & Lestinger, 1981).

In international affairs, several scholars have studied the role of reasoning, judgment, and argumentation in foreign policy decisions (Allison, 1971; Axelrod, 1977; Holsti, 1976; Jervis, 1986; Simon, 1983). Voss (1991), in reviewing this literature, observed that decision making and the reasoning underlying it are informal; individuals rely on heuristics for information that they use in cognitive processing. They generate inferences that lead to conclusions influenced strongly by beliefs or supporting reasons. In turn, conclusions and beliefs may be influenced strongly by biases related to how issues are examined. Voss (1991) provides a particularly apt description of how this process occurs:

> The individual reasoning that takes place by a weighing of pros and cons has interesting limitations in accounts of decision making. Weighing the relative strength of pro and con arguments may appear in the course of an argument, but each of the respective pro and con arguments has a weighing that is based on individual beliefs as they relate to the particular situation—beliefs that may vary considerably from person to person. Thus, beliefs play a role in the weighing process. Furthermore, the Axelrod data point to the possibility that persuasion, as typical in a debate model, may not be the form in which it most often occurs; instead, the process likely involves individuals stressing points and stating positions, with the comparing and contrasting of differing positions essentially leading to a new, quite possibly acceptable, solution, a more or less dialectical process. (p. 51)

A similar dialectical process seems to undergird patterns of reasoning typical of teaching. Research on teachers' practical knowledge (Elbaz, 1983) and their principles of practice (Conners, 1978; Marland, 1977) suggests that teachers develop rules and principles of practice based on well-developed arguments and reasons. Marland (1977), for example, described five principles that seem to guide and explain teachers' actions: (a) compensation, (b) power sharing, (c) strategic leniency, (d) progressive checking, and (e) suppressing emotions. Teachers gave reasons explaining how each principle is related to a desired pedagogical outcome. Each requires a judgment contingent on some form of practical argument. Conners (1978) replicated Marland's study, obtaining results that extended these principles and added new ones.

Elbaz (1983) described teachers' practical knowledge as rules of practice, practice principles, and images dealing with curriculum, subject matter, instruction, milieu, and self. According to Elbaz, rules of practice are short explicit statements describing how a teacher might act in typical teaching situations. They are drawn from experience, and they guide and rationalize actions. Often they are accompanied by images of how teaching should look and feel. Most important, they are based on pragmatic arguments grounded in experience.

These researchers, as well as others (Bussis, Chittenden, & Amarel, 1976; Duffy, 1977; Janesick, 1977; Munby, 1983), argue that teachers construct highly individualistic theories and beliefs grounded in a variety of complex interpretations, explanations, and reasoning about practice. Teachers' decisions and actions are grounded in theory (Duffy, 1977; Janesick, 1977; Munby, 1983), and the relationships between their theories and their classroom actions are extraordinarily complex (Argyris, 1980; Bussis, Chittenden, & Amarel, 1976; Duffy, 1977; Nias, 1987; Sanders & McCutcheon, 1986). For example, teachers who have identical belief systems often differ considerably from one another in their principles and actions. Together these studies argue that teachers construct highly individualistic theories, beliefs, and patterns of action arising from practical reasoning.

Much of teachers' practical reasoning occurs before teaching, during preparation (Borko & Livingston, 1989) and planning (Borko & Niles, 1987; McCutcheon, 1980; Yinger, 1980), but teachers also engage in considerable analysis and evaluation of their teaching during (Clark & Peterson, 1986; Conners, 1978; Leinhart & Greeno, 1986; MacKay, 1977; Marland, 1977; McCutcheon, 1980; Yinger, 1980) and after teaching (Borko & Livingston, 1989). It is probably more accurate to claim that experienced teachers prepare rather than plan (Borko & Livingston, 1989; Yinger, 1986). They prepare broad scripts or very general outlines of what they will teach, which they fill in, tune, and tailor to students' needs and performances. During interactive teaching, they improvise according to experience, knowledge of situations and role, routines, and patterns of action that play out in a continuously responsive interaction with students and circumstances. These improvisational capabilities are relatively undeveloped in novice teachers (Feiman-Nemser & Buchmann, 1986). Yinger (1979, 1986) contends that preparing general lesson guidelines is a more effective strategy for experienced teachers because classroom circumstances are often unpredictable. Well-structured lesson plans imply a degree of control and predictability that may not exist in classrooms (Borko & Livingston, 1989).

Teaching thus appears to entail complex thinking about students, events, content, and outcomes. Such thinking includes reasoning about the transformation of content into pedagogically powerful representations of knowledge tailored to students' variable needs and abilities (Borko & Livingston, 1989; Shulman, 1987). It is conducted by experienced teachers at highly abstract levels of image and thought, and is keyed to routines, situations, and cues from students.

HOW DOES PEDAGOGICAL REASONING WORK?

Classrooms are complex and dynamic environments where much on-the-spot thinking and reasoning occur during teaching. Teachers make hundreds of decisions during interactive teaching over the course of a day (Clark, 1988; Clark & Peterson, 1986; Marland, 1977; Wagner, 1984) which lead to rapid adjustments in teaching (Doyle, 1977, 1979; Peterson & Clark, 1978; Peterson, Marx, & Clark, 1978) and sometimes to significant departures from prepared plans (Clark, 1988; Clark & Lampert, 1986; Doyle, 1979). Teachers' reasoning and the actions that follow are influenced by theories and beliefs (Bussis et al., 1976; Duffy, 1977; Elbaz, 1983; Kuhs, 1980), by problem sensing and avoidance (Mitchell & Marland, 1989), and by assessments of pupils' dispositions (Yinger & Villar, 1986).

Because teachers must act spontaneously in these dynamic situations without explicit rules of practice, their thoughts and actions are based on complex knowledge structures (Berliner & Carter, 1986; Borko & Shavelson, 1990; Calderhead, 1981; Leinhardt & Greeno, 1986; Wagner, 1984). When given opportunities to examine pedagogical issues or problems, they provide detailed and often highly explicit reasons for their actions, which they predicate on (a) complex practical arguments that evolve into highly reasoned principles of action, (b) simple principles that are based on such arguments, and (c) broad professional norms, not well understood or well described (Morine-Dershimer, 1987, 1988; Rentel, 1991; Rentel & Pinnell, 1989).

Teachers, like physicians and diplomats, cannot function in these fluid and complex settings without constraints on their judgments and decisions. Borko and Shavelson (1990) assume that these constraints operate as follows:

> Given the limited information processing capabilities of the human mind, teachers, like all persons attempting to solve complex problems, construct simplified models of the actual situation and then behave rationally with respect to these simplified models. This view of teachers as operating rationally within the limits of their information processing capabilities leads to the assumption that they make reasonable (rather than rational) judgments and decisions. (p. 312)

Although teachers' decisions may be reasonable, their decisions are not unbiased. In general, several kinds of bias can affect reasoning and decision making: the omission of significant information or evidence (Kahneman, Slovic, & Tversky, 1982; Tversky & Kahneman, 1982), assuming too much, and taking a particular stance or adopting a particular framework for analyzing evidence and information (Christensen-Szalanski, 1986; Hogarth, 1980). In teaching, biases take several forms. Information about students, particularly teachers' perceptions of students' ability, strongly influences teachers' reasoning (Mintz, 1979; Shavelson & Stern, 1981). Biases about students' ability affect reasoning—particularly the reasoning that undergirds planning, the reasoning that leads to the tailoring of instruction (Shavelson & Stern, 1981), and the reasoning that relates to grouping students for instruction (Borko & Niles, 1983). Textbooks and teachers' manuals also bias planning in that teachers rely heavily on these items for content included in the curriculum (McCutcheon, 1980; Smith & Sendelbach, 1979). Institutional constraints on teachers' decision making also affect how teachers plan by altering their expectations (Borko, Eisenhart, Kello, & Vandett, 1984; McCutcheon, 1980). In fact, school board and school administration policies frequently cause teachers to alter decisions about content selection and about student discipline (Borko et al., 1984; Floden, Porter, Schmidt, Freeman, & Schwille, 1981). Although it is commonly expected that teachers' beliefs and curricular philosophies have a pronounced effect on curriculum and instruction, evidence suggests that these effects exert little direct influence on reasoning about teaching (Borko & Niles, 1982; Russo, 1978); rather, ideology may have a strong effect on teaching style (Zahorik, 1990) and on the acceptance by teachers of instructional innovations (Rich, 1990).

Planning is perhaps the most extensively studied of the contexts in which teachers reason. Teachers engage in two very distinct kinds of planning: that which occurs in deliberately formal planning periods removed from teaching, wherein teachers often write out their plans, and that which occurs spontaneously throughout the workday. Deliberate formal planning is devoted mainly to selecting curricular content and learning activities suitable for students (Borko, Livingston, McCaleb, & Mauro, 1988; McCutcheon, 1980: Yinger, 1980). How teachers think about content and learning activities varies according to the type of planning being done and upon the teacher's level of experience and expertise.

Formal written plans seem to be a subset of more comprehensive images of teaching. Apparently the purpose of images is to project a general approximation of how teaching looks and feels. Images include an array of visual and affective tones related to concrete aspects of teaching, such as activity sequences, analysis of student interactions with content, and anticipation of factors likely to impinge on instruction (Rentel & Pinnell, 1989; Smith & Sendelbach, 1979).

The bulk of teachers' planning occurs spontaneously during teaching (McCutcheon, 1980). Evidence suggests that teachers construct images of good teaching that include goals and objectives (Calderhead & Robson, 1991; Morine-Dershimer, 1979). These images appear to be abstract cognitions about the appropriateness and feasibility of action premises; also one may argue that they are metacognitions or a form of meta-awareness (Calderhead, 1981, 1989), which help to give shape and form to intangible aspects of teaching. Images also may relate aspects of teaching to affective predispositions, and may give expression to premises in practical action contexts (Calderhead, 1989; Morine-Dershimer, 1979). Images frequently are visual, but they are also reported to include affective components (Calderhead & Robson, 1991). Calderhead and Robson (1991) argue that:

> one might expect teachers in various problem-solving aspects of their work—in planning, in coping with children's difficulties, in responding to classroom incidents—to draw upon images of lessons, incidents or children to help them interpret and solve teaching problems. In fact, being able to recall images, and to adapt and manipulate these images in reflecting about actions in a particular context is possibly an important aspect of the task of teaching. (p. 3)

The concept of image appears often in the literature but remains a rather ill-defined notion both in psychology (Johnson-Laird, 1987) and in teaching (Calderhead & Robson, 1991). Still, it is a useful construct in that it aptly describes one kind of thought process equally typical of student teachers (Calderhead & Robson, 1991) and of seasoned teachers (Carter, Sabers, Cushing, Pinnegar, & Berliner, 1987; Clandinin, 1986). Just how images affect reasoning is a matter of conjecture. Research in other fields has shown that images can be a means for improving performance by functioning as a cognitive model that guides and fine-tunes performance (Cratty, 1984). In teaching, departures from visual and affective images may trigger analytic processes for identifying problems, sorting out cues, or establishing the grounds for altering routines and plans—in view of the fairly elaborate justifications that experienced teachers construct for their decisions.

Metaphors may function in the same way as images; that is, they may help teachers clarify the importance and attributes of complex experiences that are understood only poorly (Bowers, 1980; Ricoeur, 1977). For example, teachers' descriptions of their experiences include numerous metaphors of space and movement (Munby, 1986). Metaphors in this sense may help teachers capture the elusive but critical dimensions of pacing, which is necessary for students' success but difficult to establish. Image, metaphor, theory, and practice blend into a complicated dialectic that guides the direction of inquiry and evaluation of teaching (Munby, 1982, 1986; Russell, 1988; Russell, Munby, Spafford, & Johnston, 1988), and establishes the grist for analysis, prediction, quick deliberation, and improvisation in teaching (Borko & Livingston, 1989; Yinger & Villar, 1986).

Teachers also engage in reasoning during interactive teaching. Shavelson and Stern (1981) have attempted to depict teacher reasoning in these action contexts as a form of decision making. Teaching proceeds according to a plan until a classroom event destabilizes the process. Teachers then must decide whether to ignore the problem and proceed according to plan or to alter the course of instruction. If the decision is to change the course of teaching, teachers either select a dependable routine or strategy or quickly concoct a new course of action.

Serious questions have arisen about the extent to which decision-making models approximate teachers' thinking (Clark & Peterson, 1986; Mitchell & Marland, 1989; Yinger & Villar, 1986). Mitchell and Marland (1989), for example, argue that decision making provides a poor account of the many kinds of thinking that occur during interactive teaching. Their findings indicate that teachers' thinking can be represented in many ways, such as: (a) *problem avoidance*, the thinking underlying actions taken by teachers to avoid problems; (b) *teacher reactions*, the thinking underlying how best to respond in particular circumstances to individual students' needs; (c) *opportunity seeking*, the thinking underlying the distribution of opportunities for pupils to interact with the teacher; and (d) *mood assessment*, the thinking underlying the assessment of the tone of a class and the adoption of tactics designed to focus students' attention on given learning tasks. Mitchell and Marland (1989) contend that teachers' thought processes are described more aptly as *schemata* encompassing "teachers' intimate knowledge of the social and academic dimensions of classroom life and their pedagogical wisdom" (p. 127).

Typically, only a handful of actions—in fact, seldom more than two or three—are considered at specific decision or response points during interactive teaching (MacKay, 1977; Morine-Dershimer & Vallance, 1976; Peterson & Clark, 1978). In part, options are limited by the kinds of events and circumstances that provoke decisions. Students' disruptions, inattentiveness, errors, misconceptions, incomplete responses, and unsatisfactory responses gain the teacher's attention and often force the teacher to reconsider and alter initial plans (Fogerty, Wang, & Creek, 1982; Housner & Griffey, 1985; Marland, 1977; Mitchell & Marland, 1989; Warner, 1987). In these circumstances, teachers rely most often on experience-tested routines or strategies to return the situation to normal, or they rely on students' questions, misconceptions, and learning needs to suggest an appropriate course of action (Marland, 1977; Mitchell & Marland, 1989; Warner, 1987; Yinger & Villar, 1986).

Expert teachers appear to excel in this kind of impromptu thinking (Borko & Livingston, 1989; Sato, Akita, & Iwakawa, 1990); in contrast, novices spend considerable time planning or preparing to teach. Novices, however, spend their time learning or reviewing the content they plan to teach (Sato et al., 1990), whereas expert teachers reason through content to determine how best to represent it to students (Borko & Livingston, 1989; Morine-Dershimer, 1991; Rentel & Pinnell, 1989; Sato et al., 1990). Expert teachers "are rich with interpretations of classroom life" (Sabers, Cushing, & Berliner, 1991, p. 84). They are able to consider students, review subject matter, map out content, assign priorities, and establish pedagogical schemata and interactions in their planning processes; thus, they are able to comprehend events and improvise in the actual setting (Carter, Cushing, Sabers, Stein, & Berliner, 1988; Carter et al., 1987; Sabers et al., 1991; Sato et al., 1990; Strahan, 1989). Novices, conversely, have fewer schemata tied to particular contexts and pupils. Similarly, Sato and colleagues (1990), who compared expert and novice teachers in Japan, found that expert teachers can monitor their teaching from several standpoints—their own and their students'—whereas novices can view only their teaching or a student's learning, but not both. Expert teachers seem able to frame a problem, "constructing and reconstructing their thoughts in conformity with the teaching process and context" (Sato et al., 1990, p. 12).

One other important distinction between experienced and inexperienced teachers is the finding that novice teachers' approaches to problem solving are simple, sparing, and specific, with little development of rationale or argument, whereas experienced teachers' solutions to problems are abstract and are based on very full arguments (Voss, Tyler, & Yengo, 1983). Experienced teachers, more often than inexperienced teachers, give elaborate justifications for their actions, decisions, and analyses, and discuss problems within the framework of principles, procedures, and abstract imperatives (Peterson & Comeauex, 1987). Although experienced teachers are no more aware of specific features of classroom events than inexperienced teachers, they make a great deal more of those features and they carefully and extensively justify their actions and reactions (Chi, Feltovich, & Glaser, 1981; Peterson & Comeauex, 1987).

Another kind of reasoning by teachers serves to buttress their minute-by-minute decisions during interactive teaching. These decisions most often are made in the context of actions with or responses to students (Clark & Peterson, 1986). The reasoning performed by teachers in these circumstances requires them to weigh grounds and evidence for the selection of alternative courses of action (Marland, 1977; Warner, 1987). Among experienced teachers, the selection of alternatives takes place in a context of tested and reliable routines (Leinhardt & Greeno, 1986; Warner, 1987). Routines reduce the amount of information that teachers must consider and thereby reduce the complexity of teaching (Shavelson & Stern, 1981). Routines also free teachers to focus their attention on potential problems or on misconceptions on the part of students (Conners, 1978; MacKay, 1977; Marland, 1977; Warner, 1987) and on specific instructional processes (Conners, 1978; Marland, 1977; Peterson & Clark, 1978; Warner, 1987).

As noted briefly in the previous section, teachers also appear to act on the basis of practical theories (Sanders & McCutcheon, 1986) or action theories (Argyris, 1980; Marland & Osborne, 1990; Nias, 1987)—partly conscious explanations and models of teaching, intermixed with values and norms about the purposes of education, ethical considerations, students' learning, and particular contexts for teaching (Marland & Osborne, 1990). It is not clear how action theories influence teaching. Possibly by assigning priorities or preferential weights to particular routines, responses, or actions designed to meet students' needs, action theories reduce the number of alternatives that teachers must consider in reaching split-second conclusions. Interestingly but not unexpectedly, Marland and Osborne (1990) report that teachers' theories of action include expectations that dilemmas will arise in teaching, wherein teachers must choose among competing and sometimes conflicting values, beliefs, and practices. They contend that teachers' theories of action may serve as frameworks within which lessons are planned and conducted, but that they probably play a minor role, if any, in teachers' interpretations of particular classroom incidents. Action theories are deeply contextualized; they are linked to a given teacher's classroom and may be unique to each teacher.

Teachers also reflect on the process of teaching, both during interactive teaching and after class. They weigh their explanations and questions. They assess the effectiveness of practice materials and of their homework assignments, as well as the sequencing and pacing of activities and the transitions between them (Conners, 1978; Marland, 1977; Marx & Peterson, 1981; McNair, 1978–1979). Rentel and Pinnell (1989), in their content analyses of experienced teachers' after-teaching critiques, found that about 10 percent of teachers' analyses and justifications were devoted to global reflections about students' performance and classroom interactions with the teacher, and that about 46 percent focused on specific evaluations of pupils' or teachers' performances. Post lesson reflections seem to focus heavily on the success of lessons and on students' performances (Borko & Livingston, 1989; Rentel & Pinnell, 1989).

Other research shows that teachers engage in a cycle of conception and problem identification, design and elaboration, and reflection and assessment (Yinger, 1980) in which they imagine, plan, evaluate, revise, and refine their knowledge and routines. Their immediate reflections are spontaneous; frequently refer back to earlier planning; often are the basis for redirecting or steering activities and students' comments toward the goals and purposes of the lesson, and may serve as a framework within which theoretical knowledge about teaching is applied to given instructional instances and cases (Borko & Livingston, 1989; Leinhardt & Greeno, 1986; McCutcheon, 1980).

The reflections of student teachers, however, are superficial (Calderhead, 1989) and remain so despite courses and curricula intended to develop reflective thinking (Borko, Livingston, McCaleb, & Mauro, 1988; Calderhead, 1989; Feiman-Nemser & Buchmann, 1987). Calderhead (1989) attributes student teachers' reluctance to evaluate their own practice to the pressing demands of teaching. The complexities of teaching leave little capacity for evaluation and reflection, particularly in the absence of confidence and without a sufficient repertoire of routines, alternatives, and analytical skills. Russell (1988), who compared student teachers' reflections with those of experienced teachers, speculated that student teachers may not be able to reflect on their practice until after they have learned a set of routines and have achieved a level of skill in which they have a modicum of confidence. Calderhead (1989) described these difficulties succinctly:

> To be able to answer such questions as "How well did I teach?", "What were the effects of my teaching?", "What assumptions have I made in teaching this way?", "How else might I have taught the lesson?", "How will I do it next time?" require the student teacher to draw upon knowledge of alternative teaching approaches, of children's typical performance and achievement, and of criteria for judging teaching. Students may well lack the knowledge that enables the necessary comparisons and evaluations to be made. (p. 48)

Experienced teachers, however, address these questions broadly and pointedly in their self-assessments. They are the grist for much of the reasoning done by teachers both during interactive teaching and during the quiet reflection of taking stock.

HOW DO TEACHERS LEARN PEDAGOGICAL REASONING?

Evidence (Holland, Holyoak, Nisbett, & Thagard, 1987; Nisbett, et al., 1987) suggests that practical reasoning is learned through certain kinds of experiences and that it also can be taught indirectly. Nisbett et al. (1987) define practical reasoning as follows:

> Instead, the types of inferential rules that people use naturally and can be taught most easily are a family of pragmatic inferential rule systems that people induce in the context of solving recurrent everyday problems. These rule systems are abstract inasmuch as they can be used in a wide variety of content domains, but their use is confined to certain types of problem goals and particular types of relations between events. (p. 625)

Nisbett and his colleagues studied the effects of training on the use of inferential rules in statistics, in causal schemata, and in "contractual rules" underlying permission and obligation in social settings. In one such experiment, Cheng and Holyoak (1985) trained subjects to solve straightforward conditional problems, first without benefit of context and then with context. Subjects were trained to solve simple conditional problems of the form, "If p, then q"; then they were given problems to solve. For example, in a case about the deplaning of airline passengers, subjects were to indicate whether the conditional was violated in various instances of the following type: "If the form says 'entering' on one side, then the other side includes cholera among the list of diseases." Many subjects were unable to solve the problem correctly. When they were provided with a "permission" rationale—that is, when they were told that the form included diseases for which passengers had been inoculated—almost all subjects solved the problem. Similar effects were obtained in studies in which subjects generalized "the law of large numbers" (Fong, Krantz, & Nisbett, 1986; Jepson, Krantz, & Nisbett, 1985; Nisbett, Krantz, Jepson, & Kunda, 1983). Nisbett et al. (1987) interpreted these results to mean that although logical training by itself may not be generalizable, pragmatic rules that can be related to pre-existing knowledge structures do generalize.

This conclusion is further supported by results obtained in a study of the effects of undergraduate courses in formal logic on students' ability to solve problems involving conditional or biconditional reasoning (Cheng, Holyoak, Nisbett, & Oliver, 1986). No significant differences were observed between pre- and posttests in students' ability to solve conditional and biconditional problems. On the other hand, Nisbett et al. (1987) reported the results of a pair of unpublished studies, one cross-sectional and the other longitudinal, on the effects of graduate education in psychology, medicine, law, and chemistry on statistical reasoning, methodological reasoning, and conditional and biconditional reasoning. Assuming that psychology and medicine, both probabilistic sciences, would improve the ability to apply statistical and methodological rules, and assuming that both of these sciences deal with varied causal patterns involving both necessity and sufficiency, the authors expected differences favoring psychology and medicine over chemistry (where necessary and deterministic causes are emphasized), and over law (where probability is not stressed). Because law deals with contracts, they expected no differences between law, psychology, and medical students in the use of conditional and biconditional reasoning.

Initial differences in populations were insignificant, but after two years of training, effects favoring psychology and medicine were large and statistically significant for probabilistic and methodological reasoning. The expected results were obtained for conditional and biconditional reasoning. Psychology, law, and medical students improved significantly for statistical, methodological, or conditional reasoning; chemistry students did not do so. This study, conducted at the University of Michigan, was replicated at the University of California at Los Angeles for chemistry and psychology students; the results were similar. Nisbett et al. (1987) concluded:

> Our work suggests that the formal discipline rule may well be correct in essence, but that it has misidentified the knowledge structures that underlie reasoning about everyday life events. There are abstract rules and these can be trained abstractly. The rules may not be those of formal logic, however, but instead may be pragmatic inferential rules having to do with particular types of relationships and inferential goals. These structures are more specific than logical rules, but they are abstract in that they are not bound to any content domain. (p. 629)

Nisbett et al. (1987) call this kind of reasoning *pragmatic reasoning*, as contrasted with formal reasoning. The concept of pragmatic reasoning is similar, if not identical, to *practical reasoning*, a concept that originated with Aristotle but whose modern meanings have been analyzed and extended by Jarvis (1964), Toulmin et al. (1984), Green (1971, 1976), and Fenstermacher (1986). Green (1971, 1976) has long held that teaching is based on a particular form of practical reasoning. One of the major tasks of teacher education, he contends, is to prepare teachers to frame practical arguments undergirding their actions. By assisting teachers to formulate the practical arguments supporting instructional practices, and by helping them to amass evidence that bears on relevant premises, such education provides the teacher with a basis for becoming aware of his or her own practices and for judging the possible outcomes of a particular action.

Shulman (1987) suggested that teachers engage in reasoning about broad general teaching concepts and about the specific content they may be teaching. This kind of practical reasoning underlies the formulation of arguments supporting instructional practice, the accumulation of evidence that bears upon relevant instructional premises, and the basis for judging outcomes and consequences that follow acts of teaching. Shulman (1987) defined this kind of reasoning as *pedagogical reasoning*.

We have modest evidence that pedagogical reasoning can be taught and improved with coaching and practice (Rentel & Pinnell, 1987). Other research has attempted to describe the specific content of teachers' practical arguments and how these contents are altered or evolve as reasoning improves (Rentel & Pinnell, 1989). This work focused on the teaching of 12 experienced reading teachers who participated in a year-long training program to prepare them to be reading recovery teachers (teachers who provide intensive, one-on-one daily tutoring for young children who have difficulty in learning to read). For the entire training year, these teachers taught children daily in 30-minute lessons. They also met in weekly seminar sessions during which they observed each other teaching and then critiqued these observations in subsequent discussions. Each teacher was engaged in a cycle of tutoring a child while being observed by the other 11 members of the group, observing others in the group as they taught, and critically analyzing each teaching session for an hour under the guidance of a teacher leader, who raised questions about premises, grounds, backing, and warrants for arguments advanced during each critique.

This process forced participants to make their ideas explicit by expressing them verbally so that claims could be examined and refined—that is, subjected to the reasoning process. When claims were made, the leader asked participants for evidence to support or counter these statements. Participants selected the specific instances of behavior from their observations, or selected evidence and theory from their reflections, that supported their claims. A discussion leader requested and sometimes provided or pointed out evidence, or gave feedback as to whether the evidence selected by participants was relevant to their claims. The in-service course required participants to justify their decisions by relating general background theory to specific claims about individual children, or to support claims by grounding them in other evidence such as research or previous class presentations on theoretical material. In providing this backing, group members were required to move from specific instances of behavior in the cases they were examining toward more general theoretical statements about their work.

Group members were instructed to withhold judgment, to restrict conclusions to the observed evidence, and to avoid judgments and conclusions based on unsupported assumptions. The leader sometimes said, "We can't be sure," or "Let's look for more evidence." When conflicts arose, participants were expected to obtain more evidence or to argue from research and theory. They negotiated, argued, and discussed, reaching conclusions that were the result of complex problem-solving and reasoning processes. Tutoring and critique sessions were audiotaped, and the tapes were transcribed. Transcriptions were segmented into *turns*—utterances by a single speaker bounded by the utterances of other speakers. Each speaker occupied a turn slot. Two trained judges classified the statements in each turn as a claim, as grounds for a claim, and/or as backing for a claim (.94). The arguments then were segmented into propositions (Anderson, 1976; Calderhead, 1981). Propositions were assigned to one of Shulman's categories of pedagogical content knowledge or to one of six additional categories derived from arguments advanced in the critiques. The first and the last of 30 staff development sessions were compared as to frequencies of propositions.

During the initial session, propositions dealing with representation, pupil evaluation, problem representation, text representation, and theory were observed. Significant final-session decreases were observed in the number of propositions dealing with comprehension, preparation, selection, teacher evaluation, and reflection. No differences were found between the initial and the final sessions in the number of propositions classified as adaptation, problem solving, problem identification, and professional norms.

The arguments during the initial session dealt with selecting texts at appropriate grade levels, determining pupils' levels of motivation and ability, and adapting pedagogical style to pupils' psychological states. The initial discussion focused on the instructional alternatives available to the teacher, particularly the selection and use of texts. During the initial session, participants spent little time attempting to achieve an adequate representation of a problem; instead they appeared to have a problem identification schema in which "readability level of text" was one of a few high-probability alternative explanations to account for pupils' reading difficulties. In the first session, they identified almost all problems as text selection problems—texts that were too difficult for the child. Arguments about the nature of problems were resolved quickly and directly by characterizing them as "the readability of the text is too difficult" or "the pupil's lack of strategies."

During the final session, arguments about appropriate text selection almost disappeared. Problems now were identified only after considerable analysis of how the problem might be described and represented. Nearly half of the arguments during the final session set forth claims about pupils' learning strategies, pupils' misconceptions, and pupils' adaptive responses to specific structures, functions, and relationships in the text. The significant increase in *pupil evaluations* in the final session was a function of increased discourse about the interaction between pupils and specific portions of text that they were reading. References to or analyses of pupil–text interactions were employed as grounds for pedagogical claims centering on how content should be represented rather than on selecting texts at designated reading levels. During this session, arguments shifted from analyzing pupils' psychological states to analyzing how pupils represent the linguistic structure of texts. In turn, arguments about pedagogy dealt with how best to represent these structures to pupils.

These results fit rather well with other descriptions of teachers' thinking (Marland & Osborne, 1990; Mitchell & Marland, 1989; Peterson & Comeauex, 1987; Shavelson & Stern, 1981). Teachers appear to have stereotypic models of problems, linked to evasive steps designed to avoid or remedy problems. These models or schemata include information about context, features of the problem that trigger the identification of the problem, and a repertoire of responses to problems (Clark, 1988; Floden & Klinzing, 1990; Lampert & Clark, 1990; Sato et al., 1990). Teachers appear to have identifiable frames, models, or schemata through which they process and interpret the fast-paced action of classroom life (Borko & Shavelson, 1990; Doyle, 1977; Mitchell & Marland, 1989). Even in circumstances allowing ample time for reflection and planning, these experience-shaped schemata play a significant role in teachers' thinking. Training designed to increase the likelihood of teachers engaging in reasoned analysis of instructional premises appears to broaden and deepen these schemata and to produce fuller and more carefully grounded arguments about problems and pedagogical solutions to those problems.

As in Morine-Dershimer's (1988) findings, the most prevalent premises set forth by these teachers focused on the assessment of pupils' comprehension and learning, either directly from a prior lesson or from the retention of prior learning. In their practical arguments in the final session, teachers examined means–end relationships associated with their reading recovery training. A balance existed between premises about pupils' comprehension and pupils' engagement in instructional activities. Similarly, as with Morine-Dershimer's subjects, these teachers made claims about subject matter in roughly the same proportion as claims about involving pupils in learning.

It also appears that the resources around which teachers plan, the subject matter they teach, their knowledge of subject matter

(Hashweh, 1987; Stein, Baxter, & Leinhardt, 1990), and the social and theoretical dimensions of their pedagogical knowledge influence their interpretations and representations of subject matter (Mitchell & Marland, 1989; Rentel, 1988), though far less than cues in the teaching situation itself (Yinger & Villar, 1986).

Finally, a form of meta-argument—claims about pedagogical reasoning—emerged in the last training session. Claims categorized initially as reflection focused on self-adequacy and efficacy; in the final session, however, *reflection* dealt with the adequacy of pedagogical strategies, the reasoning supporting those strategies, and the quality of pedagogical arguments advanced by members of the group.

These data suggested that practical reasoning can be taught and learned, although not necessarily through direct didactic methods. Given the opportunity to relate pragmatic rules to preexisting knowledge structures through argument and discussion surrounding everyday problem solving, teachers improved their ability to reason soundly and thereby improved their teaching. As stated above, sound reasoning requires an adequate foundation of facts, principles, practical intuitions, rather complex theories, and action schemata. Constructing sound rationales for teaching—the ability to explain actions on the basis of warranted belief, sound evidence, and adequate backing (Fenstermacher, 1986; Green, 1971, 1976)—leads to the improvement in pupils' reading levels typically associated with reading recovery programs (Pinnell, Fried, & Estice, 1990).

Not all teachers succeed to the same extent. It remains unclear how the pedagogical reasoning of less successful teachers differs from that of successful teachers. A rapidly developing body of evidence argues that teachers' cognitions are deeply contextualized (Brown, Collins, & Duguid, 1989; Dreyfus & Dreyfus, 1986; Greeno, 1989; Perkins, 1989; Suchman, 1987) and that situations contribute strongly to expertise (Lampert, 1988; Lampert & Clark, 1990). What successful teachers learn from their immediate context and from their experiences with students seems likely to be the next frontier for research on teachers' cognition and reasoning (Borko & Livingston, 1989). Glaser (1984) points out that hundreds and even thousands of hours of learning and experiences are necessary for the development of expertise.

Experience contributes to expertise in at least two important ways (Kolodner, 1983). First, memories are formed incrementally. As isolated bits of information are integrated through repeated occurrences in the same context, they are related as knowledge structures. Second, practical arguments are refined and gradually come to function as a guide to reasoning processes. Teachers are able to test their premises as they repeat and extend their plans and deepen their preparation. Repeated opportunities to teach the same content provide teachers with a framework for refining their premises and for obtaining further evidence to warrant or disconfirm all or parts of their developing schemata for specific instructional contexts and circumstances (Borko & Livingston, 1989; Rentel, 1991). Over time, stock routines and principles of practice gradually emerge, built on a foundation of knowledge and reasons.

Another critical aspect of learning in general, but particularly of learning to teach, is the acquisition of an understanding of conditions under which knowledge is applicable (Anderson, 1976; Bransford, Vye, Kinzer, & Risko, 1990; Larkin, 1983; Simon, 1983). Bransford et al. (1990) suggest three ways in which access to conditionalized knowledge can be strengthened. First, understanding the conditions under which knowledge is useful enhances access to that knowledge (Adams et al., 1988; Lockhart, Lamon, & Gick, 1988). Problem-oriented learning seems to operate in this way. Solutions demonstrate graphically the utility and the value of particular knowledge (Alexander & Judy, 1988; Bransford et al., 1990; Hashweh, 1987; Stein et al., 1990). Second, the ability to define and represent problems as well as evaluate possible strategies for solving them appears to distinguish expert from novice teachers; among expert teachers, what seems most useful in solving problems is information that contributes to definition of problems and formation of hypotheses (Swanson, O'Connor, & Cooney, 1990). Third, viewing a problem from multiple perspectives facilitates access to conditioned knowledge as long as context remains stable; when context varies, however, access is weakened unless it is anchored in themes that promote sustained thinking about a problem Bransford et al., 1990; Cognition and Technology Group at Vanderbilt, 1990).

KNOWLEDGE OF SUBJECT MATTER, PLANNING, AND TEACHING

Just as an adequate knowledge base is important to problem solving, an adequate base of subject-matter knowledge is important to learning how to reason about teaching. Lack of such a base leads not only to presentation of misconceptions and erroneous information to students, but also to improper and overnarrow conceptions of how to teach (Hashweh, 1987; Stein et al., 1990). Stein et al. (1990) reported that teachers possessing only limited knowledge of subject matter often oversimplified concepts. They also ignored opportunities to provide information that was crucial to later learning or critical to helping students build relationships among concepts (Chi, Hutchinson, & Robin, 1989; Perkins & Simmons, 1988). It is also clear that teachers can evaluate children's thinking and problem solving effectively only if they possess a full understanding of the content that the children are attempting to learn (Carpenter, Fennema, Peterson, Chiang, & Loef, 1989). Their knowledge of subject matter is associated with higher achievement by pupils and with teaching that is oriented more to problem solving than to memorization and rote learning (Peterson, 1988).

In Hashweh's (1987) study of the effects of subject-matter knowledge on the teaching of biology and physics, differences in knowledge, even among experienced teachers, directly affected the quality of decisions on planning and interactive teaching. Teachers with less well-developed knowledge of biology and physics transformed content in erroneous ways, failed to adapt and tailor instruction appropriately, and failed to comprehend accurately the textbook content presented to students. Teachers with well-developed knowledge of biology and physics were more likely to detect students' misconceptions and accurate preconceptions, to exploit and improve on text content, to adapt and represent content in ways that minimized or eliminated students' misconceptions, and to interpret students' responses accurately and insightfully.

Hashweh observed that in planning their lessons, less knowledgeable teachers followed the textbook and incorporated only the activities suggested by the textbook. Misconceptions and inaccuracies in knowledge crept into their plans, even though the textbook contained correct and accurate information. More knowledgeable teachers, on the other hand, exploited their superior knowledge of biology and physics, supplementing the textbook or discarding textbook information and activities that they deemed shallow or unessential. Knowledgeable physics teachers rejected a textbook theme that they believed to be misleading, namely that systems help make work easier. Instead they organized their lessons around basic principles of work and energy. Their enrichments of the text emphasized the themes they created for their lessons. Less knowledgeable physics teachers patterned their lessons around the textbook theme, failing either to detect a weakness or to strengthen the inadequate theme in any way. Hashweh obtained similar results for knowledgeable and less knowledgeable biology teachers. In short, knowledgeable physics and biology teachers planned more coherent and more accurate lessons; the opposite was true of less knowledgeable teachers.

Hashweh's results are consistent with Leinhardt and Smith's (1985) findings from a study of expertise in mathematics instruction. Leinhardt and Smith mapped expert and novice mathemaics teachers' knowledge of fractions as reflected in the presentation segment of a lesson. They analyzed teachers' plans, determining the kinds of semantic nets (concepts and their interrelationships), planning nets (procedural and declarative knowledge organized in a sequence of actions), and flow charts (algorithmic aspects of procedure) that these expert and novice teachers produced. In keeping with other studies of expertise (Chi et al., 1981; Larkin, 1983), Leinhardt and Smith (1985) found that expert mathematics teachers had more elaborate and deeper categories of knowledge whereas novices possessed more unrelated and more separated categories. Even among experts, however, the authors observed differences in levels of mathematics knowledge. These differences led to differences in the details, conceptual level, and emphases in their presentations. As noted in Hashweh's work, experts organized their presentations around themes related to their levels of mathematical knowledge, but Leinhardt and Smith (1985) found that experts and novices alike provided incomplete descriptions of concepts and relationships, which led to the likelihood of misconceptions among students.

Although teachers must know the subjects they teach so that students will succeed, they must realize equally that "real understanding consists in a web of relationships that connect with content knowledge but also with knowledge in the problem-solving, epistemic, and/or inquiry frames" (Perkins & Simmons, 1988, p. 322). These frameworks for understanding are interdependent. Collins and Brown (1988) described four kinds of knowledge that are crucial for understanding: facts and concepts, which they call *domain knowledge*; conceptual tools, which they call *heuristic strategies*; an awareness of ongoing cognitive processes, which they describe as *monitoring strategies*; and contextually sensitive problem-solving insights, which they call *learning strategies*. Other observers (Posner, Strike, Hewson, & Gertzog, 1982) contend that conceptual growth requires certain conditions: dissatisfaction with one's current understanding, the perception that another concept is more plausible, and the extent to which a new concept implies benefits. Students also have commitments to certain approaches to learning, to standards of reasonableness, to kinds of evidence, and to beliefs about what make sense to them (Posner et al., 1982). In short, if students are to achieve confident understandings, they must be provided with multiple frameworks and perspectives within activities that provide rich opportunities for collaborative social interaction so as to trigger fundamental nonconceptual prerequisites of perception and representation (Brown et al., 1989; Smith & Neale, 1989).

Content knowledge coupled with management and organizational knowledge, the various aspects of procedural knowledge that accrue from teaching, and the depth of analysis and justification typical of expert teachers are acquired only over relatively long periods (Anderson & Smith, 1985; Smith & Neale, 1989) and in the presence of opportunities to address multiple instances of problems and solutions in stable contexts where the utility, costs, and benefits of knowing are clear. In addition to the complexity of learning what and how to teach, there is consistent evidence that for the first several years of teaching, teachers' goals remain highly stable and resistant to change (Adams, 1982; Fuller, 1969). Moreover, beginning teachers resist changing their beliefs and goals (Weinstein, 1990). Experienced teachers, however, are far more disposed to change how they think about both students and instruction and in fact, they do so (Anderson, Anderson, Mehrens, & Prawat, 1990). Shifts in teaching are triggered most often by students who create discipline problems (Anderson et al., 1990). Managing and motivating students successfully is related strongly to teachers' beliefs about their own efficacy (Woolfolk, Rosoff, & Hoy, 1990).

As teachers grow in experience, confidence, ability, and sense of efficacy, they become more adaptable and more highly motivated to change their stance toward students, teaching, and curriculum (Stein & Wang, 1988). Growth of teaching knowledge and skill is an extraordinarily complex process, apparently organized around a web of abstract beliefs, principles, and justifications about the teaching of rather specific subjects. Yet the process of growth is deeply sensitive to students and to the social and political contexts of classroom and school life. No simple description of subject mastery can capture how teachers become skilled in their craft.

In summary, although knowledge of subject matter alone cannot account for competent teaching, it is indispensable to both expert teaching and learning how to teach. It plays a significant role in planning, explanation, tailoring, adapting, and selecting appropriate content for students. It is a necessary ingredient in the reasoning that teachers employ in planning for instruction and reflecting on the outcomes of instruction. Probably a threshold of subject knowledge is a necessary foundation for learning how to teach, if (as it appears) learning to reason pragmatically is an essential component of teaching. The thresholds for various fields of knowledge are not known, but Hashweh's findings suggest that "pedagogical content knowledge" is specific to a particular science (physics, for example) and does not generalize readily to other fields of science. Similar conclusions have been drawn about the teaching of mathematics (Carpenter et al., 1989; Leinhardt & Smith, 1985) and probably could be drawn about the teaching of other subjects as well (Rentel, 1988).

These knowledge resources also must be integrated into actions that in turn must be highly responsive to the details of context, particularly the social details (Lampert & Clark, 1990). Together these resources are embedded in a complex dialectic of justifications, premises, evidence, and subtle warrants (Rentel, 1991). These arguments and premises gradually become telescoped into a seamless set of transactions between teachers and students; they are given direction by images, principles, and norms, are balanced intricately by context-sensitive routines, and are held together by continuous planning and preparation for teaching. Factors such as board policies, the clamor for educational reform, ideological movements within the profession, teachers' beliefs, and a host of other political and cultural values impinge upon these reasoning processes to bias them in one direction or another.

Are teachers' reasoning processes valid? Are their inferences valid, drawn as they are from the rough-and-tumble of practice? If these questions are addressed by standard *regularity* theories of causation (Cook & Campbell, 1979; Cronbach, 1982), only certain kinds of claims by teachers can be validated, but not the kinds of claims that teachers ordinarily make (House, Mathison, & McTaggart, 1989). Much that teachers know and assume is tacit, and often it cannot be stated in propositional or causal form (House et al., 1990). This fact does not invalidate such claims, but certainly it makes them unsuitable for assessment by regularity theories of causation.

Searle (1983) set forth a different theory of causation, known as *intentional causation*, which requires no observations other than the experience of the event. This theory applies to "human mental states, experiences, and actions that do not sit very comfortably with the orthodox account of causation" (p. 117). Searle gives the example of thirst and its satisfaction with a drink of water. The experience of drinking to satisfy thirst provides its own explanation of cause without reference to general laws. Thirst causes one to drink: drinking removes the state of thirst. This account of causation flies in the face of regularity theory assumptions: (a) causes are not observable by immediate experience, only temporal sequence, contiguity, and regularity are thus observable; (b) observations are instances of universal laws; and (c) causal regularities are independent of logical regularities. House et al. (1989) contend:

> Accepting other theories of causation, like the intentional theory, does not mean that experimental design is entirely wrong or useless. Rigorous designs may be useful for some purposes, including validating effects removed from the practitioners' view, such as long-term effects, or investigating controversial issues such as the effects of retention. But accepting such a theory means that correct causal inferences can be arrived at in other ways as well. There are means of validation other than experimental or quasi-experimental designs. (p. 15)

How does one arrive at valid causal inferences in the context of practice? And how can practitioners' causal inferences be validated? Ennis (1973) and Weir (1982) suggested nonproblematic ways to approach these questions and to determine how such processes operate. How to improve causal inference and how to help practitioners improve the quality of their reasoning remain the pressing questions.

IMPLICATIONS FOR TEACHER EDUCATION

The most direct implication of this literature on teachers' reasoning for preservice teacher preparation is that preservice teachers should be exposed to as much clinical and firsthand experience as time and resources permit, coupled with opportunities to reflect on and reason about these everyday situations. Teaching is not simply a didactic procedure. Rather, teaching encompasses both direct and indirect approaches; in nearly all circumstances it requires complex problem solving. Careful analysis of evidence and experience may be far more important in the education of novice teachers than efforts to inculcate good methodology and sound technique. Student or novice teachers who teach and observe real children being taught, or who engage in the analysis of simulated teaching (that is, cases embodying the situated complexities of teaching) should be required to analyze and reflect on these situations. In that way they can begin to acquire knowledge of alternative teaching approaches and of children's typical levels of performance and achievement, and they can begin to develop and refine their analytical skills. Thus, it follows that the analysis of first- and secondhand cases should play a pivotal role in teacher preparation programs.

It seems equally clear that clinical experiences must be articulated carefully with case analysis. In clinical settings, where situational variables can be controlled, students can grapple productively with problems, dilemmas, action premises, and hypotheses formed in first- and secondhand case experiences. Such experiences can be reexamined, viewed from multiple perspectives, and connected with solutions whose utility is obvious, or whose usefulness can be emphasized where issues are subtle or very complex. The literature discussed above suggests that linkages are best achieved by discussion and argument aimed at justifying the problems, dilemmas, premises, and hypotheses identified and clarified in clinical experiences. Analysis of this sort underscores the benefits of carefully identifying problems, gathering and weighing evidence, and justifying one's actions and premises. Most critically, linking case analysis with clinical experience tests the kinds of reasoning required by case analysis in a safe and controlled context in ways that improve the accessibility of newly acquired knowledge. Clinical experiences teach students sets of pragmatic rules for relating existing knowledge to everyday situations in socially grounded webs of justification.

Less obvious but no less valid is the implication that teacher education—classroom, field, and clinic—should be organized around themes. Teaching is extremely complex. The evidence argues that learning to teach is based on multiple experiences in many different contexts where no single answer or problem solution will suffice for long and where multifaceted issues and action-oriented thinking are not simply commonplace but are characteristic. To reduce this complexity and to enable novices to take stock of practice, themes would be useful because they help the novices anchor and frame problems by sustaining their thinking over numerous examples through various contexts.

Another implication of this literature is that if knowledge is to be accessible, it must be actionable. That is, stock routines, avoidance schemata, ongoing awareness of students, mood assessments, dual monitoring, and a wide array of other improvisational skills cannot be learned wholly in preservice programs. Those aspects of learning to teach wherein teachers "construct and reconstruct their thoughts in conformity with the teaching process and context" argue for in-service programs, similar to medical internships and residencies, conducted over the first several years of teaching. Such internships and residencies would be a distinct improvement over the current practice of assuming that preservice preparation is sufficient and that experience and state regulations are minimal guarantees of future professional growth. Surely improvisational capabilities could be developed to higher levels in less time and with fewer casualties, among both students and novice teachers, in coherent internships and residencies. Induction-year programs, though spotty and often incidental, are a start in this direction. Even so, they fall short of the systematic extended professional preparation suggested here.

An interesting implication for teacher education is present in the Nisbett et al. (1987) study of the effects of graduate education in psychology, medicine, law, and chemistry on probabilistic and conditional reasoning. Recall that the authors observed large and statistically significant increases for psychology, law, and medical students, but not for chemistry students. This study was replicated and produced similar results. This evidence suggests that novice science teachers may not fare well at framing practical arguments that depend heavily on probabilistic reasoning. Indeed, this may be the case for students in all teacher preparation programs, on the assumption that probabilistic reasoning plays a restricted or narrowly defined role in these programs. Given the pervasive role of probabilistic reasoning in teaching (risk assessment, goal setting, problem framing, and many other activities), preservice and novice teachers may need extensive exposure to probabilistic and problem-oriented reasoning. At a minimum, research ought to be conducted on the effects of the study of probability—not in the formal sense, but in the context of teaching.

Although the Nisbett et al. (1987) findings raised many interesting questions about the impact of content knowledge on pedagogical reasoning, we have strong evidence that depth of content knowledge is an essential component of expert teaching. Clearly certain threshold levels of content knowledge are foundational to effective teaching, but little is known about these values. Recall also that important nonconceptual prerequisites of perception and representation (Brown et al., 1989) are equally essential for conceptual growth. It is probably a safe bet that programs preparing secondary teachers assume that high levels of content knowledge are necessary for effective teacher preparation but also assume that there is little or no need for content and experiences detailing the impact of heuristic strategies, monitoring strategies, and contextually based problem-solving strategies on conceptual growth. Teacher education programs must provide multiple frameworks and perspectives in learning contexts that are rich in collaborative social interaction so that these nonconceptual prerequisites can develop in preservice students.

Last and most speculative are the implications for teacher education derived from the role of images in guiding the dialectic of justifications, premises, and evidence that seems intrinsic to all teaching interactions. Earlier I noted that images may be a means to improved performance. Images function as a cognitive model of complex performances. In other fields, students have employed them to guide and fine-tune their performances (Cratty, 1984). I suggested that in teaching, departures from normative visual and affective images trigger analytic, probabilistic reasoning processes that are useful in sensing problems, sorting complex sets of cues, and selecting optimal routines for given conditions or circumstances. One of their more important functions may be to clarify the import of complex experiences. They may enable teachers to capture the elusive but important dimensions of pacing, transitions, wait time, problem sensing, opportunity seeking, mood assessment, and many other social and academic dimensions of classroom interactions. These observations must be combined with the further findings that teachers monitor their teaching from several standpoints (either simultaneously or in very rapid sequence), constructing interpretations tied very closely to particular contexts and contents, and that they improvise on the basis of these interpretations.

Deliberate imaging of how teaching looks, sounds, and feels may be a productive follow-up activity not only for clinical and student teaching experiences, but also for case analyses as a way of linking probabilistic reasoning to shorthand, preconceptual representations and perceptions of teaching. If imaging is followed by opportunities to discuss actual teaching experiences from multiple theoretical and pragmatic perspectives in collaboration with others, it may promote the development of improvisational skill married to content and context. Even though imaging of this sort has led to demonstrable improvements in other kinds of complex performances, this suggested application is highly speculative. I believe, however, that this hunch is testable, and of course should be tested before it is taken too seriously.

Practical reasoning in one guise or another (clinical reasoning, informal reasoning, pragmatic reasoning, pedagogical reasoning, legal reasoning, critical thinking) increasingly has claimed attention and interest from a variety of researchers. Coupled with heightened interest in the processes of induction and probabilistic reasoning, productive new avenues of research with great potential for altering and improving teacher education now seem to be within reach. Sara Teasdale's treasure may be ours as well: we have no riches but our thoughts.

REFERENCES

Adams, L., Kasserman, J., Yearwood, A., Perfetto, G., Bransford, J., & Franks, J. (1988). The effects of facts versus problem-oriented acquisition. *Memory & Cognition, 16*, 167–175.

Adams, R. D. (1982). Teacher development: A look at changes in teacher perceptions and behavior across time. *Journal of Teacher Education, 33*, 40–43.

Alexander, P. A., & Judy, J. E. (1988). The interaction of domain-specific and strategic knowledge in academic performance. *Review of Educational Research, 58*, 375–404.

Allison, G. T. (1971). *Essence of a decision: Explaining the Cuban Missile Crisis.* Boston, MA: Little Brown.

Anderson, J. (1976). *Language, memory and thought.* Hillsdale, NJ: Erlbaum.

Anderson, C., & Smith, E. (1985). Teaching science. In V. Koehler (Ed.), *The educator's handbook: A research perspective* (pp. 80–111). New York: Longman.

Anderson, D. B., Anderson, A. H., Mehrens, W., & Prawat, R. S. (1990). Stability of educational goal orientations held by teachers. *Teaching and Teacher Education, 6*(24), 327–336.

Argyris, C. (1980). *Reasoning, learning, and action: Individual and organizational.* San Francisco, CA: Jossey-Bass.

Axelrod, R. (1977). Argumentation in foreign policy settings. *Journal of Conflict Resolution, 21*, 727–744.

Balla, J. (1980). Logical thinking and the diagnostic process. *Methods of Information in Medicine, 19*, 88–92.

Berliner, D., & Carter, K. J. (1986). *Differences in processing classroom information by expert and novice teachers.* Paper presented to the International Study Association on Teacher Thinking, Leuven, Belgium.

Borko, H., Eisenhart, M., Kello, M., & Vandett, N. (1984). Teachers as decision makers versus technicians. In J. A. Niles & L. A. Harris (Eds.), *Changing perspectives on research in reading/language processes and instruction: Thirty-third yearbook of the National Reading Conference* (pp. 124–131). New York: National Reading Conference.

Borko, H., & Livingston, C. (1989). Cognition and improvisation: Differences in mathematics instruction by expert and novice teachers. *American Educational Research Journal, 26*, 473–498.

Borko, H., Livingston, C., McCaleb, J., & Mauro, L. (1988). Student teachers' planning and post lesson reflections: Patterns and implications for teacher education. In J. Calderhead (Ed.), *Teachers' professional learning.* London: Falmer Press.

Borko, H., & Niles, J. A. (1982). Factors contributing to teachers' judgments about students and decisions about grouping students for reading instruction. *Journal of Reading Behavior, 14*, 127–140.

Borko, H., & Niles, J. A. (1983). Teachers' cognitive processes in the formation of reading groups. In J. A. Niles & L. A. Harris (Eds.), *Searches for meaning in reading/language processing and instruction: Thirty-second yearbook of the National Reading Conference* (pp. 282–288). New York: National Reading Conference.

Borko, H., & Niles, J. A. (1987). Descriptions of teacher planning: Ideas for teachers and researchers. In V. Koehler (Ed.), *Educator's handbook: Research into practice* (pp. 167–187). New York: Longman.

Borko, H., & Shavelson, R. J. (1990). Teacher decision making. In B. F. Jones & L. Idol (Eds.), *Dimensions of thinking and cognitive instruction* (pp. 311–346). Hillsdale, NJ: Erlbaum.

Bowers, C. A. (1980). Curriculum as cultural reproduction: An examination of metaphor as a carrier of ideology. *Teachers College Record, 82*, 270–271.

Bransford, J. D., Vye, N., Kinzer, C., & Risko, V. (1990). Teaching, thinking and content knowledge: Toward an integrated approach. In B. F. Jones & L. Idol (Eds.), *Dimensions of thinking and cognitive instruction* (pp. 381–414). Hillsdale, NJ: Erlbaum.

Brown, J. S., Collins, A., & Duguid, P. (1989). Situated cognition and the culture of learning. *Educational Researcher, 18*, 32–42.

Bussis, A., Chittenden, F., & Amarel, M. (1976). *Beyond surface curriculum.* Boulder, CO: Westview Press.

Calderhead, J. A. (1981). A psychological approach to research on teachers' decision making. *British Educational Research Journal, 7*, 51–57.

Calderhead, J. A. (1989). Reflective teaching and teacher education. *Teaching and Teacher Education, 5*, 43–51.

Calderhead, J., & Robson, M. (1991). Images of teaching: Student teachers' early conception of classroom practice. *Teaching and Teacher Education, 7*, 1–8.

Carpenter, T. P., Fennema, E., Peterson, P. L., Chiang, C., & Loef, M. (1989). Using knowledge of children's mathematics thinking in classroom teaching. *American Educational Research Journal, 26*, 499–532.

Carter, K., Cushing, K., Sabers, D., Stein, P., & Berliner, D. (1988). Expert-novice differences in perceiving and processing visual classroom information. *Journal of Teacher Education, 39*(3), 25–31.

Carter, K., Sabers, D., Cushing, K., Pinnegar, S., & Berliner, D. (1987). Processing and using information about students: A study of expert, novice, and postulant teachers. *Teaching and Teacher Education, 3*, 147–157.

Cheng, P., & Holyoak, K. (1985). Pragmatic reasoning schemas. *Cognitive Psychology, 17*, 391–416.

Cheng, P., Holyoak, K., Nisbett, R., & Oliver, L. (1986). Pragmatic versus syntactic approaches to training deductive reasoning. *Cognitive Psychology, 18*, 293–328.

Chi, M. T., Feltovich, P. J., & Glaser, R. (1981). *Categorization and representation of physics problems by experts and novices* (Technical Report No. 4). Pittsburgh, PA: University of Pittsburgh, Learning Research and Development Center.

Chi, M. T. H., Hutchinson, J. E., & Robin, A. F. (1989). How inferences about novel domain-related concepts can be constrained by structured knowledge. *Merrill-Palmer Quarterly, 35*, 27–62.

Christensen, C., & Elstein, A. S. (1991). Informal reasoning in the medical profession. In J. F. Voss, D. N. Perkins, & J. W. Segal (Eds.), *Informal reasoning and education* (pp. 17–36). Hillsdale, NJ: Erlbaum.

Christensen-Szalanski, J. J. (1986). Improving the practical utility of judgment research. In B. Brehmer, H. Jungermann, P. Lourens, & E. G. Sevon (Eds.), *New directions in research on decision making* (pp. 383–410). New York: Elsevier Science.

Clancey, W. J., & Lestinger, R. (1981). Neomycin: Reconfiguring a rule-based expert system for application to teaching. In *Proceedings of the Seventh International Joint Conference on Artificial Intelligence* (Vol. 7, pp. 829–836). Vancouver, BC: IJCAI.

Clandinin, D. J. (1986). *Classroom practice: Teacher images in action.* London: Falmer Press.

Clark, C. (1988). Asking the right questions about teacher preparation: Contributions of research on teacher thinking. *Educational Researcher, 17*(2), 5–12.

Clark, C., & Lampert, M. (1986). The study of teacher thinking. *Journal of Teacher Education, 37*, 27–31.

Clark, C., & Peterson, P. L. (1986). Teachers' thought processes. In M. C. Wittrock (Ed.), *Handbook of research on teaching* (Third edition, p. 255–296). New York: Macmillan.

Cognition and Technology Group at Vanderbilt. (1990). Anchored instruction and its relationship to situated cognition. *Educational Researcher, 19*(5), 2–10.

Collins, A., & Brown, J. S. (1988). *Cognitive apprenticeship and social interaction.* Paper presented at the American Educational Research Association, New Orleans, LA.

Conners, R. (1978). *An analysis of teacher thought processes, beliefs, and principles during instruction.* Unpublished doctoral dissertation, University of Alberta, Edmonton, Canada.

Cook, T. D., & Campbell, D. T. (1979). *Quasi-experimentation.* Boston, MA: Houghton-Mifflin.

Cratty, B. J. (1984). *Psychological preparation and athletic excellence.* Ithaca, NY: Movement Publications.

Cronbach, L. J. (1982). *Designing evaluations of educational and social programs.* San Francisco, CA: Jossey-Bass.

Doyle, W. (1977). Learning the classroom environment: An ecological analysis. *Journal of Teacher Education, 28,* 52–55.

Doyle, W. (1979). Making managerial decisions in classrooms. In D. L. Duke (Ed.), *Classroom management* (78 Yearbook of the National Society for the Study of Education, Part 2, pp. 42–74). Chicago, IL: University of Chicago Press.

Dreyfus, H. L., & Dreyfus, S. E. (1986). *Mind over machine.* New York: Free Press.

Duffy, G. (1977). *A study of teacher conceptions of reading.* Paper presented at the National Reading Conference, New Orleans, LA.

Eisenhart, M., Shrum, J., Harding, J., & Cuthbert, A. (1988). Teacher beliefs: Definitions, findings, and directions. *Educational Policy, 2,* 51–70.

Elbaz, F. (1983). *Teacher thinking: A study of practical knowledge.* New York: Nichols.

Elstein, A. S., Shulman, L., & Sprafka, K. (1978). *Medical problem solving.* Cambridge, MA: Harvard University Press.

Ennis, R. H. (1973). On causality. *Educational Researcher, 2,* 4–11.

Feiman-Nemser, S., & Buchmann, M. (1986). The first year of teacher preparation: Transition to pedagogical thinking? *Journal of Curricular Studies, 18,* 239–256.

Feiman-Nemser, S., & Buchmann, M. (1987). When is student teaching teacher education? *Teaching and Teacher Education, 3,* 255–273.

Feltovich, P. J., Johnson, P. E., Miller, J. H., & Swanson, D. B. (1984). LCS: The role and development of medical knowledge in diagnostic expertise. In W. J. Clancey & E. H. Shortliffe (Eds.), *Readings in medical artificial intelligence: The first decade* (pp. 275–319). Reading, MA: Addison-Wesley.

Feltovich, P. J., & Patel, V. (1984). *The pursuit of understanding in clinical reasoning.* Paper presented at the American Educational Research Association, New Orleans, LA.

Fenstermacher, G. (1986). Philosophy of research on teaching: Three aspects. In M. Wittrock (Ed.), *Handbook of research on teaching* (Third Edition, pp. 37–49). New York: Macmillan.

Floden, R. E., & Klinzing, H. G. (1990). What can research on teacher thinking contribute to teacher preparation? A second opinion. *Educational Researcher, 19*(5), 15–20.

Floden, R. E., Porter, A. C., Schmidt, W. H., Freeman, D. J., & Schwille, J. R. (1981). Responses to curriculum pressures: A policy capturing study of teacher decisions about content. *Journal of Educational Psychology, 73,* 129–141.

Fogerty, J. L., Wang, M. C., & Creek, R. (1982). *A descriptive study of experienced and novice teachers' interactive instructional decision processes.* Paper presented at the annual meeting of the American Educational Research Association, New York.

Fong, G., Krantz, D., & Nisbett, R. (1986). The effects of statistical training on thinking about everyday problems. *Cognitive Psychology, 18,* 253–292.

Fuller, F. (1969). Concerns of teachers: A developmental conceptualization. *American Educational Research Journal, 6,* 207–226.

Gauthier, D. P. (1963). *Practical reasoning: The structure and foundations of prudential and moral arguments and their exemplification in discourse.* London: Oxford University Press.

Glaser, R. (1984). Education and thinking: The role of knowledge. *American Psychologist, 39,* 93–104.

Green, T. (1971). *The activities of teaching.* New York: McGraw-Hill.

Green, T. (1976). Teacher competence as practical rationality. *Educational Theory, 26,* 249–258.

Greeno, J. G. (1989). A perspective on thinking. *American Psychologist, 44,* 134–141.

Harman, G. (1986). *Change in view: Principles of reasoning.* Cambridge, MA: MIT Press.

Hashweh, M. H. (1987). Effects of subject matter knowledge in teaching biology and physics. *Teaching and Teacher Education, 3,* 109–120.

Hogarth, R. M. (1980). *Judgment and choice.* New York: Wiley & Son.

Holland, J., Holyoak, K., Nisbett, R., & Thagard, P. (1987). *Induction: Processes of inference, learning, and discovery.* Cambridge, MA: The MIT Press.

Holsti, O. R. (1976). Foreign policy decisions viewed cognitively. In R. Axelrod (Ed.), *The structure of decision* (pp. 18–54). Princeton, NJ: Princeton University Press.

House, E. R., Mathison, S., & McTaggart, R. (1989). Validity and teacher inference. *Educational Researcher, 18*(7), 11–15.

Housner, L., & Griffey, D. (1985). Teacher cognition: Differences in planning and interactive decision ced and inexperienced teachers. *Research Quarterly for Exercise and Sport, 56,* 45–53.

Janesick, V. (1977). *An ethnographic study of a teacher's classroom perspective.* Unpublished doctoral dissertation, Michigan State University, East Lansing, MI.

Jarvis, J. (1964). Practical reasoning. *Philosophical Quarterly, 12,* 316–328.

Jepson, C., Krantz, D., & Nisbett, R. (1985). Inductive reasoning: Competence or skill? *The Behavioral and Brain Sciences, 6,* 494–501.

Jervis, R. (1986). Representativeness in foreign policy judgments. *Political Psychology, 7,* 483–506.

Johnson, P. E. (1983). What kind of expert should a system be? *Journal of Medicine and Philosophy, 8,* 77–97.

Johnson, R. H., & Blair, J. A. (1985). Informal logic: The past five years—1978-83. *American Philosophical Quarterly, 22,* 181–196.

Johnson, R. H., & Blair, J. A. (1991). Contexts of informal reasoning. Commentary. In J. F. Voss, D. N. Perkins, and J. W. Segal (Eds.), *Informal reasoning and education* (pp. 131–150). Hillsdale, NJ: Erlbaum.

Johnson-Laird, P. N. (1987). Reasoning, imagining, and creating. *Bulletin of the British Psychological Society, 40,* 121–129.

Kagan, D. M. (1988). Teaching as clinical problem solving: A critical examination of the analogy and its implications. *Review of Educational Research, 58,* 482–505.

Kagan, D. M. (1990). Ways of evaluating teacher cognition: Inferences concerning the Goldilocks principle. *Review of Educational Research, 60,* 419–470.

Kahneman, D., Slovic, P., & Tversky, A. (1982). Judgment under uncertainty: Heuristics and biases. *Science, 184,* 1124–1131.

Kolodner, J. (1983). Towards an understanding of the role of experience in the evolution from novice to expert. *International Journal of Man-Machine Studies, 19,* 497–518.

Kuhs, T. (1980). *Teachers' conceptions of mathematics.* Unpublished doctoral dissertation, Michigan State University, East Lansing, MI.

Lampert, M. (1988). What can research on teacher education tell us about improving quality in mathematics education? *Teaching and Teacher Education, 4,* 157–170.

Lampert, M., & Clark, C. (1990). Expert knowledge and expert thinking in teaching: A response to Floden and Klinzing. *Educational Researcher, 19*(5), 21–23,42.

Larkin, J. H. (1983). The role of problem representation in physics. In D. Genter & A.L. Stevens (Eds.), *Mental models* (pp. 75–98). Hillsdale, NJ: Erlbaum.

Leinhardt, G., & Greeno, J. (1986). The cognitive skill of teaching. *Journal of Educational Psychology, 78,* 75–95.

Leinhardt, G., & Smith, D. A. (1985). Expertise in mathematics instruction: Subject matter knowledge. *Journal of Educational Psychology, 77,* 247–271.

Leland, J. W. (1991). Informal reasoning in decision theory. In J. F. Voss, D. N. Perkins, & J. W. Segal (Eds.), *Informal reasoning and education* (pp. 209–224). Hillsdale, NJ: Erlbaum.

Lesgold, A. M. (1984). Acquiring expertise. In J. R. Anderson & S. M. Kosslyn (Eds.), *Tutorials in learning and memory: Essays in honor of Gordon Bower.* New York: W. H. Freeman.

Lesgold, A. M., Rubinson, H., Feltovich, P. J., Glaser, R., Klopfer, D., & Wang, Y. (1988). Expertise in complex skills: Diagnosing x-ray pictures. In M. T. H. Chi, R. Glaser, and M. Farr (Eds.), *The nature of expertise* (pp. 311–342). Hillsdale, NJ: Erlbaum.

Lockhart, R. S., Lamon, M., & Gick, M. L. (1988). Conceptual transfer in simple insight problems. *Memory and Cognition, 16,* 36–44.

MacIntyre, A. (1981). *After virtue.* Notre Dame, IN: University of Notre Dame Press.

MacKay, A. (1977). The Alberta studies of teaching: A quinquereme in search of some sailors. *CSSE News, 3,* 14–17.

Marland, P. (1977). *A study of teachers' interaction thoughts.* Unpublished doctoral dissertation, University of Alberta, Edmonton, Canada.

Marland, P., & Osborne, B. (1990). Classroom theory, thinking and action. *Teaching and Teacher Education, 6,* 93–109.

Marx, R. W., & Peterson, P. L. (1981). The nature of teacher decision making. In B. R. Joyce, C. C. Brown, and L. Peck (Eds.), *Flexibility in teaching: An excursion into the nature of teaching and training* (pp. 236–255). New York: Longman.

McCutcheon, G. (1980). How do elementary school teachers plan? The nature of planning and influences on it. *Elementary School Journal, 81,* 4–23.

McNair, K. (1978-1979). Capturing inflight decision. *Educational Research Quarterly, 3*(4), 26–42.

Mintz, S. L. (1979). *Teacher planning: A simulation study.* Paper presented at the annual meeting of the American Educational Research Association, San Francisco, CA.

Mitchell, J., & Marland, P. (1989). Research on teacher thinking: The next phase. *Teaching and Teacher Education, 5,* 115–128.

Morine-Dershimer, G. (1979). *Teacher plan and classroom reality: The South Bay study: Part 4* (Research Series No. 60). East Lansing, MI: Michigan State University, Institute for Research on Teaching.

Morine-Dershimer, G. (1987). Practical examples of the practical argument: A case in point. *Educational Theory, 37,* 395–407.

Morine-Dershimer, G. (1988). Premises in the practical arguments of preservice teachers. *Teacher and Teacher Education, 4,* 215–229.

Morine-Dershimer, G. (1991). Learning to think like a teacher. *Teaching and Teacher Education, 7,* 159–168.

Morine-Dershimer, G., & Vallance, E. (1976). *Teacher planning* (Beginning Teacher Evaluation Study, Special Report C). San Francisco, CA: Far West Laboratory,

Munby, H. (1982). The place of teachers' beliefs in research on teacher thinking and decision making, and an alternative methodology. *Instructional Science, 11,* 201–225.

Munby, H. (1983). *A qualitative study of teachers' beliefs and principles.* Paper presented at the annual meeting of the American Educational Research Association, Montreal, Canada.

Munby, H. (1986). Metaphor in the thinking of teachers: An exploratory study. *Journal of Curriculum Studies, 18,* 197–209.

Nias, J. (1987). *Seeing anew: Teachers' theories of action.* Geelong, Australia: Deakins University Press.

Nisbett, R., Fong, G., Lehman, D., & Cheng, P. (1987). Teaching reasoning. *Science, 238,* 625–631.

Nisbett, R., Krantz, D., Jepson, C., & Kunda, Z. (1983). The use of statistical heuristics in everyday inductive reasoning. *Psychological Review, 90,* 339–363.

Patel, V., & Groen, G. J. (1986). Knowledge based solution strategies in medical reasoning. *Cognitive Science, 10,* 91–116.

Paul, R. W. (1990). Critical and reflective thinking. A philosophical perspective. In B. F. Jones & L. Idol (Eds.), *Dimensions of thinking and cognitive instruction* (pp. 445–494). Hillsdale, NJ: Erlbaum.

Perkins, D. (1989). Are cognitive skills context bound? *Educational Researcher, 18*(1), 16–25.

Perkins, D., & Simmons, R. (1988). Patterns of misunderstanding: An integrative model of science, math, and programming. *Review of Educational Research, 58*, 303–326.

Peterson, P. L. (1988). Teachers' and students' cognitional knowledge for classroom teaching and learning. *Educational Researcher, 17*(5), 5–14.

Peterson, P. L., & Clark, C. M. (1978). Teachers' reports of their cognitive processes during teaching. *American Educational Research Journal, 15*, 555–565.

Peterson, P. L., & Comeauex, M. (1987). Teacher's schemata for classroom events: The mental scaffolding of teachers' thinking during classroom instruction. *Teaching and Teacher Education, 3*, 319–332.

Peterson, P. L., Marx, R. W., & Clark, C. M. (1978) Teacher planning, teacher behavior, and student achievement. *American Educational Research Journal, 15*, 417–432.

Pinnell, G. S., Fried, M. D., & Estice, R. M. (1990). Reading recovery[TM]: Learning how to make a difference. *The Reading Teacher, 43*(4), 282–295.

Posner, G. J., Strike, K. A., Hewson, P. W., & Gertzog, W. A. (1982). Accommodation of scientific conception: Toward a theory of conceptual change. *Science Education, 66*(2), 211–227.

Rentel, V. (1988). *Becoming a science teacher: First lessons.* Paper presented at the American Association for the Advancement of Science Convention, Boston, MA.

Rentel, V. (1991). *Studies of the content of pedagogical reasoning among reading recovery teachers.* Paper presented at the Japan/United States Teacher Education Consortium, Palo Alto [p.51] 1991.

Rentel, V., & Pinnell, G. (1987). *A study of practical reasoning in reading recovery instruction.* Paper presented at the National Reading Conference, St. Petersburg, FL.

Rentel, V., & Pinnell, G. (1989). *Stake that claim: The content of pedagogical reasoning.* Paper presented at the National Reading Conference, Austin, TX.

Rich, Y. (1990). Ideological impediments to instructional innovation: The case of cooperative learning. *Teaching and Teacher Education, 6*, 89–91.

Ricoeur, P. (1977). *The rule of metaphor: Multi-disciplinary studies of the creation of meaning in language* (R. Czerny, Trans.). Toronto: University of Toronto Press.

Rorty, R. (1979). *Philosophy and the mirror of nature.* Princeton, NJ: Princeton University Press.

Russell, T. (1988). From preservice teacher education to first year of teaching: A study of theory and practice. In J. Calderhead (Ed.), *Teachers' professional learning* (pp. 13–34). London: Falmer.

Russell, T., Munby, H., Spafford, C., & Johnston, P. (1988). Learning the professional knowledge of teachers: Metaphors, puzzles, and the theory-practice relationship. In P. Grimmett & G. L. Erickson (Eds.), *Reflection in teacher education* (pp. 67–90). New York: Teachers College Press.

Russo, N. A. (1978). *Capturing teachers' decision policies: An investigation of strategies for teaching reading and mathematics.* Paper presented at the annual meeting of the American Educational Research Association, Toronto, Canada.

Sabers, D., Cushing, K., & Berliner, D. (1991). Differences among teachers in a task characterized by simultaneity, multidimensionality, and immediacy. *American Educational Research Journal, 28,* 63–88.

Sanders, D. P., & McCutcheon, G. (1986). The development of practical theories of teaching. *Journal of Curriculum and Supervision, 2,* 50–67.

Sato, M., Akita, K., & Iwakawa, N. (1990). *A comparative study of experts' and novices' monitoring and its implications for rethinking teacher education in Japan.* Paper presented at the third annual conference of the Japan/United States Teacher Education Consortium, Tokyo.

Searle, J. R. (1983). *Intentionality.* Cambridge, England: Cambridge University Press.

Shavelson, R. J., & Stern, P. (1981). Research on teachers' pedagogical thoughts, jugdments, decisions, and behavior. *Review of Educational Research, 51,* 455–498.

Shulman, L. (1987). Knowledge and teaching: Foundations of the new reform. *Harvard Educational Review, 57,* 1–22.

Simon, H. A. (1983). *Reasons in human affairs.* Stanford, CA: Stanford University Press.

Smith, D. C., & Neale, D. C. (1989). The construction of subject matter knowledge in primary science teaching. *Teaching and Teacher Education, 5,* 1–20.

Smith, E. L., & Sendelbach, V. B. (1979). *Teacher intentions for science instruction and their antecedents in program materials.* Paper presented at the annual meeting of the American Educational Research Association, San Francisco, CA.

Stein, M. K., Baxter, J. A., & Leinhardt, G. (1990). Subject matter knowledge and elementary instruction: A case from functions and graphing. *American Educational Research Journal, 27,* 639–663.

Stein, M. K., & Wang, M. C. (1988). Teacher development and school improvement: The process of teacher change. *Teaching and Teacher Education, 4,* 171–187.

Strahan, D. B. (1989). How experienced and novice teachers frame their views of instruction: An analysis of semantic ordered trees. *Teaching and Teacher Education, 5,* 53–67.

Suchman, L. (1987). *Plans and situated actions.* New York: Cambridge University Press.

Swanson, H. L., O'Connor, J. E., & Cooney, J. B. (1990). An information processing analysis of expert and novice teachers' problem solving. *American Educational Research Journal, 27,* 533–556.

Teasdale, S. (1919). Riches. *Love Songs.* New York: Macmillan.

Toulmin, S., Rieke, R., & Janik, A. (1984). *An introduction to reasoning.* New York: Macmillan.

Tversky, A., & Kahneman, D. (1982). Evidential impact of base rates. In D. Kahneman, P. Slovic, & A. Tversky (Eds.), *Judgment under uncertainty: Heuristics and biases* (pp. 153–160). Cambridge, England: Cambridge University Press.

Voss, J. F. (1991). Informal reasoning and international relations. In J. F. Voss, D. N. Perkins, & J. W. Segal (Eds.), *Informal reasoning and education.* Hillsdale, NJ: Lawrence Erlbaum.

Voss, J. F., Perkins, D. N., & Segal, J. W. (Eds.). (1991). *Informal reasoning and education.* Hillsdale, NJ: Erlbaum.

Voss, J. F., Tyler, S. W., & Yengo, L. A. (1983). Individual differences in the solving of social science problems. In R. F. Dillon & R. R. Schmeck (Eds.), *Individual differences in cognition* (pp. 205–232). New York: Academic Press.

Wagner, A. (1984). Conflicts in consciousness: Imperative cognitions can lead to knots in thinking. In R. Halkes & J. Olsen (Eds.), *Teacher thinking: A new perspective on persisting problems in education* (pp. 163–175). Lisse, The Netherlands: Swets and Zeitlinger.

Warner, D. R. (1987). *An exploratory study to identify the distinctive features of experienced teachers' thinking and teaching.* Unpublished doctoral dissertation, The University of New England, Armidale, Australia.

Weinstein, C. S. (1990). Prospective elementary teachers' beliefs about teaching: Implications for teacher education. *Teaching and Teacher Education, 6,* 279–290.

Weir, E. E. (1982). *Causal understanding in naturalistic evaluation of educational programs.* Unpublished doctoral dissertation, University of Illinois at Urbana-Champaign.

Woolfolk, A. E., Rosoff, B., & Hoy, W. K. (1990). Teachers' sense of efficacy and their beliefs about managing students. *Teaching and Teacher Education, 6,* 137–148.

Yinger, R. J. (1979). Routines in teacher planning. *Theory into Practice, 18,* 163–169.

Yinger, R. (1980). A study of teacher planning. *The Elementary School Journal, 80,* 107–127.

Yinger, R. (1986). Examining thought in action: A theoretical and methodological critique of research on interactive teaching. *Teaching and Teacher Education, 2,* 263–282.

Yinger, R. & Villar, L. (1986). *Studies of teachers' thought-in-action.* Paper presented at the International Study Association for Teacher Thinking Conference, Leuven, Belgium.

Zahorik, J. A. (1990). Stability and flexibility in teaching. *Teaching and Teacher Education, 6,* 69–80.

7

CLINICAL FACULTY IN TEACHER EDUCATION: ROLES, RELATIONSHIPS, AND CAREERS

CATHERINE CORNBLETH

State University of New York at Buffalo

JEANNE ELLSWORTH

State University of New York at Plattsburgh

Among the proposed responses, if not solutions, to the variously identified problems of U.S. education and teacher education is the creation of clinical faculty positions in teacher education programs. Clinical faculty members are outstanding, experienced elementary and secondary school teachers who work with college and university[1] teacher education programs, full- or part-time, in the preparation of teachers. Their titles and specific activities vary widely. Some, for example, are cooperating teachers who

---

[1] University is used to refer to both college- and university-based teacher education programs unless noted otherwise.

have received new titles. Others teach or co-teach university teacher education courses and/or supervise preservice teachers' field experiences. Still others are involved in redesigning teacher education programs and/or in research.

We focus here on those clinical faculty members (a) whose primary university teacher education responsibilities are other than serving as a cooperating teacher or supervising preservice teachers (or simply teaching a single course without further involvement in the teacher education program), and (b) who hold a university faculty title, receive remuneration, and/or receive other university benefits, such as a parking permit, library privileges, or office space. We limit our focus for two reasons. First, we are interested in newer, if not new, roles and school–university collaboration in teacher education beyond provision for field experiences and student teaching. The now conventional cooperating teacher and supervisor roles do not meet these criteria. Second, the introduction of new clinical faculty roles and school–university relationships will make, and are making, a difference in those conventional cooperating teacher and supervisor roles and in the ways in which schools and universities work together. Therefore, it seems to us that delimiting clinical faculty as we do here would best serve the interests of significant teacher education reform.

Our purposes in this chapter are to examine the roles, relationships, and careers of clinical faculty members in university teacher education, both currently and in the past, in order to understand more clearly:

1. How clinical faculty members might contribute to the improvement of teacher education along the lines sketched by The Holmes Group (1986) and others (e.g., Carnegie Forum on Education and the Economy, Task Force on Teaching as a Profession, 1986; Goodlad, 1990);
2. The implications of the creation of clinical faculty programs for aspects of university teacher education and school-university relations; and
3. The effects of being clinical faculty members on teachers' professional lives or careers.

Our interests, then, are biographical and structural as well as programmatic.

Two key assumptions underlie our construction of this review and interpretation of the available literature, as well as our own experience with a clinical faculty program at the Buffalo Research Institute on Education for Teaching (BRIET).[2] One is that meaning or understanding is necessarily contextualized (e.g., Mishler, 1979). That is, the clinical faculty as a phenomenon cannot be understood or interpreted adequately out of its context of time and place—what Mills (1959) characterizes as the intersection of history, social structure, and biography. In this regard, one's own biography and social location also ought to be recognized as shaping the meanings constructed.

A second, related assumption is adapted from both Marx and Foucault. With Marx we acknowledge that people, including clinical faculty members and other teacher educators, make their own history, although not necessarily in circumstances of their own choosing. From Foucault we take the position that power resides not only in individuals and groups but also and perhaps more importantly in social organizations, institutions, and systems—both in their formal or authoritative roles and relationships (teacher, dean) and in their historically shaped and socially shared conceptions and understandings (teaching, teacher). In modern societies, power operates increasingly through the definition of these conceptions and understandings as well as through the definition of appropriate patterns of communication including rules of reason and rationality—that is, "regimes of truth" (Foucault, 1973). Although people fill roles, enter into relationships, and participate in the prevailing discourse (in the course of which they may perpetuate or modify them), the roles, relationships, and discourse precede the individuals who enact them. A focus only on the present or on the individual (or individuals) in isolation is misleading at best.

Knowledge of conceptions, patterns, rules, and roles is empowering. It gives access to power in teacher education and more broadly as well. Further, self-conscious knowledge enables redefinition. Knowing something of the history of teacher education, or of clinical faculty programs, or of movements for greater school–university collaboration in teacher education, for example, is empowering insofar as it enables one to understand present situations more clearly and to act on them, not merely to acquiesce or resist. Thus we are concerned with the historical context as well as the current situation with respect to clinical faculty programs.

---

[2] These assumptions are elaborated in Cornbleth (1990).

We begin by surveying the current scene—that is, the past decade—with respect to the roles of clinical faculty members and their relationships with other people involved in teacher education programs at several universities across the United States. We give particular attention to the clinical faculty program at the Buffalo Research Institute on Education for Teaching (BRIET), now in its third generation.[3] Then, to provide perspective on the present, we sketch a brief history of clinical faculty programs in U.S. teacher education. We conclude by reexamining questions of roles, relationships, and careers and by considering some implications for teacher education reform and for the teachers who serve as clinical faculty members.

THE CURRENT SITUATION

The past decade has seen the emergence of new forms of school–university partnerships for teacher education. These partnerships have created new roles or have altered or expanded existing roles for classroom teachers. Although some common assumptions or purposes undergird the programs and the associated role changes, the partnerships have taken role changes in various directions. The literature available on these programs is understandably limited, because many partnerships are relatively new or are newly under way. Systematic and/or critical considerations of clinical faculty experiences are rare.[4] Our review of approximately 20 teacher education programs that include some form of clinical faculty component reveals several reasons for the creation of clinical faculty programs and for the changes in roles and relationships that they embody.

One obvious impetus for the development of clinical faculty programs lies in the recommendations of The Holmes Group and

---

[3] If we devote more space to our own experience with clinical faculty members than to others', it is because we have more data about BRIET than is available about other programs at this time. Perhaps this chapter will prompt others to systematically document, analyze, and share their experiences with clinical faculty programs.

[4] The literature on clinical faculty programs at this time tends to be of two types. First, there are brief, bulletin board program summaries in publications such as *The Holmes Group Forum*. Second, a few more comprehensive reports have been published in teacher education journals and/or are available in ERIC microfiche. In general, these reports tend to be celebratory in tone and limited in details regarding the actual (as opposed to intended) activities, roles, and relationships of clinical faculty members.

the Carnegie report, which espouse both university–school partnerships and increased roles for classroom teachers in teacher education. A number of programs are situated in Holmes Group institutions; the reports of others cite Holmes and Carnegie influences on their initiatives (e.g., The University of Tennessee: Heathington, Cagle, & Blank, 1988). In the case of the Lynchburg College program, further impetus was provided by the Virginia Teacher Education Study report, which:

> lists "the development of closer ties between the colleges and the public schools" as a critical concern and indicates "that the colleges and universities [should] call upon experienced public school teachers and administrators to complement instruction by college faculty." (Wolfe, Schewel, Bickham, 1989, pp. 66–67)

With the initiation of new fifth-year and five-year teacher education programs, alternative routes to certification, and changes in state certification requirements,[5] substantial program redesign often is required. Universities may be looking to classroom teachers not only for the practitioner's input, but also for a more general outsider's perspective—to "stir things up," in the words of Catherine Cornbleth, director of the program at the University at Buffalo (personal communication, September 1991). Furthermore, the initiation of a new program that reflects well-publicized current recommendations offers possibilities for increased visibility and/or status, both within the university and nationally.

In addition to these general influences are others more closely related to particular program needs and goals. Some programs have been expanded to five years, others have been redesigned to include more field experiences, and teacher education enrollments once again have increased. Consequently, it might be presumed that more cooperating teachers are needed. Similarly, as programs seek to "take better advantage of the field,"[6] it seems clear that additional responsibilities may devolve onto cooperating teachers. Because the role of cooperating teachers traditionally has been undertaken for little if any remuneration beyond

---

[5] New York, for example, has mandated that since 1993 student teaching experiences must include placements at more than one school or grade level.

[6] Clinical faculty at the University at Buffalo, for example, sought to improve the field experience by restructuring teacher education to include a gradual introduction of preservice teachers to their student teaching schools and their cooperating teachers, and by clustering preservice teachers in fewer schools, in which they would form field teams of preservice and in-service teachers.

tuition waivers, it is more important than ever to seek and maintain the participation of classroom teachers as cooperating teachers. As stated in an overview of the University of Oregon's program, "it became evident that the increased role of cooperating teachers would necessitate an expanded incentives package" (Progress report to the Holmes Group, 1990). The role of clinical faculty members and associated status and perquisites are coming to be viewed as ways to offer such incentives.

A related impetus for the development of clinical faculty programs may lie in the increase in demands on university personnel in expanded or extended teacher education programs. The employment of clinical faculty members to ease overextension of the faculty and the staff is an explicit part of some program rationales. At the University of Colorado, for instance, where clinical professors may take full responsibility for teacher education courses, faculty members may be released to "do research, evaluation, consultation, or curriculum projects in the district" ("Colorado Brings Expert Teachers," 1988, p. 11). Similarly, at Lynchburg College, where clinical faculty members advise and consult with two or three preservice teachers and their cooperating teachers, "the number of contacts with a student teacher are increased and the cooperating teacher has a nearby resource person, [therefore,] the college supervisor's load can be reduced" (Wolfe et al., 1989, p. 69).

The reports of the programs we reviewed reveal three major forms of clinical faculty roles and relationships:

1. enhancement of the status of the traditional role of the cooperating teacher through title changes, increased preparation and perquisites, and role differentiation;

2. classroom teachers' involvement in teaching university courses; and

3. broad participation by classroom teachers in teacher education program planning, admissions, and other decision making.

The clinical faculty programs under consideration here include any or all of these forms, with different emphases and particulars. We address each of these forms or aspects by describing the variations and consistencies across programs and by examining the assumptions that seem to underlie them.

ENHANCEMENT OF THE TRADITIONAL ROLE

In some cases, universities have changed the title and responsibilities of the cooperating teacher. The exact title can vary—teacher in residence, visiting instructor, or faculty associate, for example—but the new titles tend to embody a shift in role emphasis toward greater status and greater or different sorts of involvement in teacher education. Consider, for example, the name change from *cooperating teacher*, which implies a role limited to cooperation with a university activity, to *clinical instructor* or *clinical faculty*, which seems to indicate that the cooperating teacher's role is somehow a part of the university activity but is undertaken in a clinical setting. That is, the name change suggests that the cooperating teacher now has a distinct role in the instruction of preservice teachers rather than simply providing a placement for the field experience. If we accept the conventional though often uncomfortable notion that university faculty members enjoy greater academic status than do classroom teachers, even the simple change of title may serve to enhance the cooperating teacher's status. Conceivably this elevation in status could alter the nature of the role of cooperating teachers, their enactment of the role, and relationships with their fellow teachers, administrators, university faculty members, and others.

Frequently coupled with title changes are efforts to upgrade the role of the cooperating teacher by the provision of "training" sessions (George Mason University, University of Virginia, Radford University) and/or increased perquisites (University of Rochester, University of Oregon). Parking privileges, faculty discounts, offices and clerical support, or library cards are commonly offered to the renamed cooperating teachers, as well as increased remuneration (University of Oregon); in some cases the additional perquisite is simply the cooperating teacher seminar itself (University of Arizona, University of Pittsburgh).

The role is dignified further by the notion that a good cooperating teacher needs skills and dispositions beyond those involved in classroom teaching. This notion also adds responsibility, if only for attending the seminars. In some cases, once prepared with increased supervisory skills, the cooperating teacher becomes (for example) a clinical supervisor (University of New Mexico) or a classroom teacher educator (Cleveland State University). In this capacity, the teacher assumes full responsibility for mentoring and evaluating preservice teachers during student teaching and receives some additional remuneration.

The courses or seminars provided for cooperating teachers most often emphasize supervisory skills, coaching, and communication, presumably to improve relations with the preservice teacher and to maximize his or her learning experience. The seminars may be broader based, however, offering such topics as "teacher thinking, classroom management and effective teaching, student cognition and motivation" (University of Arizona: Network, Inc., 1987, p. 68), issues in adult education (Lynchburg College), policies regarding degree and certification requirements (Radford University), and reflective practice (University at Buffalo).

Going a step further, some clinical faculty programs have enhanced the cooperating teacher's role through career ladder schemes (Lynchburg College, Radford University, University of New Mexico). Paralleling staff differentiation projects at the school level, these programs seek to identify the "best" cooperating teachers. They assign them to work with small groups of other cooperating teachers and their student teachers, and/or to offer mini-courses or seminars in their buildings. These seminars can be held for cooperating teachers, addressing issues that are related to field experience practices (University at Buffalo, Lynchburg College), or, as in the University of Arizona program, they may be "small-group problem-solving" sessions designed for preservice teachers.

Enhancement efforts typically have entailed only limited role change for participants. Although the responsibility for instruction may be increased, as when clinical faculty members are expected to plan and conduct seminars, the cooperating teacher role remains largely unchanged with respect to its focus on guiding and evaluating student teaching, its locus in the classroom, and its placement in an existing and externally controlled program.

The assumptions that seem to underlie these programs include a perceived need to improve and/or expand field experiences by recruiting "good" cooperating teachers and identifying and rewarding the "best." Although such programs dignify the work done by cooperating teachers, programs that enhance the role also carry an assumption of deficit. In some cases this assumption is made explicit; the faculty associate program at the University of Tennessee lists among its primary aims that of addressing the "five areas of need relating to cooperating teachers" (Heathington et al., 1988, p. 25). Similarly, the University of

Arizona focuses on "improving the selection and training of cooperating teachers" (Arizona University, Tuscon College of Education, 1988, p. 68). In other cases, this assumption is implicit in the provision of courses or seminars aimed at training cooperating teachers.

INVOLVEMENT IN TEACHING UNIVERSITY COURSES

Moving beyond the implications for role change that lie in changes of preparation and/or title, a number of programs expand the classroom teacher's role to include the teaching or co-teaching of university courses for preservice teachers; most often these are methods courses. Fellows, teachers in residence, visiting instructors, residency faculty, clinical supervisors, clinical professors, master teachers, faculty associates, clinical instructors, or clinical faculty members (to cite a few of the titles given to such people) have various degrees of responsibility for teaching courses. They may have full professorial responsibilities (University of Alabama, University of Colorado, Cleveland State University, University of Louisville, University at Buffalo) or may teach on teams with university faculty members from teacher education and/or arts and sciences (Winthrop College, University of Pittsburgh, University at Buffalo). They may have more limited roles, such as teaching demonstration lessons (Lynchburg College), or some combination of roles. In the University of Rochester's program, for example, adjunct instructors play a "relatively secondary role" in a course that deals with the "nature of the discipline," and have "primary responsibility" for a "more practical" course (Rochester "Adjunct Instructor," 1990, p. 26).

Initiatives to involve classroom teachers in university teacher education courses may be linked to the idea of role enhancement and thus to improving the supply and quality of cooperating teachers. In addition, they embody assumptions that teacher education programs will be improved if practitioners' skills and dispositions somehow are made a part of classroom knowledge and discourse in teacher education. This improvement conceivably could lie in supplementing "theory" (the province of the university) with "practice" (the province of the classroom teacher). The practicing teacher is assumed to provide an invaluable voice, that of "front line experience" (University of Tennessee: Heathington et al., 1988 p. 24) and of "those who are meeting the challenge of today's classroom" (University of Alabama: Buttery,

Henson, Ingram, & Smith, 1986, p. 66). As stated in an evaluation report on the University of Arizona program:

> Student teachers greatly benefited from the chance to hear about
> recent research and discuss its practical applications with teach-
> ers who represent, in their words, "the real world" to them. Many
> involved with the project came to believe that the clinical faculty
> supported through this project formed "the bridge" from research
> to practice, the kind of bridge that is so often discussed by [sic] so
> rarely constructed by school and university collaboration. (Arizona
> University, Tuscon College of Education, 1988, p. 18)

Furthermore, as suggested by the above excerpt, the presence
and the perspectives of classroom teachers in university classes
could improve courses by adding credibility to courses taught by
university faculty members.

In addition, it is assumed that in a school–university partnership program, the intermingling of personnel will benefit each
institution. First, universities perceive a general benefit to the
teacher education program in the fact that clinical faculty members can, for example, "gain a first-hand understanding of the
philosophy, objectives, and sequence of the preservice program"
(Cleveland State University: Takacs & McArdle, 1984, p. 12),
which they will take back to their schools. A second theme seems
to be that entering the territory of the other will help to forge and
improve cooperative/collaborative relationships. Although personnel exchanges usually take place in one direction at a time
(classroom teachers teaching at the university or university faculty in the classroom), classroom teachers and university faculty members presumably can be brought to certain understandings (and beyond misunderstandings) by experiencing teacher
education from another's perspective.

The role changes contained both implicitly and explicitly in
using clinical faculty members as university instructors go
beyond enhanced status. Although the role is still essentially a
teaching role, it now includes colleagueship with university faculty members and is undertaken in a new setting. The various
responsibilities of clinical faculty members in some programs add
up to a complex new role. For instance, University of Colorado
clinical professors are expected to teach and supervise in undergraduate teacher education, perhaps to participate in faculty
research projects, and to conduct staff development and/or in-
service sessions in their home districts. These responsibilities

have the potential to make the clinical faculty role challenging and also to restructure clinical faculty members' roles in their own schools and districts. Service as a clinical faculty member may induce role changes after the term in this position has expired. That is, clinical faculty members in some cases are expected to become a link between the school and the university, to represent university perspectives and interests in their schools.

Although the practice of using classroom teachers in teacher education classes is common in clinical faculty programs (at least half of the programs surveyed include this feature), both the university and the clinical faculty members appear to feel some ambivalence regarding this role change. When clinical faculty members are assigned to help university faculty members (University of New Mexico), of when they are given "secondary" roles in theoretical courses (University of Rochester), or when their teaching is monitored by university personnel (University of Colorado), it seems possible that the role of the clinical faculty member as teacher educator may be only partially accepted as viable by the university. On the other hand, when some University at Buffalo clinical faculty members were considering solo or team-teaching methods courses, they asked that there be a faculty liaison. This suggests a desire for transitional structures in reformulation of roles.

BROADER PARTICIPATION IN TEACHER EDUCATION

In a few cases, clinical faculty members have been invited to play more extensive roles in the teacher education program. Some clinical faculty members, for example, work on admissions boards (University at Buffalo, University of Tennessee), serve on faculty committees (University of Alabama), act as student advisors (University of Alabama), and conduct or become involved with research projects (University of Colorado, University at Buffalo, Cleveland State University). Ongoing program evaluation and input into the improvement of courses also can be a part of the clinical faculty role (University of Pittsburgh, University of Tennessee). Most of the programs under consideration have included classroom teachers on the advisory or planning committees that proposed and/or designed clinical faculty programs. The clinical faculty members selected, however, have entered roles in programs that were substantially structured before they began their terms.

In at least two cases, clinical faculty members appear to have had considerable responsibility for program redesign (University at Buffalo, Winthrop College). Although it is difficult to discern from program reports exactly how and how much the shaping of programs might be shared by school and university personnel, in these cases clinical faculty members had at least some hand in designing the programs in which they would serve. At Winthrop "the college went to public schools for assistance in program revision efforts," and selected eight residency faculty to work with college faculty members to plan and implement a new team-taught interdisciplinary core of teacher education courses (Hawisher, 1985, p. 3). Because residency faculty members were included on both the planning and the teaching teams, they participated in designing their own roles.

Clinical faculty members in the program at the University at Buffalo also worked with university personnel in redesigning the teacher education program. Both initially and as their term proceeded, each clinical faculty member defined his or her own role within each of three broad categories of participation: program redesign, research, and teaching or coteaching university courses. The role of university supervisor deliberately was not among the options offered to clinical faculty members because it would limit clinical faculty members' influence to a few supervisees (preservice teachers) and would keep clinical faculty members off campus, thus impeding the possibilities for sharing expertise and for mutual learning between university faculty members and staff and classroom teachers.

The pilot teacher education program designed by the clinical faculty members at the University at Buffalo included new or altered roles for clinical faculty members themselves. That is, through their plans for the operation of the pilot program, clinical faculty members added to their own roles such activities as serving as university liaisons to pilot schools, planning and conducting seminars for cooperating teachers, communicating the goals and practices of the pilot program to administrators, and recruiting and selecting cooperating teachers.

Redesigning programs, admitting and rejecting teacher education applicants, and conducting research not only extend the classroom teacher's traditional role in teacher education, but also create possibilities for further role changes. In some ways the assumptions that underlie the broad participation of clinical faculty members in teacher education are similar to those underlying the teaching of courses. That is, programs as well as courses could benefit from the wisdom and credibility of practice, and the intermingling of people from schools and from universities could bring about more effective and more satisfying partnerships. As an additional, related assumption, teachers might be capable of and valuable in those deliberations which shape teacher education programs. Also, in the cases of Winthrop and the University at Buffalo, it is apparently assumed that clinical faculty members will function best in roles and programs in whose design they have been involved at least partially.

HISTORICAL PERSPECTIVE

By historical perspective we mean awareness and acknowledgment of what has preceded the present situation, rather than a comprehensive record. Unfortunately, very little has been published about clinical faculty members' roles, relationships, or careers. Scattered evidence exists, however, from which one can construct a tentative, partial account. This effort is worthwhile, we believe, because even a sketchy account of precursors to the present-day clinical faculty programs can increase our understanding of how the present situation came to be and our awareness of future possibilities. History is part of the context and circumstances of teacher education; past efforts at reform included the creation of the clinical faculty. Historical knowledge, as we have suggested, is potentially empowering. It contributes to possibilities for change in ways similar to those suggested by Reid (1978) with respect to curriculum.

> In order to have an adequate sense of how a learning environment can be changed, and what features of it we need to be able to influence in order to produce change, we need research that helps us to understand how the status quo came about, what tends toward its maintenance and what conflicts and dissonances point the way to possible modifications. Such research has to take account of historical perspectives, of the meanings that participants place on events, of the social and political context of the curriculum and of the moral and ethical bases on which decisions about the curriculum rest. (pp. 35–36)

In other words, in order to change/reform teacher education, perhaps by creating clinical faculty programs, it is helpful (if not necessary) to know something of past efforts and of conditions that have encouraged or impeded clinical faculty arrangements. Further, as Elmore and McLaughlin (1988) pointed out with respect to educational reform, prior reform efforts leave a "residue" that cannot safely be discounted by contemporary reformers. The current clinical faculty initiatives, for example, follow a period of proliferation of state-level regulations, including specification of desired teacher "behaviors" and prospective teacher "competencies," which might impede creativity in redesigning roles and programs.

Finally, historical perspective reminds us that the way things are is not necessarily the way they must be. Current cooperating teacher or university supervisor roles, for example, were created in particular times and places; they are not inevitable, natural, or sacred. As we discern the circumstances of the emergence and experience of the clinical faculty, we might question reasons and motives as well as specific practices in the current revival.

Clinical faculty members, as we have characterized them, could not have existed prior to the appearance of (a) systematic or formal teacher education apart from general education and apprenticeship of some sort, and (b) teacher education in colleges and universities. Although teacher education did not become a university responsibility in the United States until the late 19th century, and did not become primarily a university responsibility until well into the 20th century,[7] the first clinical faculty members could be said to have appeared as early as 1839.

In July 1839, the first U.S. normal school opened in Lexington, Massachusetts, offering a one-year course for 12 prospective teachers (Herbst, 1989, p. 65). In October 1839, Cyrus Pierce, principal at Lexington, opened a model school serving approximately 30 students in order to provide practical teaching opportunities for his normal school students. Although we are not certain who staffed Lexington's model school initially (Pierce, his normal school students, or another teacher), the model school teacher(s) appear to have been the first clinical faculty members. In addition to teaching elementary school students, they supervised the normal school students' field experiences and taught their methods classes (Troisi, 1959). The model schools associated with normal schools provided the prototype for the laboratory schools associated with university teacher

---

[7] Not until after World War II did the majority of U.S. elementary and secondary teachers hold at least a bachelor's degree. Today most U.S. teachers have a master's degree or its equivalent in graduate credits.

education programs, such as those at the Universities of Chicago and Pittsburgh. Presumably, laboratory school teachers continued to teach some teacher education classes as well as supervising prospective teachers' field experiences, including student teaching.

In the first half of the 20th century, classroom teachers' involvement in university teacher education seems to have declined. Factors influencing this decline appear to include the increasing specialization of educational tasks and roles and the discontinuation of many laboratory schools. In addition, schools of education sought status within their universities by aping the arts and sciences and distancing themselves from the schools and school people they presumably served (Clifford & Guthrie, 1988; Judge, 1982). Increasing specialization meant, for example, that laboratory and public school teachers (increasingly, the public schools provided the placements for student teaching) might take preservice teachers into their classrooms while growing numbers of college and university faculty taught methods classes and supervised student teachers. Specialization also meant that administrative positions proliferated and teachers' roles narrowed.

By the late 1940s and 1950s, however, a revival of a form of clinical faculty became evident. A major contributing factor seems to have been the significant increase in the school population after World War II and the concomitant demand for teachers and for teacher education faculty to prepare them. The shortage of college and university teacher education faculty members and the perennially limited funding of schools of education prompted a search for adjunct (inexpensive, part-time, temporary) faculty to meet immediate needs. At the same time, prospective teachers increasingly were placed in public schools for field experiences and extended student teaching, largely because the laboratory schools, which were decreasing in number, could not provide enough field placements for an increasing number of prospective teachers. The rising educational levels of elementary and secondary teachers also seem to have contributed to their acceptability as cooperating teachers and, soon after, as clinical faculty members.

In the 1950s it was not uncommon to find public school teachers supervising student teachers and teaching university teacher education classes, more or less as clinical faculty members. Such an arrangement, according to one account, "keeps the supervising teacher involved in both theory and practice and conceivably helps to overcome the frequent criticism made by students in education that the courses are too theoretical" (Troisi, 1959, p. 22). Thus, clinical faculty members not only staffed but also apparently enhanced the credibility of university teacher education programs.

Another form of clinical faculty program evident in the 1950s was the exchange or "rotation plan," whereby experienced classroom teachers spent one or a few years teaching prospective teachers in a university teacher education program while university education faculty taught in their school classrooms. This arrangement was seen to enhance the capacity of both university and school faculty and thus the education of elementary and secondary school students and of prospective teachers. In addition, it was seen to improve communication between university and school personnel, to contribute to "respect and appreciation for each other's roles," and to provide more coherent teacher education programs (Troisi, 1959, p. 22).

Although Conant (1963) often receives credit for the idea of clinical faculty or clinical professors, calls for greater involvement by classroom teachers in university teacher education were apparent in the late 1950s.[8] Ruman and Curtis (1959), for example, writing in the 38th Yearbook of the Association for Student Teaching (later to become the Association of Teacher Educators), called for "professionally prepared" cooperating teachers to "become participating members of the internal planning, implementation, and evaluation of the total teacher education program" (p. 111). They noted that teachers

> working in the laboratory aspects of the teacher education program have a tremendous contribution to make, and their potential must be recognized and utilized. Further, such status will replace the present attempts to give off-campus supervising teachers somewhat superficial status through such means as tuition exemptions and placing their names in the college catalog. (p. 111)

More specifically, Ruman and Curtis recommended that school–university partnerships to strengthen teacher education should involve classroom or cooperating teachers in activities such as planning teacher education programs and particular

---

[8] We found no evidence of widespread response to such calls in the 1950s, 1960s, or 1970s.

courses, teaching parts of on-campus teacher education courses, participating in the evaluation of teacher education programs, and serving on university policy-making committees.

In addition to bringing cooperating teachers' expertise on-campus, Ruman and Curtis suggested that the cooperating teacher might well "serve as a liaison person between the college or university and the public school in developing and maintaining close working relationships" (p. 113). The authors' enthusiasm for such school–university partnerships is tempered only by concern that participating cooperating teachers be adequately prepared for the task through education as well as practical experience.

Questions regarding the appropriate preparation of teachers, cooperating teachers, and clinical faculty members have long been debated, as have the "best" kind of student teaching experience and the roles of school and university personnel in relation to student teaching (e.g., Hughes, 1982; Shaver & Wise, 1988). Preparation of cooperating teachers for supervisory and more extended roles, particularly through in-service education, was the focus of the 45th Yearbook of the Association for Student Teaching (Association, 1966). The literature of the past 30 years reflects the ambivalence of university personnel: They recognize the desirability of classroom teachers' involvement in teacher education beyond the conventional cooperating teacher role but have misgivings about the adequacy of teachers' academic and professional education—for which, ironically, they are at least partially responsible. Conant's message is illustrative in this respect. In *The Education of American Teachers*, Conant (1963) called for specialized methods courses before student teaching, to be taught by

> the "clinical professor of education," prepared by training to understand what the other specialists have to say, and inclined to listen to them, and prepared by continuing experience in the elementary or secondary school to demonstrate in concrete teaching situations the implications of expert judgment. (p. 140)

Note that Conant's clinical professor is to be a conduit for specialists' advice and "expert judgment." The value of the teachers' craft or experiential knowledge is acknowledged only implicitly, if at all. Conant assumes that knowledge generated by "scientific" research and interpreted by experts (presumably university faculty researchers) is to be applied rather directly in practice; further, such knowledge can be transmitted from experienced to prospective teachers for application in their classroom practice with little or no regard for the particularities of time and place.

Conant's (1963) clinical professors would also supervise prospective teachers' student teaching and would conduct seminars to "amplify and extend what the cooperating teacher is teaching" (p. 144), review textbooks, and consider significant trends in the field. Conant says of secondary teacher education, "Most important of all, he [the clinical professor] can and should keep the subject-matter departments in the college or university alert in regard to what a future high school teacher needs to know" (p. 144).

With respect to clinical professors' formal status and obligations, Conant recommended that they be designated "full" professors with salaries equal to those of other professors, serving either part-time or full-time. Further:

> Clinical professors need not hold the Ph.D. degree and would not be expected to make contributions by research and writing. They would be generally recognized as superb teachers of children or youth and as skilled teachers of college students. Such persons might well be given term appointments of, say, three to five years, either taking leave from their school teaching positions or, if possible, serving both the university and the school at the same time. They would be under an obligation to renew continually their experience in the classroom, either by serving both the university and the school at the same time or by returning to the school classroom every few years. (pp. 143–144)

Conant's clinical professor would bridge but maintain a separation between university research and theory, on the one side, and classroom practice, on the other.

Events in the 1960s relevant to clinical faculty members' roles, relationships, and careers are represented in *The Clinical Professor in Teacher Education* (Hazard, 1967), the report of a conference funded by the Carnegie Corporation of New York and held at Northwestern University in 1966. According to the foreword to the report, written by B.J. Chandler, Dean of Northwestern's School of Education:

> The imperative need for innovations in staffing for teacher education programs is increasingly recognized, and a growing number of universities and school systems are developing and testing new patterns. The clinical professorship, a significant innovation, is receiving considerable attention, and already has been established

in a number of leading universities in cooperation with nearby school systems. This new position was recommended by Dr. James B. Conant in 1963 in his book, *The Education of American Teachers*. At a conference of representatives from fourteen leading universities held at Northwestern University in 1964, John Goodlad elaborated a concept of the clinical professorship. In October of 1966, a two-day working conference at Northwestern, which involved scholars and leaders from a dozen universities and various organizations, analyzed and projected plans for clinical professorships.[9,10]

Noteworthy in this statement is the absence of reference to precursors to Conant's clinical professor in prior educational literature and practice.[11] This omission can be viewed as a sign of educators' lack of historical perspective, and perhaps also of university educators' tendency to distance themselves from lower status state college teacher educators and their programs. In earlier years, clinical faculty and advocacy of clinical faculty members' roles had been associated with state colleges.

In his introduction to the Northwestern report, Hazard (1967) noted that conference participants seemed to agree that "clinical professors are more than student teaching supervisors," but did not agree on what their role might or should be. "Simply renaming the supervisors 'clinical professors' and the traditional practice teaching 'clinical experiences' will not strengthen weak programs or make relevant the irrelevant." Proposals for the clinical professor's role ranged from organizing field/clinical experiences at participating school sites to reshaping educational research—in addition to supervising student teaching. With respect to research, it was suggested that

> his major strength may be in supervision and expert teaching, [but] the clinical professor nevertheless should have the ability to conceptualize, to construe, and to reflect upon the practice of teaching itself. This ability is highly relevant to his work and would provide ample equipment for valuable clinical research in educa-

---

[9] The only examples described in the report are Harvard University, Northwestern University, and the University of Maryland.

[10] We have tried, but without success, to find a published report of the 1964 conference and Goodlad's conception of clinical professors.

[11] In a 1967 paper, Conant credits Robert Bush of Stanford with introducing the term clinical professor into educational discussions but does not cite him as a reference. He credits himself with popularizing the phrase (Conant, 1967, p. 142).

tion. The clinical professorship might be an opportunity to reform
educational research and to produce some research that is relevant
to classroom problems. (Fretwell, 1967, p. 72)[12]

Papers included in the Northwestern report offer glimpses of
the creation of clinical professorships at Northwestern University
and the University of Maryland. Of particular interest here is
Bolster's account of his experience as Harvard University's first
clinical professor, which began in 1964 with a dual assignment
at Harvard and the Newton, Massachusetts public schools.[13] Because Bolster's is a first-person account, because he addresses
questions of relationships as well as of role, and because his
experience has significant parallels with our experience in a clinical faculty program at BRIET some 25 years later, we find it
worthwhile to present his views in depth rather in than summary
fashion.

Bolster (1967) traces the sources of Harvard's clinical professorship to dissatisfaction with the nature and supervision of the
field experience component of the secondary M.A.T. program
begun in the 1930s. The part-time apprenticeship became a full-
year internship, and "a new faculty role explicitly oriented toward
the clinical component of teacher training" (p. 88) was created.
Bolster notes that the position was created "independently of Dr.
Conant's report . . . but agreeing with many of its conclusions"
(pp. 88–89).

Because the problems that the position was intended to
address were not fully understood, the role was "deliberately left
vague" with the expectation that "the first clinical professor was
to define and implement optimum conditions of practice teaching
in one of the subject fields [history and the social sciences] and
to integrate the practicum more logically with the other elements
of the program" (p. 88). Bolster goes on to describe the evolution
of the role in practice during his first two years and to comment
on problems "which seem to be inherent in its implementation"
(p. 89).

Bolster's clinical faculty role came to focus on field supervision
of Master of Arts in Teaching (M.A.T.) interns and school cur-

---

[12] Through the 1960s, none of the literature that we found relevant to clinical
faculty members was written by women, and clinical faculty members were
referred to consistently as "he."

[13] Although clinical faculty members may have written of their experiences,
Bolster's is the only self-report we have encountered in undertaking this review.
Interestingly, the only subsequent publication by Bolster that we found was a
1983 article in the *Harvard Educational Review* about research on teaching. At
that time Bolster was identified as "Harvard University, Emeritus."

riculum development in history and the social sciences. The evolving role was shaped by "assumptions about how one aids novices to become competent teachers" (p. 89). Two of these assumptions were that there exist "little reliable empirical data on teaching effectiveness" and that "effective teachers seem to operate in a variety of modes. . . . Consequently, it is neither possible nor desirable to construct a precise set of teaching styles which can be transmitted to any novice as a basis for teaching competence" (p. 89). This first pair of assumptions seems to anticipate and oppose the translation of the process-product research of the 1960s and 1970s into prescriptions for presumably generic, effective teaching behavior. A second pair of assumptions seems to foreshadow the interest in reflective practice (Schön, 1983) and pedagogical content knowledge (Shulman, 1986) of the 1980s and 1990s. Resembling reflection was the assumption that teaching can be analyzed, and that teachers can learn to analyze their teaching behavior critically in ways that lead to improved teaching. Resembling pedagogical content knowledge was the assumption that

> Knowledge of subject matter is necessary but not sufficient to competence in teaching. In general, the more competent a teacher the more he knows about what he is teaching, but it is also critical that he be able to select and organize from what he knows and to deal with content in such a way that students can make use of his experience to enlarge their own range of awareness. (Bolster, 1967, p. 90)

Bolster's activities during the course of the two-year M.A.T. program included (a) acting as social studies department head at Newton High School, a position that involved selecting cooperating teachers, overseeing their supervision of interns, and generally coordinating their work during a six-week summer session; (b) conducting a summer seminar for both cooperating teachers and interns which dealt with teaching methods and materials; (c) coteaching a more theoretical two-semester course for interns, titled "Curriculum and Methods in History and the Social Sciences," with education faculty members; (d) engaging in other faculty activities such as research, supervision of advanced graduate students, and university policy making; and (e) supervising two or three interns at Newton High School, who were teaching two new courses in a program "being jointly developed" by Newton High School teachers and faculty members from three area universities (including the clinical professor who also taught a section of one of the new courses). The meshing of curriculum development, demonstration, and supervision, Bolster observes, provided "the most systematic and productive contact between clinical professor and intern" (p. 92).

The problems identified by Bolster as inherent in his evolving role pertain to time, "institutional focus," and continuity. First, the clinical professor's many and varied activities made tremendous demands on time and energy. Bolster describes the role as follows:

> Given the basic assumptions we have made about how one aids novice teachers to develop competence—that our most productive knowledge about teaching is the result of intuitive reflection on specific performances, that individuals have unique teaching styles which can be made more effective by analysis, and that knowledge of subject matter and skill in selecting and organizing it imaginatively are both essential to effective practice—all of these functions seem to be necessary. If the clinical professor is to keep his intuitive perceptions sharp and be able to apply them effectively to the analysis of teaching, he needs the reinforcement that comes from continual performance as both teacher and critic. If he is to help others become effective instructors in his discipline, he must keep informed of new knowledge in his subject area and save time to worry about logical and creative ways to apply this knowledge in the school curriculum. If he is not to deal solely with old perceptions but to develop new insights into teaching and curriculum development, he needs to remain in dialogue with his professional colleagues in both the university and the school and employ some of his efforts in research and development. (p. 93)

Second, with respect to "the ambivalent institutional focus of the role," Bolster points to the difficulties of being "a participating member of the faculties of both a university and a school . . . [of] the need to fit . . . into the bureaucratic structures of two different institutions, each of which has its traditional model of a faculty member" (pp. 93–94). Specifics cited by Bolster include (a) scheduling difficulties, in view of the traditional secondary school expectation of "systematic accounting for a teacher's time and activity" and the "somewhat less rigid but nevertheless confining university schedule" (p. 94), and (b) the uncertainty of status and varying degrees of acceptance by peers at both the school and the university, because the clinical professor does not fully meet the traditional expectations of either institution—for example, with respect to scholarly publications or cafeteria duty.

The third problem area, personnel turnover or continuity in the clinical professor's role, derives from the complexity of the role and the difficulties noted above. How might promising candidates be selected and prepared for such a demanding role?

Bolster's suggestions for responding to these problems are particularly relevant to current interest in reforming teacher education by means of restructuring school–university roles and relationships to foster more productive collaboration. In effect, he recommends redefining the clinical faculty role and setting rather than trying to combine aspects of existing school and university positions within existing organizational structures. "Our problem," he concludes,

> is not that the worlds of the university and the school cannot be joined, but rather that by positing the existing institutional arrangements for the clinical training of teachers we have necessarily limited the potential effectiveness of the clinical professorship by insisting that it be created by means of minor *ad hoc* modifications of the existing structure. . . . Rather than being centrally concerned with protecting their traditional functions, the school and university must focus together on the problem of providing the best teacher training possible and rebuild the existing model of the clinical professorship as radically as may be necessary to make it an effective means to that end. (Bolster, 1967, p. 96)

At that time at Harvard, the two modifications to the clinical faculty role and relationships under consideration, as described by Bolster, seemed to foreshadow current notions of professional development schools and clinical faculties. In one of the proposed modifications, interns would be clustered at a smaller number of schools where the clinical professor would "direct the work of resident supervisors [i.e., selected cooperating teachers], developing them into a teacher training faculty within the school . . . [by not having to teach classes on a daily basis or directly supervise interns] he would be freed from the present limitation of having his activity tied closely to the lock step of the school's schedule" (p. 97).

In the second modification, valued research would be redesigned to include "clinical research projects." Such research would focus on "problematic clinical situations and would not only aim at the analysis of specific contexts but would also contribute to our understanding of the processes of teaching and supervision in general" (p. 98). Clinical research would be distinguished by its "emphasis on the generation of new knowledge from a specific classroom situation" (p. 98). Three additional benefits existed in addition to the value of what Bolster describes as clinical research for informing the understanding and practice of teaching and teacher education. Clinical research "would provide a focus for his [the clinical professor's] own scholarly efforts which are consistent with the major purpose of his role—the improvement of the clinical training of teachers" (p. 98), a means of facilitating the clinical professor's efforts to bridge university research and school practice, and providing a setting in which to identify and prepare future clinical professors.

Bolster ends his enlightening account by anticipating the continuing evolution of clinical faculty roles and relationships. Optimistically he notes that "redefinition in light of experience is at the heart of what we mean by the concept 'clinical' " (p. 99).

Bolster's vision and optimism, however, seem not to have been widely shared or supported at the time. We found no evidence that the clinical faculty concept was realized or institutionalized during the 1970s or early 1980s. Several factors seem to account for the demise of this idea. Important among these were declining enrollments in elementary and secondary education and in teacher education, school and university budget cuts, and faculty retrenchment. The general political conservatism of the period also may have discouraged clinical faculty initiatives. The clinical faculty concept did not reemerge until the mid-1980s, when interest in education and teacher education was revived in part by a series of reports calling for various reforms.

Revival of the clinical faculty idea since the mid-1980s seems to have been spurred by increasing teacher education enrollments and associated needs for field placement and staffing, by the need of university teacher education for credibility through close association with the realities of classroom practice, and by reform reports calling for school-university collaboration in teacher education (e.g., the Holmes Group's *Tomorrow's Teachers*, 1986; *Tomorrow's Schools*, 1990), as well as by teachers' demands and the needs of school districts. Teachers' demands for professionalization and professional recognition have included calls for a greater say in the preparation of new entrants into teaching. Increasing numbers of school districts are seeing the need both to provide strong veteran teachers with new opportunities in order to minimize possibilities of burnout and to support improved education of the new teachers they will be hiring. In addition, despite long-standing tensions between schools and universities, formal affiliation with a university teacher education program could enhance a school district's status as well as a university's credibility. It also would provide continuity that could ease the logistics of arranging field placements for the once again increasing numbers of prospective teachers (in several schools or districts for one teacher education program; in others from several teacher education programs).

With the benefit of this brief historical excursion, we return to the present and reexamine the clinical faculty experience. First we offer a critical reexamination of clinical faculty members' roles and relationships in their context of time and place, including connections between knowledge and power in teacher education. Then we explore the question of clinical faculty members' careers, drawing primarily on an ongoing study with BRIET's first-generation clinical faculty members. We conclude with a brief consideration of future possibilities for clinical faculty initiatives.

REEXAMINATIONS

In the past, the *clinical* in *clinical professor* or *clinical faculty* appeared to refer to the setting in which clinical faculty members worked, namely the schools. Today, *clinical faculty* is being interpreted more broadly to encompass bringing the experience of the school into the university as well as working for the university at school sites.

Historically, with few exceptions, the clinical faculty role consisted primarily, if not solely, of supervising student teachers. The supervisory role of university-appointed clinical faculty members apparently originated in the assumption that elementary and secondary school teachers, as cooperating teachers, might share their classrooms with prospective teachers for student teaching, but that most teachers were not (and could not and/or should not) be in a position to guide and evaluate student teaching. Such supervision has been viewed as a university prerogative or responsibility. University supervision seems logical if the university is held responsible for the preparedness of new teachers. The assumption of university prerogative, however, also can be regarded as reflecting an increasing specialization or division of educational labor wherein the university presumably has a superior capacity to prepare teachers and evaluate their teaching. By present standards, lines between school levels (elementary, secondary, undergraduate, graduate) and between school-university and teacher-administrator roles were blurred in the mid-19th century. By the early 20th century, however, the dividing lines were clearly drawn, and the now familiar hierarchies were in place. The role of clinical faculty member as supervisor can be seen as a means of linking the separate camps while maintaining the separation—as well as meeting the university's needs for staffing and credibility.

In the 1980s and 1990s, at graduate research universities, doctoral students who are experienced teachers frequently supervise prospective teachers' field experience, including student teaching. Supervision by such students meets staffing needs for teacher education and maintains university control while providing graduate students with professional experience and support. Consequently it is not surprising that what we call "enhancement" of the traditional cooperating teacher role is currently a more common clinical faculty arrangement than is field supervision.

Clinical faculty roles that involve teaching in university teacher education courses also can be viewed as simultaneously bridging and maintaining another historically constructed separation—in this case, the presumed dichotomy between university-based theory and research on the one hand and classroom practice on the other. In our review of the present situation, we noted that clinical faculty members not infrequently were described as "helping," "assisting," and "playing a secondary role" in more theoretical courses. Such terms clearly communicate an assumption of the superiority of university-generated knowledge. University versions of theory and research are held to be more valuable, both in general and for teacher education, than is teachers' craft or experiential knowledge. Although the value of the latter is recognized with increasing frequency and commitment, it is not yet accepted fully within the university as having equal standing. Further, even clinical faculty members, who are thought to be above the average classroom teachers—to be wiser, more capable—rarely are expected to engage in educational or teacher education research. Recall Conant's comments in this regard, for example.

Relationships between clinical faculty members and other school and university participants in teacher education programs vary with the program, the setting, and their joint history. In an analysis of roles and relationships in BRIET's pilot teacher education program, which was designed by clinical faculty members and which incorporated several new or modified roles, Ellsworth and Albers (1991) identified four major issues or sources of tension: role overlap, disjunctions in perceptions of roles, persistence of traditional roles, and power and authority. Conflict ensued when perceived role responsibilities overlapped or "when players' own role perceptions failed to coincide with others' perceptions of their role" (p. 25). These difficulties can be viewed as temporary, to be worked out as a new program is clarified and refined. More important are the persistence of traditional role perceptions and the expectations and questions of power and authority.

With respect to traditional roles, Ellsworth and Albers (1991) noted that cooperating teachers:

> may be only partially reconceptualizing their role in the direction of becoming teacher educators. That is, cooperating teachers appear to be applying the mentor model of one-on-one experience-based problem-solving to the new structure of the Field Team, rather than significantly restructuring their role toward that of the teacher educator, linking particular events with broader concerns and working with more general issues as a group. (p. 27)

Similarly, several clinical faculty members at least initially appeared to have difficulty in seeing themselves in roles other than as cooperating teachers or supervisors of student teaching.

Individuals are not blank slates onto which new roles and relationships are drawn. Expectations for new roles and relationships interact with and are modified by preexisting conceptions and experience. Nor do many people seem comfortable in creating new roles and relationships for themselves.

Tensions between school and university personnel with respect to power and authority took several forms in the BRIET program, from questions of the agenda for Field Team meetings to the more sensitive question of who shall evaluate preservice teachers (Ellsworth & Albers, 1991, p. 28).

> While there were few major disagreements regarding the evaluations, cooperating teachers raised the issue again and again in on-campus seminars—who "has the final say" in the decision of a "final grade" for the preservice teacher? TEAs [teacher education associates, aka university supervisors], while apparently willing to defer to the cooperating teachers, were still ultimately responsible for submitting the reports. And, while usually willing to defer, TEAs occasionally felt that they could not. . . . It becomes quite clear that the question of the "final say" in evaluation exposes

another issue—that of whether the university or the field is the authority on issues of teaching—whether the scholar or the practitioner "knows best." (p. 28)

Debate about evaluation of preservice teachers focused on who would do the evaluating, not on the criteria or the basis for the evaluation. (The conflict was resolved, at least for the time, by making the final say a joint responsibility of the cooperating teacher and the TEA. Any disagreement was to be resolved by the BRIET Associate Director for the Program, a tenured university faculty member.)

Questions of power and authority appear to be salient to relationships in other school–university partnerships involving clinical faculty. Despite apparent commitment and statements of high hopes and good feelings, university faculty members appear to be ambivalent regarding the capacity of classroom teachers to play a greater part in teacher education programs. Ambivalence is evident in the shape of most clinical faculty roles and in the language used to describe them. Subservience to the university, including its faculty and its norms, is implicit, if not explicit, in most accounts of clinical faculty programs. Perhaps most telling in this regard is that with very few exceptions, clinical faculty members have not had much say in shaping their roles and relationships. The roles and relationships have been created for them, usually by university personnel.

Another way in which the university dominates "partnerships" involving clinical faculty members, intentionally or otherwise, is by establishing relationships with individual teachers to serve as clinical faculty members rather than with the schools or districts from which clinical faculty members are to be selected. Individual teachers, especially if they are few in number or come from different schools or districts, are rarely in a position to seriously challenge university organization, faculty groups, or campus norms. Further, although this perception is changing, teacher education has been regarded as university turf, both literally, in terms of physical location (except for university supervised field experience), and in terms of responsibility. Clinical faculty members are expected to accept the university milieu and to serve as a liaison or link between school and university; in effect, they are to be bicultural.

Entering roles and relationships created by others, as individuals from a lower status organization and without benefit of that organization's support, clinical faculty members are at a structural disadvantage in relation to university faculty members in most teacher education programs. Although not without bargaining power, clinical faculty members have less formal power and authority in the teacher education setting than do university personnel. In addition, although clinical faculty members' practical knowledge is valued, typically it is viewed as supplementary to university-generated knowledge. Acquisition and application of university knowledge by clinical faculty members seems to be prerequisite to acceptance as an academic equal. In other words, to gain power in the teacher education partnership, clinical faculty members must become more "like us."

We believe that both university and school personnel involved in teacher education partnerships with clinical faculty programs would benefit from examining the assumptions underlying their structural arrangements, including roles and relationships, operating procedures, and norms. Teacher education reform also might benefit from examination of the implications and the likely consequences of current and emerging practice. One category of consequences is the impact of being a clinical faculty member on a teacher's professional life or career. Very little is known about the career implications of a clinical faculty members' experience. Consequently we offer only a partial, tentative account, based primarily on interviews with BRIET's first generation of seven clinical faculty members at the end of their 2 1/2-year terms in late spring 1991.

The career impact of experience as a clinical faculty member, we expect, would be influenced in part by what clinical faculty members brought to the experience and what they expected from it. We obtained pertinent information from data gathered from BRIET clinical faculty members' applications in the fall of 1988 and from interviews in the spring of 1989, which were part of a research project about knowledge-in-use. All of the clinical faculty members were career teachers, averaging more than 20 years' experience. They had master's degrees, and were involved in education and/or teacher education beyond classroom teaching, and had served as cooperating teachers. Four were or had been team leaders or department chairs; six had experience in leading staff development activities in their district or teaching teacher education courses at area colleges. Other experience included statewide curriculum development and union activity.

The following reasons for applying for a clinical faculty position were mentioned by more than one clinical faculty member: seeing a need for improvement in teacher education, believing that classroom teachers should be involved in teacher education, and being excited by the idea of the schools and the university working together. Other reasons included a desire to recruit and help new teachers and an assumption that the experience would be interesting. One individual saw being a clinical faculty member as a way to "be involved with the profession" and to continue to teach instead of becoming an administrator. Another related her interest in "evolving" beyond "my classroom," sharing her learning, and gaining status. Becoming a clinical faculty member provided "the next step."

Although the BRIET clinical faculty experience was not without frustrations, 2 1/2 years later, the clinical faculty members described it very positively as an opportunity for personal learning (especially about teacher education) and growth (especially as a teacher and a teacher educator), for making a contribution to teacher education and the teaching profession, and for meeting and working with a diverse group of educators. Apart from particular activities in which clinical faculty members became involved and the satisfaction they derived, several individuals stated explicitly that it was important to them that the partnership was "real." One clinical faculty member commented that for a long time she had wondered why schools and the university couldn't "have a relationship beyond just on paper." In this program, she said, they do have a relationship—"we're partners." Another mentioned her initial skepticism that "real control" of the teacher education program would be shared with clinical faculty members and her surprise to find that "they really meant it." The recognition and acceptance implied by the "reality" of the partnership seemed very important to the clinical faculty members.

The partnership experience, together with the specific opportunities and activities that clinical faculty members both created and fulfilled, seems to have had a considerable impact on their professional lives. Although that impact remains to be played out and documented, some preliminary indicators can be provided now.

Of the seven first-generation BRIET clinical faculty members, only one said explicitly that she accepted the desirability as well as the inevitability (given the agreements between the university and the school districts) of her clinical faculty appointment's coming to an end and being passed on to another person. Even though she did not want to leave, she said she considered it important that the "old" make way for new members and new ideas. At the other extreme, only one individual expressed bitterness, saying "Now we feel all this teacher education stuff and now we're done" and "my turn is up." Three of the clinical faculty members expressed a mixture of resignation and regret that their term was ending.

A particularly salient theme in the clinical faculty members' comments is the question "Where do we go from here?" Is the clinical faculty experience merely a "blip" on their career paths? Do they simply return to their former roles and situations as classroom teachers, perhaps with a sense of renewal and with appreciation of the recognition that they had something to offer? Or has the clinical faculty experience brought about changes that cannot be and perhaps should not be reversed? What are the responsibilities of participating universities and school districts in this regard?

At present, we have little information on the school districts' perspectives. The turnover of clinical faculty members was designed to spread the benefits of staff development and to maintain vitality in the program. Only one school district administrator expressed concern that the district would need to provide further opportunities for former clinical faculty members because they wouldn't be satisfied with merely returning to their roles as classroom teachers; consequently, they might leave the district for more challenging professional opportunities elsewhere.

From the university side, we anticipated a growing network of school-based colleagues in teacher education. We expected that former clinical faculty members would continue to work with us as cooperating teachers, as liaisons, and in various consultant roles. Although we encouraged all first-generation clinical faculty members to "make an offer" as to how they might continue to work with us, and although several expressed strong interest, only three thus far have made explicit proposals to continue to work with BRIET in specific ways; these have been accepted with provision for release time and/or remuneration in return. Yet, we are haunted by the concern that we have intervened in these people's lives in ways that carry further responsibilities.

We found a related theme in the end-of-term comments of first-generation BRIET clinical faculty members; this concerned using the knowledge they have gained regardless of or in spite of their official positions or formal roles. Beyond the feeling that they were being "put out to pasture with an awful lot of knowledge, an awful lot that we can offer," clinical faculty members expressed uncertainty about what they could do next. They believed that there ought to be more than the opportunity to be a cooperating teacher. One clinical faculty member said that she plans to work with cooperating teachers at her school, regardless of the college or university whose prospective teachers they have agreed to work with, to share what she has learned from her clinical faculty experience. Other clinical faculty members envision themselves as continuing to work with BRIET in some way, but have not yet indicated ways in which they might make a difference in their school or district.

Ironically, perhaps, if the BRIET experience is at all representative, school–university partnerships involving clinical faculty programs may be exerting more immediate effects on the universities than on the schools, despite the previously noted power imbalance favoring the university. Examples of such effects include changes in the form, substance, and direction of university teacher education programs as well as new roles and relationships within the university. Over time, increasing tensions and changes in roles and relationships might be expected in the schools, as more experienced teachers have clinical faculty experiences and as more new teachers experience reformed teacher education programs in which clinical faculty members play key roles. Increasing numbers of new and experienced teachers, for example, may come to expect and perhaps to demand treatment as professionals, with greater autonomy and more responsibility both for teaching and learning and for the school conditions that shape professional practice.

Our intent in this review of clinical faculty programs in teacher education has been less to critique past or current efforts than to point to broader implications and future possibilities. Both this review and our own direct experience with BRIET indicate that clinical faculty programs are worth pursuing. Benefits are to be gained by the participating schools and universities, by faculty members in both organizations, and by prospective teachers and their future students.

Although not without risk, new configurations offer significant possibilities for reform of teacher education and teaching. A key to realization of this potential is organizational involvement of schools and districts, not merely the participation of individual teachers who serve as clinical faculty members. Without changes in the conditions of teaching in elementary and secondary schools, for example, reformed teacher education and better prepared teachers can make very little difference in the education provided to young people.

REFERENCES

Arizona University, Tuscon College of Education. (1988). *The University of Arizona Cooperating Teacher Project. Final report: Project portrayal.* Program assessment report; Practice profile [p.54].

Association for Student Teaching. (1966). *Professional growth inservice of the supervising teacher* (45th Yearbook of the Association for Student Teaching). Cedar Falls, IA: Author.

Bolster, A. S., Jr. (1967). The clinical professorship: An institutional view. In W. R. Hazard (Ed.), *The clinical professorship in teacher education.* Evanston, IL: Northwestern University Press.

Bolster, A. S., Jr. (1983). Toward a more effective model of research on teaching. *Harvard Educational Review, 53,* 294–308.

Buttery, T., Henson, K., Ingram, T., & Smith, C. (1986). The teacher in residence partnership program. *Action in Teacher Education, 7,* 63–66.

Carnegie Forum on Education and the Economy, Task Force on Teaching as a Profession. (1986). *A nation prepared: Teachers for the 21st century.* Washington, DC: Author.

Clifford, G. J., & Guthrie, J. W. (1988). *Ed school: A brief for professional education.* Chicago, IL: University of Chicago Press.

Colorado brings expert teachers to campus as clinical professors. (1988). *Holmes Group Forum, III,* 11.

Conant, J. B. (1963). *The education of American teachers.* New York: McGraw Hill.

Conant, J. B. (1967). Joint appointees as supervisors of practice teaching: A summary. In W. R. Hazard (Ed.), *The clinical professorship in teacher education.* Evanston, IL: Northwestern University Press.

Cornbleth, C. (1990). *Curriculum in context.* London & New York: Falmer Press.

Ellsworth, J., & Albers, C. (1991). *Roles and relationships in the field team.* Unpublished paper, BRIET, SUNY at Buffalo, NY.

Elmore, R. F., & McLaughlin, M. W. (1988). *Steady work: Policy, practice, and the reform of American education.* Santa Monica, CA: RAND.

Foucault, M. (1973). *The order of things: An archaeology of the human sciences.* New York: Vintage.

Fretwell, E. K., Jr. (1967). Discussant. In W. R. Hazard (Ed.), *The clinical professorship in teacher education.* Evanston, IL: Northwestern University Press.

Goodlad, J. I. (1990). *Teachers for our nation's schools*. San Francisco, CA: Jossey-Bass.

Hawisher, M. (1985). *Winthrop College transformed curriculum*. ERIC Document Reproduction Service.

Hazard, W. R. (Ed.) (1967). *The clinical professorship in teacher education*. Evanston, IL: Northwestern University Press.

Heathington, B., Cagle, L., & Blank, M. (1988). Seeking excellence in teacher education: A shared responsibility. *Teacher Educator, 23,* 19–29.

Herbst, J. (1989). *And sadly teach: Teacher education and professionalization in American culture*. Madison: University of Wisconsin Press.

Holmes Group. (1986). *Tomorrow's teachers*. East Lansing, MI: The Holmes Group.

Holmes Group. (1990). *Tomorrow's schools*. East Lansing, MI: The Holmes Group.

Hughes, R., Jr. (1982). Student teaching: The past as a window to the future. In G. A. Griffin & S. Edwards (Eds.), *Student teaching: Problems and practices*. Austin: Texas Research and Development Center for Teacher Education.

Judge, H. S. (1982). *American graduate schools of education: A view from abroad*. New York: Ford Foundation.

Mills, C. W. (1959). *The sociological imagination*. London: Oxford University Press.

Mishler, E. G. (1979). Meaning in context: Is there any other kind? *Harvard Educational Review, 49,* 1–19.

Network, Inc. (1987). *A compendium of innovative teacher educaton projects* (pp. 30–31). Andover, MA: Author.

Progress report to the Holmes Group. (1990). *Far West Regional Holmes Group Conference*. Seattle, WA.

Reid, W. A. (1978). *Thinking about the curriculum*. London: Routledge and Kegan Paul.

Rochester "adjunct instructor" reflects university collaboration. (1990). *Holmes Group Forum, IV,* 26–27.

Ruman, E. L., & Curtis, D. K. (1959). The supervising teacher in future teacher education programs. In E. J. Milner (Ed.), *The supervising teacher* (38th Yearbook of the Association for Student Teaching). Cedar Falls, IA: The Association.

Schön, D. (1983). *The reflective practitioner: How professionals think in action*. New York: Basic Books.

Shaver, J. C., & Wise, B. S. (1988). *Winners need trainers: Looking at cooperating teacher educators*. Paper presented at the conference of the Southeastern Regional Association of Teacher Educators, Lexington, KY.

Shulman, L. S. (1986). Those who understand: Knowledge, growth in teaching. *Educational Researcher, 15,* 4–14.

Takacs, C., & McArdle, R. (1984). Partnership for excellence: The visiting instructor program. *Journal of Teacher Education, 35,* 11–14.

Troisi, N. (1959). Development of the supervising teacher's role. In E. J. Milner (Ed.), *The supervising teacher* (38th Yearbook of the Association for Student Teaching). Cedar Falls, IA: The Association.

Wolfe, D., Schewel, R., & Bickham, E. (1989). A gateway to collaboration: Clinical faculty programs. *Action in Teacher Education, 11,* 66–69.

Author Index

T

U

V

W

Y

Z

SUBJECT INDEX